"Sharing the biblical reflections of leadership guru J. Robert (Bobby) Clinton, Reese and Lane ably communicate the insights gained from a lifetime of study. Their book imparts life-changing ideas. Reflecting on the patterns of growth in others, the book deepens our understanding of how to develop leaders. *Deep Mentoring* moves the needle toward maturing leadership!"
C. Douglas McConnell, Fuller Theological Seminary

"Words have to become flesh for us to understand them. While my life and library are full of books, at their best they only take us so far, a little way along the way. Everything we learn that forms us—from throwing Frisbees to doing justice—we learn over the shoulder and through the heart. In *Deep Mentoring,* Randy Reese and Rob Loane have given us the gift of a different sort of learning. Skillfully drawing in the visions of wise and good teachers over the centuries to their own years of paying attention to what matters most, they set forth a way of learning that is also a way of life."
Steven Garber, The Washington Institute for Faith, Vocation & Culture, and author, *The Fabric of Faithfulness*

"*Deep Mentoring* is a breath of fresh air for churches and Christian leaders weary of business leadership axioms and growth principles. I highly recommend reading this book but even more strongly encourage Christian mentors to prayerfully ponder the wise guidance provided for the important work of guiding others and begin to pay attention to the way that God grows his people toward maturity in Christ. As you read, be prepared to slow down."
Rob Peterson, senior pastor, Thornapple Evangelical Covenant Church, Grand Rapids, Michigan

"Sometimes we can't see because what we're looking for is too obvious. Sometimes we can't see because we're moving too rapidly past what we need. Sometimes we don't see because we settle for something less too quickly. *Deep Mentoring* opens the door to a centuries-deep practice of apprenticeship in Jesus' way of forming leaders. Reese and Loane invite us to linger at that table of formation, which begins with the practice of learning to pay attention to the presence of God in everything. Let's face it: we need help for holy seeing and sacred listening. *Deep Mentoring* gives us that help."
Dr. Keith R. Anderson, president, The Seattle School of Theology and Psychology

"I have to believe that whether you are a seasoned Christian leader or one just starting out, *Deep Mentoring* will provide enough food to feast on for years to come! In this book, Randy Reese and Rob Loane provide substantive content and guidance along with probing questions and vivid examples that demystify the critical but often-ignored task of developing others."
Beth Booram, congregational consultant, spiritual director, speaker and author, *Awaken Your Senses: Exercises for Exploring the Wonder of God*

"*Deep Mentoring* is a must-read for anyone in leadership, a valuable tool for those mentoring the next generation of leaders as well as a helpful guide for those seeking mentoring. It has lots of great examples and ideas for building strong, effective mentoring relationships that will change lives as mentors and mentees learn to notice God's work in their lives."
Elizabeth "Betsy" Glanville, Ph.D., assistant professor of leadership, School of Intercultural Studies, Fuller Theological Seminary

"Reese and Loane have crafted an engagingly perceptive exploration of ways to help others find God's creative and redeeming purposes in the midst of the realities of their lives. In a thoughtful yet accessible personal style, drawing on their own rich experience in leadership formation, the authors remind us that Christian calling and vocation—whether as ministers, teachers, farmers or mechanics—is discovered in who we are as the persons God has made us to be, not in idealized spiritual notions of who we think we should be as followers of Christ. With grace and wisdom, they lead us carefully into the deep and refreshing waters of following Christ in life as it is."

Stephen Brachlow, professor of spirituality and church history,
Baptist Theological Seminary at Richmond, Richmond, Virginia

"There is a hunger inside churches that leaves adults wanting more—more conversations and encouragement, deeper listening, better questions and a model for finishing well with Christ. Randy Reese and Rob Loane describe this hunger and provide a path for discipleship and leadership development that only courageous and patient adult leaders will follow. My own experience with these processes after five years inside the local church is transforming our ministry goals, deepening our commitment to each other and slowing us down. We are recovering our Christ followership for the good of others, but we needed a path to get us there."

Pamela K. Edwards, Ph.D., Adult Spiritual Formation, Cedar Valley Community Church, Waterloo, Iowa

"More than any other element, the church of today is desperate for leaders to be shaped to not merely do more stuff but to be men and women who are living a life of formation in Christ. How does one live a formative life while living a sacrificial life? And how do we guide others in this lifestyle? Randy and Rob's service to us in this book is to provide a road map of sorts for the formative life in Christ."

Scott E. Shaum, director of staff development, Barnabas International

"With wide-ranging knowledge and with voices steeped in experience, we have been given a gift in this book! You are holding in your hands a guide to how a leader is made. This is not a shallow guide offering tips and techniques; it is a profound tool to help you understand how the soul of a leader is shaped. This book is set to become the go-to book on leadership development. I simply loved it! I was inspired, helped, equipped and motivated! You will be too!"

Stephen W. Smith, founder, Potter's Inn, and author, *The Lazarus Life, Soul Custody* and *The Jesus Life*

"*Deep Mentoring* presents a much needed broader exposure of the already-proven but largely unknown ministry of VP^3. I have seen firsthand as a pastor more than a hundred lay leaders and ministers have their lives changed by going through this process of spiritual formation. This book, while thoroughly grounded in Scripture and good theology, is really about application of the gospel and the implications of the gospel for how we live our lives (see Eph 2:10, which may be called the theme verse of the VP^3 process). Few things are needed in the contemporary church more than the deep exercise of seriously and honestly asking the three questions that form the threefold 'vantage point' of this process described in *Deep Mentoring*: 'Who is God?' 'Who am I?' and 'What am I to do with my life?' Read this book and taste the process, and then run to get your church involved in the most effective ministry and leadership development tool/discipline/process for the local church I have ever come across."

Dr. Vic Gordon, senior pastor, Kenwood Baptist Church, Cincinnati

"At the heart of this book is the conviction that leadership formation involves 'the simple act of paying attention to another.' Simple? It sounds revolutionary—except that it is an ancient and true way. You do not have to read this book to pay attention to another. Just do it. But as you do you will find *Deep Mentoring* a most helpful guide, rich in ideas, experience, sources and practices. I plan to recommend it to the leaders of our own mentoring community. I heartily commend it to you."

Leighton Ford, president, Leighton Ford Ministries

DEEP MENTORING

Guiding Others on Their Leadership Journey

RANDY D. REESE AND ROBERT LOANE

Foreword by EUGENE PETERSON

IVP Books

An imprint of InterVarsity Press
Downers Grove, Illinois

InterVarsity Press
P.O. Box 1400, Downers Grove, IL 60515-1426
World Wide Web: www.ivpress.com
E-mail: email@ivpress.com

InterVarsity Press® is the book-publishing division of InterVarsity Christian Fellowship/USA®, a movement of
students and faculty active on campus at hundreds of universities, colleges and schools of nursing in the United States
of America, and a member movement of the International Fellowship of Evangelical Students. For information
about local and regional activities, write Public Relations Dept., InterVarsity Christian Fellowship/USA, 6400
Schroeder Rd., P.O. Box 7895, Madison, WI 53707-7895, or visit the IVCF website at <www.intervarsity.org>.

Scripture quotations, unless otherwise noted, are from the New Revised Standard Version of the Bible, copyright
1989 by the Division of Christian Education of the National Council of the Churches of Christ in the USA. Used by
permission. All rights reserved.

While all stories in this book are true, some names and identifying information in this book have been changed to
protect the privacy of the individuals involved.

"Whatever Is Foreseen in Joy" by Wendell Berry is copyright ©1998 by Wendell Berry from A Timbered Choir.
Reprinted by permission of Counterpoint.

Cover design: Cindy Kiple
Interior design: Beth Hagenberg
Images: BZB/Getty Images

ISBN 978-0-8308-3789-2

Printed in the United States of America ∞

Library of Congress Cataloging-in-Publication Data has been requested.

P   20   19   18   17   16   15   14   13   12   11   10   9   8   7   6   5   4   3   2   1

Y   29   28   27   26   25   24   23   22   21   20   19   18   17   16   15   14   13   12

CONTENTS

FOREWORD

The North American church is in desperate need of this book. For at least fifty years, leadership in the church has been functionalized and depersonalized into programs that have steadily eroded the very core of the Christian life, which ought to be a life of trinitarian-shaped intimacy and community. This work is the antidote for that damaging trend. As I read what Randy Reese and Rob Loane have provided in these pages, I silently imagine a contrasting scenario that makes clear, in a negative way, just how critical this book is for the Christian community, its lay leaders and its clergy. This scenario causes me to appreciate how significant this book's impact can be.

In my scenario I substitute "athlete" for "Christian." Between the lines I imagine myself as young, wanting in the worst way to be an athlete, a basketball player. When the announcement is posted for tryouts for the basketball team, I am ready and eager, my imagination fired up. From that moment on, my coach will be the key leadership person in everything I do.

In contrast to the kind of leadership development I read about in *Deep Mentoring*, I see myself with my friends gathered in a room with a movie screen. Every day the coach shows up (he never learns our names), directs us to set up chairs and take our places with notebooks. We suit up and he instructs us in the skills we need to acquire to play the game: dribbling, passing off, lay-ups, free throws. He explains the history of the sport, makes sure we know the rules of the game and shows us video clips of various players to inspire us. Then, after an hour (he is very punctilious about the hour), we are dismissed. We shower and go home. We never handle a basketball, never set foot in a gymnasium, never play the game together. But we know the rules and can talk a good game.

I'm exaggerating, I know—but not as much as many may think. The language of telling people what to think and what to do dominates most leadership paradigms in the church, with very little, if any, mentoring attention given to the actual details of being a Christian in the home and workplace.

There are, however, serious efforts being made up and down the line to "re-dig the wells the Philistines have filled" and to recover a leadership of companionship and a spirituality of relationship. They are making a difference. *Deep Mentoring* ranks among the very best of what is being done—a skillful, imaginatively written and strategically placed blessing for all of us who care about the actual nuts-and-bolts living of the Christian life in these times.

Eugene H. Peterson
Professor Emeritus of Spiritual Theology
Regent College, Vancouver, B.C.

ACKNOWLEDGMENTS

We are grateful for the company of such good people who have helped make this book move from an idea and challenge to a published work. We are well familiar with our own shortcomings to be able to pull this sort of thing off on our own, and so we want to say thank you to those who have provided timely wisdom, encouragement, resources and perspective along the way.

We want to especially thank Dr. J. Robert (Bobby) Clinton for his decades of research, teaching and mentoring. His painstaking work of noticing the detail of God's shaping activity in the lives of hundreds of people has lent validity to his leadership emergence theory. He is a rare person who knows how to notice, listen and prescribe what is timely for one's development as a follower of Jesus and for maturing in the work of leadership. It is a hard thing to entrust others with your life's work. Thanks, Bobby, for entrusting us to do what we could.

Such a project is boosted when foundations believe in the need for good resources. We want to thank the Tyndale Foundation and the Kharis Foundation for their gracious support and foresight of a completed work when it was just an idea.

The board and staff at VantagePoint[3] have been supportive and gracious for us to step away from our regular responsibilities in order to stay focused and get the manuscript done. Thanks Curt, Rich, John, Pam, Doug, Vic, Gerry, Lavern, Jamie, Kay, Brian, Emily and Jessica for your belief in us.

We are grateful for the sharp pencil of Gary Deddo and the rest of the InterVarsity Press team and for their belief that the concepts and approach in *Deep Mentoring* could provide a timely help to learners in the broader Christian community. Thanks for taking the risk.

We also want to make special mention of those who have given us timely insights to help strengthen *Deep Mentoring*. Doug McConnell, for your initial challenge to write the book, and for your gentle-yet-firm accountability. Bob Freeman, for your confirmation that the book was heading in the right direction. James Houston, for being our guide on the journey, helping us catch glimpses of the mystery and love of God through the way you live. Eugene Peterson, for your teaching and prophetic voice, and for emphasizing the importance of the *way* we do what we do in Jesus' name.

I (Rob) recognize that the time invested a decade ago with the Joshua Foundation for Christian Mentoring has been so instrumental to my own thinking, writing and living. Much of its influence echoes throughout this book. I am so grateful to the Lord for the many gifts of family and friendship along the way. Chief among these gifts is my wife, Sarah. Thanks, Sarah, for the way you surprise me and notice me and love me so generously. It is such a good journey together. I love you.

I (Randy) love the way I am loved by my wife, Susan, and my son, Liam. Other than my salvation in Christ, they are the best gifts my life has received. Susan, you continue to be the "real deal" of what it means to live and love well. Thanks for grinding my coffee beans. Liam, you're the man! Thanks for not thinking I'm too weird for staring at the mystery of who you are.

INTRODUCTION

A walloping great congregation is fine and fun,
but what most communities really need is a couple saints.
The tragedy is that they may well be there in embryo, waiting
to be discovered, waiting for sound training, waiting
to be emancipated from the cult of the mediocre.

—MARTIN THORNTON, *SPIRITUAL DIRECTION*

God is in the business of raising up leaders and
intervening in their lives to develop them for carrying
out his purposes. Jesus still calls people to follow him
and influence many others.

—J. ROBERT CLINTON, *LEADERSHIP EMERGENCE THEORY*

Sometimes it's not the *what* that we are after, but the *how* and the *who*.

I (Randy) learned the importance of this in my early years apprenticing to become an electrician. The plan was to take over my stepfather's electrical company. I had gotten a taste of the electrical trade doing odd jobs around the shop after high school was out each day and during the summer months. Becoming a journeyman electrician seemed an appealing vocation. What made the choice seem like a sure thing at the time came in large measure from what I had noticed about the electricians lives. During coffee breaks I would hear them talk to one another, from what seemed to be a place of confidence and enjoyment about the complex electrical challenges they were up against that day. There was no shortage of solutions given amid the coffee and apple fritters, along with a good dose of teasing and laughter. The trade seemed to pay decently too, which made the choice all the easier.

There was a certain pride for the trade that I learned while being apprenticed under what I considered some of the best electricians in Western Canada. I had come to respect, and also fear a bit, Gordy Heron, Mike Muse, Frank Lecce, Bernie Epp and Wayne Guigon. They all possessed a remarkable ability to draw out of me what they somehow seemed to know was there. They saw in me an ability to become good at a craft they had mastered. Although there was much to get done and many deadlines to meet, there always seemed to be time to show me the right way to make the electrical connections, debrief what I had learned and invite me to participate with the them on more advanced and higher voltage assignments.

The way I learned was through careful apprenticeship—*with them*, four years' worth, not given to haste or oversight. I learned the way they learned. Several years later I have come to realize that what has stuck with me from my apprenticeship with Gordy, Mike, Frank, Bernie and Wayne was not *what* but *how* they taught me. They were concerned about developing good electricians, and I had become empowered to be one of them because of their careful attention.

I have long since hung up my electrical tool pouch (except for when the word gets out among friends that I used to do that sort of work), but the concern for how we invest in the formation of others has stuck with me and is a significant piece of my own sense of calling.

Other vocations in which an apprenticeship of sorts is required practice a similar passing-it-on approach for the craft they belong to—fishing, nursing, teaching, cooking, plumbing, masonry and cabinet-making, to name a few. New learning methods may help, but a quicker way seems absurd to those women and men who are gifted in the art of passing on their trade to others. Sometimes there are simply no shortcuts to learning. And sometimes the most effective way to learn a craft well is to have someone pass it on to you.

I was out for an early morning run in August 1995, anticipating the important day ahead, the day I would get to meet the faculty at Fuller Seminary. This was an important thing given the fact that I needed a faculty person to sponsor me into one of their doctoral programs. A few years earlier I had read a book called *The Making of a Leader* by J. Robert Clinton, and I was hopeful that somehow I could get to frame a doctoral study under his mentorship.

On my run I prayed one of those pushy sorts of prayers, the kind where you know you've hit the end of yourself and there is nothing in you to make it work. It has to be done by a gust of the Spirit. And so I prayed, "Lord, today we are to meet the faculty at a luncheon. If possible, could you please put me at the same table as Dr. Clinton? Amen."

I showered and headed to Fuller. The class I had just before noon ran late, and consequently I was then late in getting to the luncheon with the faculty. The room was packed, and I became disappointed. I thought I had lost my chance to meet Dr. Clinton. I picked up my sub sandwich, bag of chips and drink, and wove my way through the crowded room to the table in the back corner with one chair remaining. An elderly gentleman stood up, held out his hand and greeted me, "Hello. I'm Dr. Robert Clinton, who are you?"

I sat down staring at him but not saying a word. Clinton looked at me and said, "Young man, are you okay?" I then rather sheepishly introduced myself to "Bobby" and his good wife, Marilyn, and asked, "Do you mind if I share with you my prayer from this morning?" After I told the story, Bobby said, "Well Randy, I believe this morning you had a type 1, awe-inspiring destiny process item." I was glad he could not see the words in my head at the time. But I knew as awkward as his tag phrase seemed, he nailed my experience right on the head!

After the luncheon, Bobby asked if I could give him a ride home, where we could visit more about what I wanted to study. For some reason he reminded me of Don Buhr, a mechanic I used to work with in the Yukon, a tough character who always had a half-used oil rag hanging out of his back pocket, and an expert mechanic. Bobby took me to his office and showed me his "hero board," which had on it a mixture of old pictures of men and women, most of whom I did not know but wanted to get to know, as he described their influence on his life. He then asked me who my heroes were, what concerned my heart and what I wanted to do about it.

At the end of an hour or so visit, Dr. Clinton said to me, "I like your story, and see the Lord has given you something significant to be about. I think you need to study with me. Would you mind if I became your sponsor mentor into the doctoral program?" To which I replied, "I would like that very much."

Much of the formational concern reflected in this book has grown out of the relationship that began that day and developed as Dr. Clinton walked alongside me, apprenticing me in my doctoral work in the area of Christian leadership development. And it is his research and guidance that has provided an underlying structure for our discipleship and leadership development processes at VantagePoint[3].

A couple decades before that August luncheon, J. Robert Clinton was first grabbed by Hebrews 13:7-8: "Remember your leaders, those who spoke the word of God to you; consider the outcome of their way of life, and imitate their faith. Jesus Christ is the same yesterday and today and for ever." In light of the many contemporary leadership examples of failure around him, these words deeply concerned him. They drew him into a comprehensive study of the life stories of thousands of leaders, men and women who influenced people toward God's purposes.[1] Clinton's studies drew on biblical examples, historical figures and contemporary lives. Through the use of grounded theory, Clinton distilled from their stories common themes and patterns that seemed to reflect God's shaping activity in their lives. In his research he *remembered* their unique stories and *considered the outcome of their way of life*.

What Clinton found to be true and hopeful is that God is deeply concerned with our formation and is creative enough to use the varied circumstances of our lives to shape us into who he wants us to be and what he wants us to do. His work has helped us see how our unique life

---

[1]J. Robert Clinton, *Leadership Development Theory* (Ph.D. diss., Fuller Theological Seminary, 1988).

stories matter to God, and that it is within our story and in light of the stories of those around us where God matures us. Also hopeful and timely about Clinton's findings is that they affirm that we become good at the leadership formation of others by paying attention to and joining in what God is already up to in peoples' lives. And the way we do this is by coming alongside others as a guide and a friend.

Sometimes it's not just the *what* that we are after but the *how* and the *who*.

OUR CONTEXT AND CONCERNS

We come to you from a few contexts and with a few experiences along the way. At the present time we "hang our hats" at a ministry called VantagePoint³, where we are committed to providing churches and organizations transformative processes that help them foster depth in and empowerment of their adult believers. A secondary context for Randy has been teaching from time to time in the areas of leadership development and change in a doctoral program at Fuller Seminary, and in the past he has served in pastoral roles in local churches, as well as teaching and administrative roles at Sioux Falls Seminary. For a number of years Rob served at Biola University as a resident director and then instructor of Bible and spiritual formation classes. Those experiences, along with his time at Joshua Foundation for Christian Mentoring, has stirred a concern for finding simple and creative ways to deepen people's spiritual conversations with one another. Over the years we have taught each other what it means to walk in honesty and hopefulness as we follow Jesus; even more important, we have learned a good deal about friendship.

Much of our VantagePoint³ work has involved finding ways to integrate spiritual formation, leadership development and adult learning dynamics into learning processes that help others pay attention to the good work God is up to in their lives and in the lives of those they walk with in their local communities. We recognize a growing need across the landscape of the larger Christian community, a need often heard while having a cup of coffee with a local pastor in Edmonton or while listening to an amazing servant of the Lord who stewarding the missiological burn in his soul while living and learning in Turkey, or even while sitting across from a college student who is trying to make honest sense of her emerging adult faith. So many people are longing to mature and serve in Jesus' name, but even beyond that they also desire to learn *how* to teach others to go and do likewise. The potential is astounding. Listening to these men and women, and the many others like them living in North America and across the globe, has led us to believe that paying attention to the formation of others is a lifelong work, which holds in tension our growing with our serving—our followership and our leadership. The Spirit's faithful shaping work in our lives seems to be concerned with both ends of the tension.

We are also convinced that leadership development in Jesus' name is a *slow and deep work*. Amid the hectic pace of normal life and ministry today, the thought of slowing down in order to pay attention to the formation of others is a hard sell. We want the brightest and the best to be able to hit the ground running. And even if we do invest in them developmentally, it is mainly so we can get more mileage out of them. Sadly, many well-intended servants of the Lord are so driven to get things done for God that they neglect both themselves and the people they serve. It is no wonder that many followers of Jesus today feel as though they have been reduced to "functionaries for God," as James Houston puts it.[2] Such discoveries can be so very confusing, even despairing. But there are many others who are in search for better and more faithful ways to invest deeply in others. Their lives seem to challenge the more conventional understandings of Christian leadership. Much more than simply getting done what needs to get done as efficiently as possible, they care deeply about who people are becoming along the way. Listen in on some of their stories and challenges:

> Kim Cho represents a large mission agency seeking to reach out to Muslims in various places of the Arab-speaking world. Her mission requires people with a strong sense of calling and a willingness to sacrifice in order to serve remote regions in foreign lands. No one could accuse Kim of having a small vision to help fulfill the Great Com-

---

[2]James M. Houston, *Living a Mentored Life* (Vancouver: Regent College Audio Series, 1994).

mission. She has, however, had some painful lessons in learning that as grand as her vision may be, it will be short lived unless she invests in the ongoing care and development of those who follow her.

Keith represents a church in small-town Iowa that has exponentially grown in numbers over a relatively short amount of time. Keith knew the system would feel the stress of the growth unless they found a way to identify and invest in the leadership development of their people. The investment has not only strengthened the system but has precipitated a wave of ordinary people leading various ministry endeavors.

Pam represents someone who has a deep concern for the spiritual formation of her community. She was well schooled in knowing the importance of adult discipleship, but needed to find a process to help facilitate the learning. Pam also needed to find a way to invite the people to realize they too could become change agents in the various contexts God has placed them. For many of the people in her community, the notion of *leadership* conjures up more negative perceptions than positive.

Chris represents someone known for his uncanny ability to "call out" people from within his local congregation. He believed in them, and did his best to encourage them to live more fully for Jesus. Helping people believe in themselves was a good start. What Chris needed was a way of understanding how to walk a little farther down the road with them in their learning. He was in search of a careful approach in order to appropriately prescribe learning that would be timely for their development and growth.

Carla represents a small mission organization with a big impact. Carla's heart is full of love and courage as she goes to high-risk areas around the globe in order to rescue those who are marginalized and in danger. Carla has identified a handful of other women to join her "dispersed order." Other than provide her small team with plenty of places to serve, Carla knows it will be important to find ways to pay attention to their formational needs. Carla knows her time in this particular work will be limited, and wants to see the work continue and expand through them.

Kent and Mike represent a tag-team pastoral effort in a church that has gone through some remarkable transformation over the past twenty years. By using a seeker-sensitive strategy they grew the church to over sixteen hundred people. Then they encountered Dallas Willard, who asked them a series of simple yet pointed questions: "What kind of people are you developing?" "Are they more loving, kind, joyful?" "What kind of life are you inviting people to?" Their honest response of no sent them on quite a trajectory—growing the church from over 1,600 to around 750. Willard has been mentoring them in a fuller understanding of the Great Commission, especially the "teaching them to obey everything I've taught you" part. Their depth, however, is in much better proportion to their width.

Jorge represents a "big L" type leader who years ago felt led to pastor a small, declining church. Over the past decade the church has turned around to become one of the fastest growing churches in Lima, Peru. Jorge has spotted a number of church planters from within the congregation who have been able to replicate what he has done. Jorge—a gifted leader—has largely built the success of the ministry around his abilities and charisma. He knows leadership development is important, and that's why he's kept it focused on future church planters. However, taking the time to invest in the growth of others in the congregation seems too costly and may jeopardize the momentum they are experiencing in reaching out to the community with the gospel.

These stories reflect the need and central concern of this book. We trust that because you hold this book in your hands you too share a similar need and concern for your own context. *How can we participate in the deepening and empowering of those given to the work of leadership?* We are careful in our use of words like *leader* and *leadership*, mainly due to the negative connotations these two words have acquired in recent years. The overuse of these words has also precipitated premature questions like, Am I or am I not a leader? or What exactly is good leadership? For our purposes we will suspend judgment on who is or isn't a leader and come at it from the assumption that although some do possess a special gift of leadership, we want to offer hope to a wider group of us who desire to be faithful to Jesus, who believe we have been given something unique to be and do, and who know that in order to do what we have been given to do it will involve serving and influencing others toward a more hopeful way.

In recent decades there has been much discussion about the shortage of leaders: "We need more leaders." "If only we had a real leader." "Where can we find good leaders?" "Why are people running the other way from leadership positions?" "How do we develop leaders?" These statements or questions have been volleyed around in a variety of settings. We believe that one of the primary causes of this leadership struggle is the failure to notice those around us. Too many of us have been looking for "the leader" to come riding in on a white horse to rescue us, all the while overlooking the many lives right in front of us.

This book is for those who want to learn ways to notice and walk alongside others who want to grow into maturity in Christ (Eph 4:13) and to live more fully into the hope and invitation of Ephesians 2:10: "We are what he has made us, created in Christ Jesus for good works, which God prepared beforehand to be our way of life."

At some point in our faith journey we wake up to the fact that God has already been at work in our lives, loving us, preparing us and re-aligning us toward a way of life and service that befits who we really are. Then the questions become, What are those good works God has given me to do? and Does my way of life reflect those good works? If we need more influencers, they are right before us. And therein lies the challenge and the problem. Paying attention to those persons before us will confront our own paradigms of how we do ministry, as well as the organizational systems around us.

At the close of the two-day retreat, Autumn approached me (Randy) to express her gratitude for the solitude time woven into the schedule. Sometimes it's hard to be still with eighty-five others. I was both encouraged and saddened at her story. Her life of twenty-eight years had already seen too much for one person. A mixture of neglect, abuse, poor choices in her later teens and a surprising turn toward being caught by God's love. "I was captured by a love that changed everything."

Autumn shared how grateful she was for learning at her church that she not only could be used by God for some good things but should be expecting God to do so. Her heart broke for young teenage mothers who were left to fend for themselves and their new babies. Her pastor thought it would be a no-brainer for the senior pastor and others on the leadership council to bless Autumn's proposal for a new ministry through the church to care for these neglected women and babies. Continuing to tell me the story, Autumn had a puzzled look on her face as she said, "The leadership of the church felt like my idea didn't fit within the existing ministries of the church, and encouraged me to get connected to a social agency in the city who did that sort of thing."

Autumn followed her heart and began to care for those who needed her love and attention. Others noticed Autumn's work and offered space, supplies, education and finances to help her out. Some confirmed a similar beating within their hearts and joined the effort. Even the local media did a feature segment on the evening news about Autumn's story and the twenty-two young mothers and babies being cared for.

Not doing a very good job of holding back the tears, Autumn said, "I never thought God would be so good to me. To trust what was in my heart seemed so small and insignificant, almost embarrassing to say out loud. I am so glad I listened and followed." Our conversation ended with her sharing how her senior pastor contacted her after he saw the news clip that one night. Autumn said, "He congratulated me and asked if I would be interested in having my ministry become a part of the church. I told him thanks, but for now, things seemed to be going okay." I found myself grateful for the Lord's working in and through Autumn, and disappointed at the shortsightedness of her senior pastor.

Are we noticing others within our contexts, and *how* are we approaching their learning and formation? Are we making related decisions based primarily on expediency and efficiency for the sake of the mission? What might happen if we approached people in our contexts with a genuine concern to invest in them as persons—in the learning they may uniquely need in order to be true to the beating within? Noticing God's good work in others will challenge our way of doing things for God. Like you, we have noticed how little attention has been paid to apprenticing others like Autumn to do those "good works . . . God prepared beforehand to be [their] way of life" (Eph 2:10).

There is a need for a subtle but critical paradigm shift—moving from an *enlisting way* of ministering in our communities to more of an *investing way* of ministering. So much of our leadership culture is dominated by the need to enlist volunteers for the various activities of the church. This sort of work begins with "a slot to fill" and then the hard recruiting work of finding people to fill those many slots, whether they are ushers or Sunday school teachers or building committees members. The work of enlisting others will always be part of our leadership culture, but what if our primary attention was given to people investment?

Investing suggests we need to begin with paying attention to and honoring the good work God is already doing in people's lives. And then we ask, What does this person need in order to grow more fully into a kingdom way of life? It suggests an equal if not greater concern for the kingdom work they are designed for than the work we ourselves may have been given to do. In fact, deepening and empowering others may well be the more mature work we have been invited to consider (Eph 4:12). We know these people when we run into them. They are persons who help us discover more of who we were meant to be because they have taken the time to notice. If we move intentionally in the investing direction, not only will the nondevelopmental nature of our organizations and churches surface, but our imagination and energy for who we could become and what we could do in Jesus' name will be ignited.

WHAT IS THIS BOOK ABOUT?

The last thing the planet needs is another book about leadership. Much has already been written. This book, however, is about leadership formation. It is an invitation to cross the bridge from *leading* others to *developing* others as leaders, and to do so by *noticing* the already-present shaping activity of the Spirit of God in the lives of persons in our communities. We can *learn* from those leaders who have come before us. Their stories can teach us about the journey of faith and what it means to finish well. This book is designed to help us see and embrace our role as a *guide* alongside others in their formation.

We are fundamentally concerned with how we can better participate with God in the work of leadership formation. Consequently, when we approach the work of developing leaders from a Christian vantage point, we discover that before we start talking too quickly about notions of leadership, *discipleship is the first order of business.* In fact, it may well be the same sort of work. With this in mind, our work has a broader application than for just the obvious leader types.

It also includes those who might never have considered themselves leaders, but who, in their more honest moments, confess a desire deep within to be faithful to do the good works God has been stirring within. So our concern for leadership development finds itself squarely rooted in the ongoing process of making disciples.

We also share a deep concern with *the means* we use to develop others, as well as *the ends* or goals of their formation.[3] In this respect, we must pay attention to how Jesus developed others. He had a way of stopping the music in order to notice someone, or seizing a teachable moment on the way to somewhere, or giving to others a work to do long before they were "ready." But he was always *with* them in the everyday curriculum of their life stories. Our life stories are sacred because they are written in partnership with God's Spirit. We become aware of their holy significance when we come to see them as a gift from God to be stewarded, enjoyed and celebrated. Frederick Buechner puts it this way, "I think of my life and of the lives of everyone who has ever lived, or will ever live, as not just journeys through time but as sacred journeys."[4]

Learning from those who have come before us will help us in our efforts to faithfully walk alongside others. It is here that J. Robert Clinton's research will prove to be very instructive. We are grateful that he has given us permission to utilize his research and theory throughout this book. In both unpacking and applying the theory we don't want to lose the richness of the whole by looking too closely at the parts, as can sometimes become the case when we discover a new map, typology or system. We can at times try to corset everything and everyone into the new thing we have discovered. Developmental maps and models can have a valuable place in walking alongside others. Maps can be helpful in finding our way. But the real deal is to visit the places the map describes.

Clinton's "leadership emergence theory" is a map that invites us to consider the "something more" that God may be doing with, among and through us. We have utilized leadership emergence theory as an

---

[3]Eugene H. Peterson, *The Jesus Way: A Conversation on the Ways That Jesus Is the Way* (Grand Rapids: Eerdmans, 2007).

[4]Frederick Buechner, *Sacred Journey: A Memoir of Early Days* (San Francisco: HarperCollins, 1982), p. 6.

undergirding framework for our own ministry at VantagePoint[3], where a primary focus has been in the deepening and empowering of adult believers. Although Clinton's study was primarily focused on the lives of persons in vocations of ministry (pastors, missionaries, denominational leaders, biblical leaders and leaders from various cultural backgrounds), we have applied his theory for lay leadership development and have found it applicable in the leadership formation of over seven thousand people. Our hope is that you will find his theory helpful for your own context and purposes.

Developmental theories and maps serve a vital purpose, but *what we desperately need more of today are wise men and women who are willing to become guides for others along the way.* They are people who have had the courage to walk faithfully and honestly ahead of us, and can help us explore the places the map describes. The essence of a guide is to ensure that others will follow in a manner appropriate for their learning and the journey ahead. Not all have the confidence or courage to be a guide, and some have falsely believed they can get people "there" by simply telling them where and how to go, and what to watch out for as they do. *So much of what passes for leadership development today lacks interpersonal investment,* life upon life. Simply telling others where they must go won't cut it. The journey must be shared. Guiding requires a mentor's heart. We desire to help you not only become a better guide but to pay attention to certain conditions or dynamics that can help cultivate an environment conducive to the growth, change and empowerment of others.

THE STRUCTURE

Our learning together will be divided into three parts. The first part, "Noticing God's Already-Present Action," responds to the question, How are we noticing people in our midst? Chapter 1, "Paying Attention," explores four conditions we may find ourselves in as we claim to do God's work, and how the simple act of *noticing* can cause a timely realignment in *how* we do what we do in Jesus' name. Chapter 2, "A Storied Way," discusses how we are shaped by God throughout our lives. Each of us possess a wonderful and purposeful story in which we can learn more fully who God is, who we are and what God has given us to do in his kingdom. We can discover much if we take the time to edit our lives.

Part 2, "Learning from Those Who Have Come Before Us," addresses the question, What can we learn from those who have come before us? Chapter 3, "Foundation: A Beginning," explores the critical importance of the "once upon a time" of our life stories. Some of us don't recognize the importance of the early chapters and God's sovereign presence in our lives until we are well into the story. Our beginnings are where our character is formed. Chapter 4, "Preparation: Finding Our Way," describes how we grow through exploration and discovery of how God has gifted and is shaping us for service. Chapter 5, "Contribution: Leading Out of Who We Are," invites us to consider one of the more pivotal discoveries of our formation—that God is more concerned with our being (our character) than our doing (our competencies and achievements). This paradigm shift provides us a fresh set of lenses through which to hone in on our service. The leadership we provide derives from a deepened character, a renewed sense of the power of the Spirit and a more focused fit between our calling, giftedness, responsibility and context of service. Chapter 6, "Multiplication: Finishing Well," allows us to consider how endings have the power to ask fresh questions of beginnings. Our time spent shifts toward investing in the formation of others—noticing and calling out the good work God has been doing in the lives of those around us, and, as appropriate, teaching them what we have learned from a lifetime of faithful service in Jesus' name.

Part 3, "Guiding the Formation of Others," surfaces the question, How can we become guides alongside others in their formation? Chapter 7, "Imitating Jesus' Way with Others," invites us to see the life of Jesus Christ as the unique model worthy of imitation. Does our way of doing ministry line up with the manner in which Jesus walked with his apprentices? To imitate Jesus' way of forming the next generation of followers and leaders, we would do well to learn how to be a guide—a mentor for others. Chapter 8, "Christian Leadership Formation: The Nature of Our Work," our final chapter, invites us to consider the nature of our leadership-formation work. We will discover that when we are concerned with the formation of others, ours is a deepening work, a particularizing work, a hospitable work, a patient work. Process must come alongside content if our desired goals are transformation, faithfulness and empowerment in Jesus' name.

AN INVITATION

From the ministry contexts we have served over the past years, we have developed the following convictions, which will be woven throughout the book. We invite you to consider them as you continue to be faithful to the good work God is doing in your own life and as you consider the formation of others.

Shape the person and you stand a much greater chance of shaping everything else. This was a challenge given to us by James Houston, founder and chancellor of Regent College in Vancouver, as we began our work. After a dozen or so years of experience, we have noticed time and again how change in a small group of people begins to leak out and impact their local community.

Discipleship and Christian leadership development are inextricably linked and together make a slow and deep work. Those who promise impressive growth through simple and easy steps are simply selling an illusion. Some things simply cannot be learned quickly. Apprenticing people toward Jesus' way eventually establishes what it means for them to influence others toward God's purposes. In this regard, discipleship and leadership development are seamless.

Igniting a grassroots renewal is possible. Although there are important things to be said for vision from the top or a "speed of the leader, speed of the team" approach, if we desire the work of the Spirit in our midst these are sometimes overrated. Igniting more people toward an Ephesians 2:10 way of life will precipitate significant movement in a local setting. Beware of lighting fuses.

A Christian approach to leadership formation requires a ministry of paying attention. If it is true that God uses people, events and particular circumstances over time to shape us, our role in guiding others toward growth and maturity becomes a ministry of noticing where God is at work and then partnering with him in the learning endeavor.

Conditions can be cultivated in order for local communities to become significant places of learning and growth. Although formal education is important, it is not the only means of learning. Igniting a thirst for learning happens when we help people make a connection between truth and life—in the ordinary places where life is lived.

As you continue to read you will no doubt "find yourself" in the following pages. A story will recall one of your own. A principle will cause you to think about your own formation or lack thereof. But we also want you to keep in mind those persons who are under your care, influence and tutelage. How will you invest more particularly in their formation?

As you sink into the book we hope that (1) the ministry of *paying attention* would become for you a primary way of how you do what you do, (2) you will become more aware of the lessons learned from those who have come before us, and (3) you will value the role of being a guide for the leadership formation of those in your setting. They and we need you.

> Come to me, all you that are weary and are carrying heavy burdens, and I will give you rest. Take my yoke upon you, and learn from me; for I am gentle and humble in heart, and you will find rest for your souls. For my yoke is easy, and my burden is light. (Mt 11:28-30)

Part One

Noticing God's
Already-Present Action

1

PAYING ATTENTION

From the time we were children we were told to "pay attention,"
as if this were the simplest thing in the world. But in fact
attentiveness is one of the most difficult concepts to grasp and
one of the hardest disciplines to learn. For we are very
distractible people in a very distracting world.

—LEIGHTON FORD, *THE ATTENTIVE LIFE*

What do you think? If a shepherd has a hundred sheep, and one of
them has gone astray, does he not leave the ninety-nine on the
mountains and go in search of the one that went astray?

—MATTHEW 18:12

The emergence of a leader is a life-time process in which God
both sovereignly and providentially is active in the spiritual
formation, ministerial formation, and strategic formation
of a leader. All of life is used by God to develop the
capacity of a leader to influence.

—J. ROBERT CLINTON, *LEADERSHIP EMERGENCE THEORY*

In 1905 the Grand Trunk Railroad was beginning to wend its way
through southeastern Saskatchewan. Along the newly laid tracks, one
particular community was given the name Ituna; today it has a popu-

lation of around seven hundred. It is said that Ituna got its name because the letter "I" was next in the alphabet—the last few communities had already been named Fenwood, Goodeve and Hubbard. It is also believed that Ituna got its name from Rudyard Kipling's story "Puck of Pook's Hill." In that story, Kipling tells of a wall built by the Romans to keep out the Scots. The wall spanned what is now the English countryside from Segedunum on the east coast to Ituna on the west, and still exists today. In any event, the hardworking and rugged Itunians appreciate the peculiar history of their town's name.

The railroad brought with it opportunity for Anglo-Saxon and Ukrainian settlers to clear the bush and squat on the land with the hope of someday making a livelihood from their new farms. Purchase of the land was made official when the settlers could put up a building or two within three years and come up with the $10 to pay for their 160 acres.[1]

Many of those early farms remain in the same families that had the courage and fortitude to settle the land all those years ago. These are hardworking folks who still pride themselves on an honest day's work and a type of farming that keeps the land clean. Their commitment to farming and their love for the land has also brought with it a lifestyle of simplicity and frugality. All this may sound admirable, but a visit to the local coffee shop and some discreet eavesdropping would reveal fatigue with the farming way and hope that someday a stroke of luck might come along—often expressed as a hope for the winning ticket in "Lotto 649." The stories of complaint turn into stories of dreaming— dreaming of what life and farming would be like if "only luck would come our way."

Recently, on some of the same family farms in the Ituna area, mining companies were given permission to do exploratory testing for various types of underground mineral deposits. These mining prospectors soon became the brunt of much coffee shop banter, conversations which were mainly a mixture of disbelief and offense that someone from outside Ituna could tell them something new about their land. However, these conversations soon took on a different character

---

[1]"History," *Intuna, Saskatchewan, Canada*, www.ituna.ca/History.html, 2007.

when, to the utter shock of the farmers, the mining prospectors discovered diamonds on their properties.

There are seasons in our lives when, like those Ituna farmers, we find ourselves wondering, *Is this as good as it gets?* Or from time to time we may hold onto a secret wish: *If only luck would come my way.* Our lives are often lived in the tension between being dutiful to what we have been given to do (raise kids, till the land, pay the bills, etc.) and dreaming for another way of life that is more true to what we hope our life could someday become by God's grace. In Ephesians 2:1-10 the apostle Paul addresses this hope for another way of life. He shares some very good and "lucky" news with the community in Ephesus. He writes that they have been delivered from the life that they once lived, a way of life that really was death (v. 1). But now God has "made us alive together with Christ" (v. 5). He then elaborates on this new way of life:

> By grace you have been saved through faith, and this is not your own doing; it is the gift of God—not the result of works, so that no one may boast. For we are what he has made, created in Christ Jesus for good works, which God prepared beforehand to be our way of life. (vv. 8-10)

God had already deposited something greater under the surface of their lives. These gracious deposits included first and foremost a *salvation* to a restored and ever-growing relationship with God—a relationship that would have implications for every aspect of their lives. Second, these gracious deposits included a promise of being uniquely designed by God to participate in the work he does, the *good works* which were to become *our way of life*.

It is sadly misguided to think of these *good works* as being primarily of concern for apostles, pastors or missionaries. This Ephesians 2:10 way of life is good news for all followers of Jesus. *You have been created for good works.* Consider how this is such good news for those persons in your setting or sphere of influence, those who are wondering, struggling, maybe even yearning to believe that there might be so much more going on in their lives beyond what they experience on the surface. We enter a whole new dimension of development when we begin to care deeply about inviting others into a personal exploration of how God has been graciously preparing them for *a good works way of life*. We each would do well to become prayerfully attentive to this question, How might God want us to invite others in our midst to dig below the surface of their lives and discover what is already there? If we had the courage to do so, our efforts would most surely bring with them an alignment toward a new way of life for these folks and for our community—a *good works* sort of life as surprising as diamonds in Ituna.

But so long as our leadership formation lacks this below-the-surface exploration work, it makes sense that we will then continue to struggle in our efforts. Why is it that in so many pockets of the church (broadly speaking), it's a struggle to get people below the surface and empowered to live an Ephesians 2:10 way of life? We don't have to poke around too much in this regard before we begin to sense that something is not quite right.

AN ABSENCE OF NOTICING

When things go unnoticed for too long, bad things begin to happen. A leaky roof turn into a major repair of an entire wall; unattended weeds eventually squelch the growth of the vegetables; a "not that big-a-deal" lump over time becomes cancerous; an undisciplined child later in life lacks a healthy sense of boundary and hurts others; another great work opportunity equates to high blood pressure and joyless life; one more late-night meeting away bears the fruit of a distant spouse. Time has a way of forcing things to get the attention they need. Many in our culture have lived with a deep sense of *unnoticedness* for too long. And it is time for us to take notice.

Jesus tells a story of a person who was traveling from Jerusalem to Jericho. Along the way the person gets attacked, brutally beaten, robbed and left on the side of the road to die. Three people traveling the same road come across this dying man. The first two, as Jesus tells it, are ostensibly good, righteous people in their community who, when seeing the man, "pass by on the other side." But the third person, a Samaritan, a hated outsider in that neck of woods, sees the man on the side of the road, feels compassion for him, reaches out and rescues him, providing all that he needs and more (Lk 10:29-37).

It is a most familiar story of neighborliness. Three portraits or pictures emerge in the story: a portrait of need (*on the side of the road*), a portrait of avoidance (*passing by on the other side*) and a portrait of compassion (*the Samaritan's kindness*). And these three pictures can certainly take us in many good and fruitful directions. In particular, they challenge us to personally identify with the thrust of Jesus' story within our set of circumstances, people and places. We must ask ourselves: Where are our roads from Jerusalem to Jericho today? Are we noticing those in our setting? How do we *pass by on the other side* when we encounter such need?

In the *New York Times* bestseller *Tuesdays with Morrie*, journalist Mitch Albom tells us of a special person, his mentor and favorite college professor, Morrie Schwartz. The book recounts the final year of Professor Schwartz's life, as he shares himself with Mitch, a former student and now Detroit sports journalist. Mitch's reflections upon Morrie's life, influence and death have been, for many, a simple reminder of the profound influence one person can have on another. Among all the stories of this enchanting man there is one in particular that lingers. Mitch writes:

> The Morrie I knew . . . would not have been the man he was without the years he spent working at a mental hospital just outside Washington, D.C. . . . Morrie was given a grant to observe mental patients and record their treatments. While the idea seems common today, it was groundbreaking in the early fifties. Morrie saw patients who would scream all day. Patients who would cry all night. Patients soiling their underwear. Patients refusing to eat, having to be held down, medicated, fed intravenously.
>
> One of the patients, a middle-aged woman, came out of her room every day and lay facedown on the tile floor, stayed there for hours, as doctors and nurses stepped around her. Morrie watched in horror. He took notes, which is what he was there to do. Every day, she did the same thing: came out in the morning, lay on the floor, stayed there until the evening, talking to no one, ignored by everyone. It saddened Morrie. He began to sit on the floor with her, even lay down alongside her, trying to draw her out of her misery. Eventually, he got her to sit up, and even to return to her room. What she mostly wanted, he learned, was the same thing many people want—someone to notice she was there.[2]

---

[2]Mitch Albom, *Tuesdays with Morrie: An Old Man, a Young Man, and Life's Greatest Lesson* (Port-

Mitch's recollection of Morrie's kind response to this suffering woman paints a powerful and resonating picture. There are a tremendous amount of people today who on the outside appear fine, but whose inner suffering is reminiscent of this woman's experience: *What she mostly wanted was the same thing many people want—someone to notice she was there.* Whether sitting across the table from a lonely and confused high school student, or a midcareer professional who has just been laid off, or a pastor who has been serving faithfully for years but wonders if anyone sees his need, one so often hears "between the lines" a deep and painful sense of unnoticedness.

Psychologists tell us that much pathology and mental disease result from the experience of being unnoticed, especially early in life. Our communities, in their many forms, somehow do not notice and care for the person in the way he or she is designed to be noticed. Consequently, early on, people internalize the pain of this unnoticedness. Over time they learn to compensate for this pain in many different ways. Some become high achievers. Others become very skilled at entertaining or pleasing others. Some withdraw. Others addictively attach themselves to someone else. All of them ache for someone or something that will address their deep sense of unnoticedness. We have to wonder, as we sit in church or a coffee shop or as we walk through the supermarket, how many of the people around us feel isolated and overlooked? That is, inwardly, do they seemingly lie facedown on the tile for hours ignored by everyone? Are they longing for someone to pay attention in simple and very human ways?

As we notice our own world, we see a collective overlooking that runs rampant through society. So much of our contemporary life involves the experience of being the stranger, and this is sadly even the case in our Christian communities. We have been going to malls and hospitals and universities and airports and sporting events and even churches where the vast majority of the people we are surrounded by— we do not know. Anonymity characterizes so many of our social interactions. And these impersonal dynamics perpetuate and even aggravate

land: Broadway Books, 1997), pp. 109-10.

the already internalized unnoticedness of so much of our lives.

Mother Teresa of Calcutta said, "Do small things with great love," and it seems that what is needed today is this sort of challenge, resonating through our many daily interactions, everyday conversations and community life. Who are the people we are already surrounded by, the men and women on the edges of our attention, with whom God might be inviting us to walk more closely? Perhaps they are in our neighborhoods; perhaps they sit next to us in Sunday morning worship or report to us in our mission. Amid our fast-paced and independent lives, many are beginning to wonder why things are as they are and hope for a better way—a way that imitates the Samaritan's mercy and courage (Lk 10:30-37) by intentionally slowing down and walking compassionately with others.

Jesus' way of noticing *the other*, not from behind a pulpit, lectern or computer screen, but up close and personal, confronts how we so often go about doing what we do for God. Although Jesus had a lot to accomplish in his rather short time on earth, his approach was unhurried and compassionate—inviting people, often one at a time, to sink more deeply into the truth of their lives. Sharon Daloz Parks tells us that this sort of attentiveness requires "a seeing heart." She elaborates, "Paying attention, as the phrase suggests, requires an active investment of self— and a certain vulnerability to the phenomenon at hand. It asks us simultaneously to be awake, to be present, to observe, to see, to listen, to hear, and to feel."[3]

If we are concerned with the leadership formation of others, and if we desire to imitate Jesus' way, then we must pay attention with *a seeing heart* to those around us. But this sort of seeing and noticing with compassion is not easily cultivated in today's world. There are cultural conditions that frustrate such an investment in and attentiveness to the other. Four conditions in particular are worth mentioning. Each of these reflects a different aspect of what we find normal today. And it is this "normal" that must be resisted if we are to live and serve and develop others in Jesus' name.

---

[3]Sharon Daloz Parks, *Leadership Can Be Taught: A Bold Approach for a Complex World* (Boston: Harvard Business School Press, 2005), pp. 244-45.

Condition 1: Skimming the surface. In September 1999 we were invited by James Houston to attend the International Consultation on Discipleship in Eastbourne, England. The conference addressed the question of how the global church is doing in its discipleship efforts. John Stott was the keynote speaker for the conference. He began his address by sharing a startling thought from his friend J. I. Packer, whose concern for the church, particularly in the West, was that it seemed to be suffering from a "1000 miles wide but a ½ inch deep" syndrome. As he continued his talk, Stott echoed his friend's concern.

> I wonder how you would sum up the Christian situation in the world today. For me, it's a strange, rather tragic, and disturbing paradox. On the one hand, in many parts of the world the church is growing by leaps and bounds. But on the other hand, throughout the church, superficiality is everywhere. That's the paradox. Growth without depth.
>
> No doubt God is not pleased with superficial discipleship. The apostolic writers of the New Testament declare with one voice that God wants his people to grow up and grow into maturity in Christ.[4]

And his perspective on our superficiality is not a solitary one. Richard Foster introduced his landmark evangelical book *Celebration of Discipline* with the observation that "Superficiality is the curse of our age. The doctrine of instant satisfaction is a primary spiritual problem. The desperate need today is not for a greater number of intelligent people, or gifted people, but for deep people."[5]

Foster argues that "surface living" will not sustain us for the long haul if we are to remain faithful to Jesus. We must move into the depths. We are hard pressed to find a time in history when the church has gone more places, has activated more efforts, has provided more resources and has proclaimed the gospel more widely than in the past several decades. Yet there is rising from among all this activity a realization that we are just skimming along the surface. As Gordon MacDonald looks around the church he concludes

---

[4]Siang Yang Tan, *Full Service: Moving from Self-Serve Christianity to Total Servanthood* (Grand Rapids: Baker, 2006), p. 135.
[5]Richard J. Foster, *Celebration of Discipline: The Path to Spiritual Growth* (San Francisco: Harper & Row, 1978), p. 1.

that our branch of the Christian movement (sometimes called Evangelical) is pretty good at wooing people across the line into faith in Jesus. And we're also *not bad* at helping new-believers become acquainted with the rudiments of a life of faith: devotional exercise, church involvement, and basic Bible information—something you could call Christian infancy.

But what our tradition lacks of late—my opinion anyway—is knowing how to prod and poke people past "infancy" and into Christian maturity.[6]

Many people are discovering that kingdom growth requires much more than a surface-level approach. But how is this accomplished when so much of what is offered today by way of discipleship and leadership formation are simplistic tips and techniques, and quick fixes? Just a quick glance around our communities reveals that people's lives are more often a reflection of the superficiality of our culture than of the freedom and power of the gospel. How then are we actually helping people to mature into lives of greater compassion, integrity, wisdom and service in Jesus' name?

Many leaders are longing to live with greater understanding and faithfulness to God. Amid the complexity and busyness of their lives, they are hoping for more out of their life with God than what they are currently experiencing. They are asking questions of the heart as well as the hands, character as well as action. And their development requires an investment of time and attention, prayer and community that can too often get put to the back burner due to the tyranny of the urgent. Other leaders are hoping to simply succeed or get by with what they already know. Self-sufficiency, pride and fear in their lives result in a posture of indifference or even resistance to growth. Sadly unless something wakes them up from this self-deceptive slumber, they will cheat both themselves and the communities they serve. In either case, the conditions today are certainly not favorable for deepening people's lives. The hopeful news is that this was as much a countercultural work in the apostle Paul's day.

---

[6]Gordon MacDonald, "Leader's Insight: So Many Christian Infants," *Leadership Journal*, October 1, 2007, www.christianitytoday.com/le/currenttrendscolumns/leadershipweekly/cln71001.html.

> We must no longer be children. . . . But speaking the truth in love we
> must grow up in every way into him who is the head, into Christ, from
> whom the whole body, joined and knitted together by every ligament
> with which it is equipped, as each part is working properly, promotes
> the body's growth in building itself up in love. (Eph 4:14-16)

We must stand alongside the many other followers of Jesus Christ who
over the centuries have encountered Paul's challenge to the community
in Ephesus. Men and women who confessed faith in Jesus have discovered their lives to be too often fearful, preoccupied and superficial
well into their faith journeys. And amid these hard discoveries they
graciously encountered God's Spirit inviting them afresh *to grow up in
every way into Christ.*

In our more honest moments we may have the courage to realize that
part of the problem of investing in the formation of others is not really
the different excuses we offer but that we ourselves may be living very
superficially in our relationships with God and others. Do we possess a
spiritual maturity capable of holding up the work we have been given to
do? It seems as though the time has come for the plow to sink deeper
into the soil of discipleship.

Condition 2: One size fits all. There has also been a prevalent tendency in adult discipleship and leadership formation efforts to adopt
one-size-fits-all approaches. In large measure this tendency is simply a
reflection of our larger culture. We are relentlessly approached as part
of a market in which we purchase certain goods or services. Mass ad-
vertisements customize their pitch to speak to our needs and wants,
given our purchasing power. And within this stream of things for sale
are a seemingly endless supply of how-to solutions to identified
problems. How to install a sink, how to raise a middle child, how to
plant a garden, how to train a horse, how to pray, how to read a book,
how to restore a 1962 Nova, how to use a computer operating system.
Such resources are wonderfully helpful for technical or mechanical
things. They are able to offer proven techniques and methods for complexities that are beyond the consumer's skill set.

These all-pervasive how-tos have revealed a tremendous appetite
and market, and in turn have shaped our expectations for general solu-

tions to all our problems. We are conditioned to think that if there is a problem, it can be solved with the correct technique or method. In many cases this assumption is accurate, but certainly not in all. In reality the most deeply human concerns (e.g., community and meaning, work and family and purpose) cannot be squeezed into generalized solutions. In such attempts the people and the challenges involved tend to get reduced to something less than what they are. The complexities of people and relationships, thinking and feeling and deciding, culture and setting, demand a profoundly nuanced and particular work. These complexities require an approach that honors the unique person and the unique setting. No matter how much our communities demand a simple, pragmatic solution, sometimes we must be willing to say no because it will not be adequate. In this regard Christian leadership formation must be an act of cultural resistance.

We certainly share themes and contexts with others, but each life is not identical to any other. In this sense we are *originals*. It is at the beginning of life and at the end of life that we most often recognize this originality. Beside the crib of a baby girl or at the bedside of an ailing grandparent, the unrepeatable nature of a human story is impressed on our hearts. We are awakened to the preciousness of a person as we hold the tiny fingers or caress the weathered and trembling hand. But day to day, we too easily overlook the precious and particular reality of our neighbor who has been created in the image of God. And consequently our communities suffer.

The default approach of some congregations and organizations in dealing with people is more often than not to reduce them to their lowest common denominator and then to reach out as broadly as possible in order to attract as many as possible. Frequently, such places are on a quest for the right programs or techniques (small group curricula, more Bible studies, satellite-fed conferences, another good book or two) to meet the demand. It would be rather refreshing to discover a congregation or organization that intentionally chose to have as their default a more particular way of noticing and addressing the learning and formational needs within its community. How do we come to value an economy of "leaving the ninety-nine for the one" when it comes to the formation of others? A generalizing, one-size-fits-all approach can certainly perpetuate overlooking people—who they are uniquely, their particular dreams and hopes, and what could happen through them if they were noticed, invited and empowered.

Perhaps our thinking and efforts have become clouded by what James Houston calls "a culture of experts." We have turned over the practice of the Christian life to the opinions of the experts rather than trust the work of the Spirit among the rest of us. Houston writes,

> What we have subtly been doing in this professional approach to ministry is substituting techniques and technology for love. Even worse, it is the loss of God in daily life that promotes the demand for human expertise. We have become a culture of "experts" because we need authority figures in our lives to replace the divine authority our culture has now denied.[7]

Expertise is certainly no substitute for love in this sanctifying and formative work. And we must prayerfully learn this reality repeatedly as we seek to help others develop along the way. Our work is not grounded or authorized by our professionalism or expertise or technique, but by God's loving way with us and through us. What if ordinary men and women discovered that they too had a significant role to play in God's ongoing restoration story? If we believe that they have already been invited and prepared by God for a *good works way of life* (Eph 2:10), then they are among us—waiting to be noticed, invited and empowered. And the Spirit of God goes ahead of us in this process.

Condition 3: Means toward ends. So much of our leadership work nowadays results in using people instrumentally to some greater end. Consequently, our visions, our missions, our strategies, our efforts to help people in general can subtly begin to devalue particular human lives. We use people for "larger, nobler" purposes, in which they are reduced to functions or roles in our efforts. In our world, in which human life is so often devalued, we need to be particularly conscious of the ways our activities can devalue human life. So whether we are looking for volunteers, putting together a team or developing a building project,

---

[7]James M. Houston, *Letters of Faith Through the Seasons* (Colorado Springs: Cook, 2006), 1:175.

people are never to be viewed or used simply as resources or capital, as we might speak of things like money or two-by-fours or vehicles.

"What will *we* get out of this initiative?" was the response that came from Pastor Bob. This question made some sense since Bob had to carefully steward his senior leadership team. The thought of having two of his staff invest a relatively large amount of time each week tending to the learning of eighteen to twenty people seemed an obvious misuse of staff resources. Especially since these two team members had the responsibility of providing oversight for the adult educational programming for the 2,800 people who attended Church of the Savior. Moreover, the congregation recently voted to "leverage its impact" by purchasing several acres in a high visibility location in order to build a multimillion-dollar facility, a resource they felt was necessary in order to further reach out to those in need. All initiatives in the church within the next two years were to focus on two things in order to fulfill its vision of growth: (1) enhance the worship services, and (2) teach people how to share their faith with others. After a while Pastor Bob made his decision known. They would need to find more efficient ways to develop their leaders due to the impending work that needed to get done.

There were moments we wished we had more honesty and courage to respond to someone like Pastor Bob with what we really think. That didn't come until several meetings and encounters later with "Pastor Bobs" in many other places. Bob's (and, unfortunately, many others just like him) truer question was, How can I get more out of my people in order to do all the work that we have to do?

There is an economy-of-scale way of thinking that seems to have become an acceptable norm for those in leadership positions like Bob's. It is a way that suggests we must cut corners where we can in order to expand. The cost must decrease while the output must increase, and of course, all of this for good kingdom purposes. This economy-of-scale line of thought can also explain away why some ministries that have figured out how to get larger, become successful and shortly thereafter become our templates and models for what "effective ministry" should really look like for everyone, everywhere.

From time to time it is a good practice to question not only where we are going but how we are getting there. We have grown accustomed to seeking immediate results by whatever means can generate them. And although we would not think of ourselves so cold or indifferent or exploitive as to use people as a means to an end, our practices often reflect otherwise. Eugene Peterson poignantly observes that we have too often imitated our culture in *how* we do Jesus' work. He states,

> The ways Jesus goes about loving and saving the world are personal: nothing disembodied, nothing abstract, nothing impersonal. Incarnate, flesh and blood, relational, particular, local.
>
> The ways employed in our North American culture are conspicuously impersonal: programs, organizations, techniques, general guidelines, information detached from place. In matters of ways and means, the vocabulary of numbers is preferred over names, ideologies crowd out ideas, the gray fog of abstraction absorbs the sharp particularities of the recognizable face and the familiar street.
>
> My concern is provoked by the observation that so many who understand themselves to be followers of Jesus, without hesitation, and apparently without thinking, embrace the ways and means of the culture as they go about their daily living "in Jesus' name."[8]

We don't have to travel far to hear the stories of people feeling tired and used by employers, communities and churches. There is no shortage within Christian communities today of people feeling overworked and undernoticed.

We tend to pay attention to the formation of others in the same ways we ourselves have been developed. For many those means have been mostly at a distance—from someone speaking behind a pulpit or lectern, from someone strategically leading behind a board table, from someone behind a nicely ordered set of doctrines—but rarely *with* someone, life upon life. In contrast, Clinton's extensive study of Christian leaders who finished well noted two important observations in their development: (1) they viewed relational empowerment as both a means and a goal of ministry, and (2) they viewed leadership selection

---

[8]Eugene Peterson, *The Jesus Way: A Conversation on the Ways That Jesus Is the Way* (Grand Rapids: Eerdmans, 2007), p. 1.

and development as a priority function in their ministry.[9] For many of the things we put our hand to, there simply are no shortcuts, no quick fixes and no seven simple steps. Leadership formation is one of those things. *It begins with the simple act of paying attention to another.* Developing others is a slow work—and the way we get there is a relational way that honors the person. It is a way that invites walking alongside another at a pace that allows for careful noticing to take place.

Condition 4: Faster ways. In his book *In Praise of Slowness*, Canadian journalist Carl Honoré explores what he sees as one of the central and unchallenged assumptions of our modern society: "do everything faster." He recounts an awakening moment in his own hurried life when he was waiting for a flight home from London. While trying to pass the time by flipping through a newspaper, Honoré noticed an article titled "The One-Minute Bedtime Story." Initially the concept attracted him. Night after night of struggling with putting his son to bed, exhausted by this two-year-old's objections of "you're reading the story too quickly" or the cries for yet "another story," Honoré admitted an irresistible draw to the possibility of somehow accelerating this nightly ritual. He writes,

> To help parents deal with time-consuming tots, various authors have condensed classic fairy tales into sixty-second sound bites. . . . Rattle off six or seven "stories," and still finish inside ten minutes—what could be better? Then, as I begin to wonder how quickly Amazon can ship me the full set, redemption comes in the shape of a counter-question: Have I gone completely insane? As the departure lineup snakes towards the final ticket check, I put away the newspaper and begin to think. My whole life has turned into an exercise in hurry, in packing more and more into every hour. I am Scrooge with a stop watch, obsessed with saving every last scrap of time, a minute here, a few seconds there. And I am not alone. Everyone around me—colleagues, friends, family—is caught in the same vortex.[10]

---

[9]J. Robert Clinton, *Leadership Emergence Theory: A Self-Study Manual for Analyzing the Development of a Christian Leader* (Altadena, Calif.: Barnabas Publishers, 1989), p. 432.

[10]Carl Honoré, *In Praise of Slow: How a Worldwide Movement Is Challenging the Cult of Speed* (San Francisco: Harper, 2004), p. 2.

Honoré explores how modern life expresses this "cult of speed" in a variety of areas—food, urban life, medicine, sex, work, leisure, raising children. He sets his sights not against the modern technological life as a whole but rather against the all-pervasiveness of this "do everything faster" ethos. He goes on to say,

> The problem is that our love of speed, our obsession with doing more and more in less and less time, has gone too far; it has turned into an addiction, a kind of idolatry. . . . And yet some things cannot, should not, be sped up. They take time; they need slowness. When you accelerate things that should not be accelerated, when you forget how to slow down, there is a price to pay.[11]

And yet some things cannot, should not, be sped up.

We are busy, busy people. We are up to so many things, packing in our schedules as tightly as we can. Sometimes we even wear our busyness like a badge of honor. Some of us have even mistakenly equated busyness with significance. Or at least we find the inverse to be true—if I am not busy, then I am not significant. And it has been a long time since we can recall actually choosing to be busy, choosing to be in such a hurry. This busyness is just normal living in our neck of the woods. We live in the wake of this unchallenged assumption: *do everything faster.* And we have long forgotten how to *slow down.*

Nothing quite erodes our capacity to pay attention and invest deeply in another's life than day after day, month after month, year after year of hurried and hectic overactivity. Such a pace shrinks our imaginations, forfeits our joy and forces a defensive posture in all our relationships. Moreover, James Bryan Smith has recently stated, "The number one enemy of Christian spiritual formation today is exhaustion. We are living beyond our means, both financially and physically."[12] We are simply not designed to flourish at this pace. And if we never challenge this do-everything-faster assumption, then any effort that involves a deepening of relationships will appear to be a waste of our time.

---

[11]Ibid., p. 4.

[12]James Bryan Smith, *The Good and Beautiful God: Falling in Love with the God Jesus Knows* (Downers Grove, Ill.: InterVarsity Press, 2009), p. 33.

Our adult discipleship or leadership formation efforts must take into account this compelling (but profoundly distorting) expectation of *faster ways*. Most people, whether pastor or congregation, will be looking for shortcuts and quick fixes. We must resist the pressure to squeeze our formation efforts into an efficient shape. Paying attention to the growth of another necessitates much patience and perseverance. It requires "a long obedience in the same direction."[13] As with the prior three cultural conditions, our guiding and mentoring others in Jesus' name must be countercultural work; we must resist the impulse to accommodate this developing work to a culture that knows so very little about being formed into Christlikeness.

PAYING ATTENTION

These four cultural conditions implicate both our work and our person today. They have a way of skewing our attention, and even damaging our ability to cultivate the soil for the growth, learning and transformation of others to occur. And so we must grow aware of the ways we have been *skimming the surface* in the formation of others, or adopting *one-size-fits-all* approaches to how we guide those persons in our midst, or how we may have used people as *means toward ends*, or how we may become rushed and impatient with our approaches (*faster ways*). We must be vigilant of the way these four conditions do their work of distraction and erosion in our communities.

The leadership formation of others is a slow and deep work, and it is fundamentally a work of paying attention. We certainly get to participate and are even invited to place our signature on these *kingdom letters* (2 Cor 3:2-3) but our efforts must rest on the understanding that the primary shaping activity belongs to the Spirit of God. It is both an honoring and an exploratory sort of work, a work that demands we notice. After hearing a sermon one day, Barbara Brown Taylor describes how she left noticing the world differently:

---

[13]"A long obedience in the same direction" is a quote from Friedrich Nietzsche and title of Eugene Peterson's book *A Long Obedience in the Same Direction* (Downers Grove, Ill.: InterVarsity Press, 1980).

My friend's words changed everything for me. I could no longer see myself or the least detail in my life in the same way again. When the service was over that day, I walked out of it into a God-enchanted world, where I could not wait to find further clues to heaven on earth. Every leaf, every ant, every shiny rock called out to me—begging to be watched, to be listened to, to be handled and examined. I became a detective of divinity, collecting evidence of God's genius and admiring the tracks left for me to follow.[14]

Becoming "detectives of divinity" means looking for evidence, listening to the clues and asking questions in order to better know what is really taking place. Learning to guide the leadership formation of others is a similar work—we become detectives in search of the work God has already been up to in the lives of those before us. Detective work is a slow process requiring focused attention; so too in our work. We can learn from the stories of those who have come before us—what they encountered, how they matured, how they led and how they finished. Because we are dealing with the complexity of a person, our approach must be an honoring one that sets aside any notion of getting the job done by a carefully calculated schedule. In working with electricity there are times when electricians need to do their work with the electricity still on, still "live." Learning to guide the leadership formation of others is a live, electricity-still-on sort of work, one that requires alertness and respect and care.

The place where we pay attention to God's shaping activity is in the *story*. We are a storied people who are a part of the storied way of God. It is in the particularities of ordinary lives where we find the clues to what God has been up to. Kathleen Norris's *Quotidian Mysteries* invites the reader to consider the importance of paying attention to this ordinary, everyday stuff of life in order to discover the presence of God. She defines *quotidian* as that which occurs every day, belonging to the commonplace, the ordinary. Norris writes,

---

[14]Barbara Brown Taylor, *The Preaching Life* (Boston: Cowley, 1993), p. 15.

The Bible is full of evidence that God's attention is indeed fixed on the little things. But this is not because God is a Great Cosmic Cop, eager to catch us in minor transgressions, but simply because God loves us—loves us so much that the divine presence is revealed even in the meaningless workings of daily life. It is in the ordinary, the here-and-now, that God asks us to recognize that the creation is indeed refreshed like dew-laden grass that is "renewed in the morning" (Ps 90:5), or to put it in more personal and also theological terms, "our inner nature is being renewed every day" (2 Cor 4:16). Seen in this light, what strikes many modern readers as the ludicrous attention to detail in the book of Leviticus, involving God in the minutiae of daily life—all the cooking and cleaning of a people's domestic life—might be revisioned as the very love of God. A God who cares so much as to desire to be present to us in everything we do.[15]

Our leadership formation is fundamentally *a quotidian mystery*, a set of dynamics and people and events that are immersed in God's loving way with us. And we must pay attention to these many little things in our lives that often seem incidental and insignificant. For God is at work among us. So then our question, *How can we participate in the deepening and empowering of those given to the work of leadership?* begins with an invitation to wake up and pay attention with *a seeing heart* to the God-immersed lives of those many Oscars, Kims, Sarahs, Seons, Marios, Jimmys and Autumns in our communities. It is a deeper and more empowering vision for change.

REFLECT ON YOUR LIFE

- Reflect on the impact of the four culture conditions on your own life and ministry: What stands out to you?

- Who in your life is paying attention to your soul and your own formational needs? What do you suppose they are noticing?

- What does it mean for you to grow in your attentiveness, to become a "detective of divinity"?

---

[15]Kathleen Norris, *The Quotidian Mysteries: Laundry, Liturgy and "Woman's Work"* (Mahwah, N.J.: Paulist Press, 1998), pp. 21-22.

REFLECT ON YOUR CONTEXT

- Which of the following best expresses the leadership development need in your setting:
  - ‣ We are growing so fast we need more leaders.
  - ‣ Our current leaders lack spiritual maturity and depth.
  - ‣ We want to carefully cultivate a leadership development culture.
  - ‣ Our people need to learn how to live more missionally.
- What are the challenges to leadership development in your setting?
  - ‣ We have been too busy as leaders to develop others as leaders.
  - ‣ We lack know-how and a process to develop people well.
  - ‣ It's hard to get our adults to invest in their ongoing learning.
  - ‣ We are afraid if we make leadership development a priority we will take our eye off the ball of evangelism and mission.
- How well are you investing in adult spiritual formation in your setting?
  - ‣ Although we could always learn more, we do an excellent job.
  - ‣ Our people seem pleased but also long for something more.
  - ‣ We are doing the basics, but it simply isn't enough.
  - ‣ A majority of our adult believers lack spiritual maturity.

2

A STORIED WAY
What We Learn from Editing Our Lives

To be a person is to have a story to tell.

—ISAK DINESON

*The education of a leader is a complex thing. Certainly, talent
matters. But even the most naturally gifted still have a lot to
learn, and one of the most important things a leader needs to
learn is what he or she stands for: what he is made of, what she
believes in, what lines he will not cross. Crucible events and
relationships have the potential to reveal what a leader stands
for. Sometimes the revelation is immediate and obvious,
but it can just as easily take years to figure out. The key
is being able to notice, to be open to learning. . . .
We need to find ways to leverage the critical formative and
transformative experiences that men and women
have in their own lives that can reveal to them
who they are and where they stand.*

—ROBERT THOMAS, *CRUCIBLES OF LEADERSHIP*

*When you look on leadership development in terms of life's processes,
you quickly realize who the academic dean really is. It is God.
Each of us has the leadership courses that are individually
tailored for us by the Academic Dean.*

—J. ROBERT CLINTON, *THE MAKING OF A LEADER*

Jesus' way with others always offers an alternative to our culture's dominant ways of relating, one that seeps into every crevice of our relationships with one another. As we detailed in chapter 1, there is an awful lot of "passing by on the other side" that makes for normal relational life today. We simply miss one another—whether it is because we are moving too fast, we are fixated on our own agenda or any other variety of reasons. Whether conversing over a cup of coffee with an acquaintance, discussing plans around a conference table with co-workers or sitting at the kitchen counter with our teenage daughter, how are we paying attention to each other in a manner reflective of Jesus' way? How are we noticing these people in our midst?

The Gospels reveal a person who was intimately involved in the lives of the people he encountered. Whether it was the crowds that swarmed him, the enemies that challenged him and ultimately killed him, or the friends and followers who stuck with him, Jesus was immersed in a network of relationships. *Jesus was with people.* His life touched theirs. His head, hands and heart were available to those he lived with. He walked the journey with them as a friend. He was not distant, but lived in their stories, and he invited them to live in his. In considering how Jesus lived out his mission by forming and developing his learning community of disciples, we must not overlook this most obvious element: *personal relationship.* He had many other options available to him, but he chose to live out his purposes by *being with* his followers, life upon life.[1]

The cultural conditions have certainly changed since Jesus' first-century ministry, but the work of developing others still holds this inherent invitation, the invitation to *be with* others. There is no way of getting around this. It is a life-upon-life work. And a crucial way we can truly be with others today in a manner that both supports and challenges them to grow up into Christ is to *prayerfully pay attention with them to their life stories.* For it is amid the particularities of our lives that we discover, in part, God's character and transforming work in the world. The slow and deep work of developing others in Jesus' name,

---

[1]This theme is pervasive throughout the Gospels (e.g., Lk 5:30; 19: 1-10; 24:13-35; Jn 1:14; 1:35-39; 21:1-14).

amid our relentlessly impersonal culture, requires that we make space to explore the uniqueness of each of our stories. *It is a storied way.*

THE LIFE STORY FRAMEWORK

It was a Saturday afternoon in late January over twenty years ago when I (Rob) sat down at my kitchen table to complete my final college application. I had every intention of rushing through the application because I had a basketball game to get ready for later that night. But the fourth essay question slowed me down a good bit. Essay 4 went like this:

> Imagine it is your seventieth year and you have just completed your 457-page autobiography. Please submit page 221.

The *difficulty* of the question stopped me in me tracks. I struggled all afternoon trying to find something to put on page 221 of my life story. I can barely remember today how I answered the question. I think I wrote something about playing or coaching basketball, since that dominated my horizon of interest when I was seventeen. It was an awfully stressful couple hours spent cramming together an adequate response, the details of which I have long since forgotten.

But the *creativity* of the question has marked my memory. I answered a fair amount of college application questions that year, but only that one sticks with me today. *My life is a story.* Until that moment I had never imagined my life or anyone else's life as a story. Story was a framework for fiction and film, or so I thought. Over the years since that Saturday afternoon, I have discovered that this story framework offers more than just a clever way to describe our lives. It actually reflects the way we experience life. Each of our lives forms a narrative with themes and plot and characters and twists and tensions and disappointments and surprises. Daniel Taylor writes, "Seeing our lives as stories is more than a powerful metaphor. It is how experience presents itself to us. By better understanding story, and our role as characters, we can live more purposefully the kind of life that will give our own story meaning."[2]

---

[2]Daniel Taylor, *Tell Me a Story: The Life-Shaping Power of Our Stories* (St. Paul: Bog Walk Press, 2001), pp. 3-4.

Story *"is how experience presents itself to us."* Or as others have summed it up, "story is how we think of ourselves."[3] And as such, it can provide a very constructive way of making sense of our lives. We all have a unique story that is unfolding. Or, if you like, we *are* a unique story. Who we are today or tomorrow is inextricably linked with what has come before: our culture, family, circumstances, choices, location and so forth. A great deal of our life is behind us, yet we still look ahead wondering what might become of our stories.

Few greater gifts can be given to a person in today's largely anonymous and hurried social reality than an honoring awareness of his or her particular life story. Cistercian monk Michael Casey puts this so eloquently:

> It is my belief that in Western society we tend to underestimate the depth of human experience. We are more at ease dealing with objective facts and overt happenings than in opening toward what is beneath the surface. Undoubtedly this complicates life. One finds beneath a cheery, well-adjusted façade a vulnerability and a history of hurt. In the short term it is easier to interact by assuming a surface calm. Mostly we do not want to listen to pressures building up inside others; we prefer to hope they will muddle through, and (anyhow) we have enough worries on our own account. Perhaps the most necessary of all skills today is the timeless knack of being able to listen to others, allowing them to tell their story, knowing that telling it will ease their burden and help them become stronger.[4]

Casey points out that there is far more going in our lives than we tend to acknowledge or even recognize ourselves. We can live such distracted and superficial lives. Waking up to the depth and possibility of the life that we already live invariably requires the caring and discerning presence of others. As we come alongside others, we are invited by God to become living reminders of this startling reality—their story is unique and it matters deeply to God and to us.

---

[3]Richard L. Hester and Kelli Walker-Jones, *Know Your Story and Lead with It: The Power of Narrative in Clergy Leadership* (Herndon, Va.: Alban Institute, 2009), p. 9.
[4]Michael Casey, *Toward God: The Ancient Wisdom of Western Prayer* (Liguori, Mo.: Liguori/Triumph, 1996), p. 134.

For a number of decades now scholarship has demonstrated the developmental significance of taking a life story approach with adult learners. Research has found that utilizing a narrative approach on the journey with adult learners can be beneficial in a few ways. A story framework serves to

- invite the adult learner into a learning process
- foster connectivity for the adult learner
- offer objective choice for the adult learner[5]

A story framework serves to invite the adult learner into a learning process. We can live so unreflectively, always hoping to survive with what we already know. Yet if life teaches us anything along the way, it is that we still have so much more to learn if we are to flourish as people. We will not be able to get by without a good bit more learning. In this sense life is always preparation for more life. Yet how often do we sit with friends or colleagues and ask them, "What are you learning?" Why is this question brought up so infrequently as adults? Perhaps it is due to our common linkage of learning with formal schooling. Perhaps the question seems too childish or too self-disclosing. For whatever the reason, sometime in our growing up many of us got out of the habit of asking each other, and even ourselves, what we are learning. And sadly, for many of us, this has translated into a *diminishment* of paying attention to our life with God and others. And consequently, we are diminished as persons.

We need to find ways or processes to awaken ourselves or others from the slumber of conventional ways of living that are rooted in borrowed convictions, second-hand experiences and inattention. Thoughtfully looking back on our lives with a narrative perspective can launch us into a dynamic learning process. Remembering the critical incidents in our lives has a way of inviting us to consider related points from the rest of our stories. Paying attention to others' stories and how they have made meaningful sense of their lives challenges the learner to consider

---

[5]These three points were adapted from Randy Reese, *A Philosophy of Education for Leadership Development Through the Leadership Center Training Model* (Ph.D. diss., Fuller Theological Seminary, 2003), p. 85.

related points from his or her own story. And as we place our experience in an ongoing life-long learning perspective, potential has a way of being unlocked and discovered. Or as Steve Garber captures it, it is when "we understand that the deepest lessons are not learned in textbooks, but instead are discovered as learning meets life."[6] This sort of narrative learning process—*where learning meets life*—precipitates a thirst for more truthful and coherent ways of living.

A story framework serves to foster connectivity for the adult learner. Our modern lives can be so fragmented. Discontinuities abound between past and present, life at home and at work, understandings of self and neighborhood and world. Robert Bellah says,

> It is often said that people today find themselves "fragmented and exhausted." We rush from work to family to school to recreation to church, if there is time for church, shifting gears and changing personalities, it would almost seem, each time we move from one context to another. . . . [W]e jump into our cars and rush from one impersonal location to another, always hoping we can find a little solace at the end of the day at "home." But at home most of us spend several hours in front of a television set watching things jump around from drama to comedy to sports, always interrupted by incessant advertisements, in a way more chaotic than the rest of our lives.[7]

We survive by piecing together as many things as we can. Or we organize things into neat compartments to manage our dissonance. We struggle to make sense of life in a way that adds up to some sort of semicoherent whole. But for many of us, life remains a collection of pieces and parts that don't seem to all fit together or even mostly fit together. And we are fatigued.

Looking at our lives with a narrative orientation serves to foster connectivity amid these many discontinuities. It provides conditions to help us make greater sense of past and present experiences, and thereby

---

[6]Steven Garber, *The Fabric of Faithfulness: Weaving Together Belief and Behavior During the University Years* (Downers Grove, Ill.: InterVarsity Press, 1996), p. 102.

[7]Robert N. Bellah, "Max Weber and World-Denying Love: A Look at the Historical Sociology of Religion," *Journal of the American Academy of Religion* 67, no. 2 (1999): 279-80, quoted in Christian Scharen, *Faith as a Way of Life: A Vision for Pastoral Leadership* (Grand Rapids: Eerdmans, 2008), p. 15.

invites us to interpret our lives within the framework of a larger story. Consequently, we can begin to envision life more developmentally, rather than haphazardly as a collection of positive and negative experiences. And in turn this allows us to see and reflect on others' lives developmentally as well.

Coupled with prayerful reflection and the caring feedback of community, paying attention to our stories can provide a sharper picture of God's sovereignty at work among the everyday stuff that makes up our stories. We begin to sense that God creatively shapes and forms and redeems the good, the bad and the confusing things in our lives.

A story framework serves to foster objective choice for adult learners. "Is it possible for people to miss their lives in the same way one misses a plane?" Walker Percy asks in his novel *The Second Coming.* With his character Will Barrett—a lonely widower, recently retired from a very successful business career—Percy confronts us with a person who has confused all the activity of his life for genuine movement or growth. Such confusion has led Will Barrett, late in his life, to wonder whether he has "missed" his life.

> Not once in his entire life had he allowed himself to come to rest in the quiet center of himself but had forever cast himself forward from some dark past he could not remember to a future which did not exist. Not once had he been present for his life. So his life had passed like a dream.[8]

Will Barrett awakens to the illusions of his life and to the emptiness of his heart. And this unrest emerges from within him like an invitation— an invitation to step back and pay attention.

We are not passive spectators in our own lives, though many of us, like Will Barrett, try to live that way. Learning and growth requires being alert and responsive in one's world. By using this life story framework, we can step back and take a more objective look at the *what, when* and *who* of earlier chapters, thus both confirming what has taken place as we've matured, and confronting what is needed for further maturity. Educator Marsha Rossiter argues that *a narrative ori-*

---

[8]Walker Percy's character Will Barrett, quoted in Eugene H. Peterson, *Reversed Thunder: The Revelation of John and the Praying Imagination* (New York: HarperCollins, 1991), p. 192.

entation to adult development provides a more objective perspective from which adults can make decisions or choices for growth. She writes:

> The point is that the very act of telling or writing the story of one's own development enables a person to step back from it, to reflect on it, and to make choices about how to interpret it and how to change it. This— making choices about one's life narrative—is the key to understanding the power of telling one's own story. To be the teller or author of a story is to have authority over it—to choose what to tell and how to tell it, to determine the kind of story that it will be. This connection between authority and authorship makes the telling of the self-narrative empowering and potentially transformative.[9]

According to Rossiter, reflecting on our lives as a life story provides a way to understand our roles not just as actors but even authors in our unfolding stories. We are participants who can make choices and chart new directions. And this discovery can make all the difference in someone's life by instilling a renewed sense of empowerment and motivation. Daniel Taylor affirms,

> We are co-authors as well as characters. Few things are as encouraging as the realization that *things can be different* and that we have a role to play in making them so [italics added]. This is possible only if we are real characters not passive victims or observers. Seeing ourselves as active characters in new and healthy stories carries the power to transform lives.[10]

"Things can be different." This looking back provides perspectives that foster choice, even change in our present and future. Specifically, we can compare our narratives with the lessons learned from those who have gone before us and finished faithfully. If we believe that God is coauthoring our stories, then reflecting on the processes through which the Spirit has worked in our lives can facilitate a better understanding of what God may be up to in the rewriting of our stories. For when we prayerfully pay attention together to our lives, the Spirit of God invites and empowers us to greater cooperation with God's way in the world.

---

[9]Marsha Rossiter, "Understanding Adult Development as Narrative," *New Directions for Adult and Continuing Education* 84 (winter 1999): 83-84.

[10]Taylor, *Tell Me a Story,* p. 3.

Understanding our lives as stories or narratives certainly offers a number of directions for considering Christian leadership development. But of primary importance in this chapter is this reality—a developmental mindset with others requires a storied approach. *If we are going to walk alongside others, seeking to pay attention with them to what God is up to in their lives, then we must pay attention to the story of their lives.*

A DOUBLE KNOWLEDGE

The sort of attention to our stories that we have been suggesting is akin to the attention that Paul suggests when he exhorts the young pastor Timothy to "pay close attention to yourself and to your teaching; continue in these things, for in doing this you will save both yourself and your hearers" (1 Tim 4:16). Beyond getting all his doctrine and teaching in order, Paul challenges Timothy at the level of personal character. *Pay close attention to yourself, Timothy!* One may object to Paul, saying, "Isn't that a bit selfish?" or "Should I really be thinking about myself like that?" Consider: Is this attention any more self-centered than a pilot taking care to practice and gain confidence in his or her skills before taking passengers for rides in a plane, or any more selfish than an athlete training prior to competing, or a soldier drilling before going to war?

Engaging in the work of serving God and others without proper inward preparation and guidance is as spiritually foolish as climbing a challenging mountain without proper preparation is physically dangerous. There have been many "causalities" because leaders have failed to heed Paul's exhortation *to pay attention to yourself*—pay attention to your person, your character. We can be dreadfully self-deceived in matters of our own heart and true beliefs. Self-deception is one of the defining features of sin. But God's Spirit is working and stirring and healing at our heart level. We will not remain faithful to God over the long haul if we do not take seriously God's holy work in us.

One of the realities that emerges from the testimony of those who have walked with the Lord before us is that a heart to know God more intimately requires an openness to discover oneself more truthfully. There was an understanding among the early church fathers that true knowledge in the life of faith is always "a double knowledge." That is to say, knowledge of God and knowledge of ourselves are inextricably linked together in the life of faithfulness to God. Consider these later voices:

- *John Calvin (1509-1564):* "Our wisdom, in so far as it ought to be deemed true and solid wisdom, consists almost entirely of two parts: the knowledge of God and the knowledge of ourselves. . . . The knowledge of God and the knowledge of ourselves are bound together by a mutual tie."[11]

- *Bernard of Clairvaux (1090-1153):* "Know yourself and you will have a wholesome fear of God. Know God and you will also love God. You must avoid both types of ignorance, because without fear and love, salvation is not possible. Without knowledge of self, we have no knowledge of God."[12]

- *Julian of Norwich (c. 1342- c. 1416):* "For our soul is so deeply grounded in God and so endlessly treasured that we cannot come to knowledge of it, until we first have knowledge of God, who is the Creator to whom it is united. . . . And all of this notwithstanding, we can never come to the full knowledge of God until we first clearly know our own soul."[13]

- *Blaise Pascal (1623-1662):* "To know God and yet know nothing of our own wretched state breeds pride; to realize our misery and know nothing of God is mere despair; but if we come to the knowledge of Jesus Christ we find our true equilibrium, for there we find both human misery and God."[14]

- *Augustine (354-430):* "Grant, Lord, that I may know myself that I may know thee."[15]

---

[11]John Calvin, *Institutes of the Christian Religion*, trans. Henry Beveridge (Grand Rapids: Eerdmans, 1989), p. 37.

[12]Bernard of Clairvaux, quoted in James M. Houston, *In Search of Happiness* (Oxford: Lion, 1990), p. 189

[13]Julian of Norwich, quoted in Margaret Guenther, *The Practice of Prayer* (Cambridge, Mass.: Cowley, 1998), pp. 111-12.

[14]Blaise Pascal, quoted in Houston, *In Search of Happiness*, p. 189.

[15]Augustine, quoted in David Benner, *The Gift of Being Yourself* (Downers Grove, Ill.: InterVarsity Press, 2004), p. 20.

One wonders whether the perceived shallowness that seems to pervade much of the church today is in part due to our knowing many of the right answers, yet failing to integrate those answers into the reality of our daily lives. Somewhere along the way many Christians have abandoned this notion of a "double knowledge" dynamic in the Christian life. David Benner points out,

> Christian spirituality involves a transformation of the self that occurs only when God and self are both deeply known. . . . Though there has never been any serious theological quarrel with this ancient Christian understanding, it has been largely forgotten by the contemporary church. We have focused on knowing God and tended to ignore knowing ourselves. The consequences have been grievous—marriages betrayed, families destroyed, ministries shipwrecked and endless numbers of people damaged.[16]

There are many Christians floundering in their spiritual lives today because they have, in one form or another, failed to appreciate the interrelationship between knowledge of God and knowledge of self. Either they have falsely equated Christian maturity with a self-actualizing journey that ignores the horizon of God's character and work, or they have reduced their "growing up into Christ" into a heady exercise that equates biblical IQ with genuine sanctification. Benner continues,

> Focusing on God while failing to know ourselves more deeply may produce an external form of piety, but it will always leave a gap between appearance and reality. This is dangerous to the soul of anyone—and in spiritual leaders it can be disastrous for those who lead.[17]

A growing faith always involves recognizing our proclivity to choose appearance over reality. We must resist the temptation to deny the reality of our own hearts. When it comes to our hearts, we must—as Paul put it—*pay attention.* But this sort of attention must always be exercised in combination with an increasing attention and trust in God's holy and gracious character. *The life of faith in Jesus always involves a double knowledge.*

---

[16]Benner, *Gift of Being Yourself,* pp. 20-21.
[17]Ibid., p. 21.

One of the blessings of my (Rob) tenth-grade geometry experience was that the answers to the odd numbered questions could be found in the back of the book. So I always found the homework much more pleasant on those evenings when the odd questions had been assigned. I didn't have to wrestle as hard with the questions if I knew already what the correct answer was. On those dreaded evenings when the even numbers were assigned, my confidence was often shattered. I wasn't such a math phenom when I didn't have the ease and security of "the back of the book." My illusions were shattered.

For a significant portion of the church we attempt to live our Christian life, as it were, from "the back of the book." We grow up in the church developing a very high Bible IQ, getting rewarded in Sunday school with pieces of candy for answers like "sin," "Calvary," Jesus," "forgiveness," "heaven" and so on. What becomes rather disillusioning in adulthood is that "these answers we know from Scripture" and "the questions we have in our life" are not really matching up well. This is profoundly confusing. *Why do I feel like I am still searching when I thought I already knew what I was looking for? Why in the context of so many answers do none of them seem to satisfy or address me deeply? Why is it that my persistent struggles seem so ill fitted to the biblical answers that I have learned? What am I doing wrong?* We begin to discover that only even-numbered questions are assigned in our adult spiritual formation.

In many cases we can become stuck in our Christian lives not because we are ignorant of Scripture but because we are ignorant of our own hearts. We have failed to appreciate that true and godly wisdom always involves a double knowledge. The task that then lies ahead for our development is that we must begin to grow into the questions of our life. The biblical answers that we already know cognitively must be personalized and learned, that is, take on a shape particular to our life story. The prevailing impulse of our mentoring of men and women, both young and old, is to give answers, when the truer need may be *a consistent presence*—a patient listening—that helps others begin to grow into the central questions and deep need of their story. So, in our work of Christian leadership development, we must afford opportunities for others to "grow into their questions" in the light of a growing knowledge of God's character and work.

PERSPECTIVE: *The Life Stories of Others*

This deep mentoring in Jesus' name requires that we make space to explore the uniqueness of others' life stories. And these explorations can be greatly enhanced by learning from those who have come before us—those who have walked faithfully before us can offer perspective to our unique journeys.

Perspective. We often need perspective amid the pressures of the present and anxieties about the future. We need another point of view from which we consider our situation, our stories. When we struggle to understand what God might be up to in our lives or when we grow tired along the way, it is helpful to see what the Spirit was up to in others' lives during similar chapters. Their insights or experiences can enable us to become more hopeful and wise, as well as to gain a measure of preparedness for the journey ahead.

Seafaring explorers in the sixteenth century set out through unchartered waters, risking their lives against many dangers, in search of the New World. Absolutely essential to their journey was the records they kept. Alister McGrath explains the importance of such record keeping.

> The seaways to the New World destroyed many who had hoped to conquer them. Those who returned had learned the secrets of the routes and recorded them in a small book—the rutter. Rutters were the key to the secrets of the world's seaways and the best hope for a captain who wished to return home alive.
>
> A rutter was basically a book in which the ship's pilot recorded every detail of the voyage so that his steps could be retraced safely. It related exactly how he got to his objective and how he returned home. The rutter was priceless because it contained the detailed navigational records of someone who had been there and lived to tell others of what he found and how he got there. The rutter related how the pilot had steered for so many days on such and such a bearing and what he had encountered along the way. The location of dangerous shoals, the bearings of

landmarks such as headlands, the depths of channels, the location of safe harbors—all were meticulously recorded. Anyone getting hold of these rutters would be able to retrace the steps of those who had been there before and gain access to the riches that lay ahead.[18]

Wisdom suggests that we would do well to learn from those who have come before us, but we need *a rutter.* That's what the writer of Hebrews had in mind when he talked about those amazing persons of faith who have gone on before us—those men and women whose lives we are to remember and imitate (Heb 13:7). In many respects the work of J. Robert Clinton provides us a rutter of the life stories of those who have come before us—how and when God's shaping work took place within their lives, what it meant for them to follow and strive toward holiness, what they learned along the way, how they invested in the formation of others and how they navigated through the journey in order to faithfully finish well a lifetime of service. Taking notice from this rutter of sorts doesn't preclude the importance of the uniqueness of our own journey or that of others. Instead it can help us know what to anticipate and how to navigate accordingly. Here are some foundational elements to Clinton's theory and research, which can provide us the needed perspective for our journey.

THREE UMBRELLA CONCEPTS (P, T, R)

Foundational to Clinton's discoveries is that there are three concepts that compose Christian leadership development: (1) God's *processing* or shaping activity in a person's life, (2) over *time* and (3) a person's *response* to God's shaping action. Let's briefly explore each of these three in order to see how they can inform our reflections on developing others in Jesus' name (see fig. 2.1).

(P) God's **processing** *events in a person's life.* When we talk about the *processing* or *shaping* that God does in our lives, we are primarily referring to God's sovereign role in our development. There are critical incidents in a person's life through which God shapes him or her. These

---

[18]Alister E. McGrath, *The Journey: A Pilgrim in the Lands of the Spirit* (New York: Doubleday, 2000), pp. 33-34.

Christian Leadership Development = *f* (P, T, R)

f = a function of

P = God's processing events (shaping events) in the person's life

T = God's development of the person over time

R = the person's response to God's shaping action

Figure 2.1. Christian leadership development

incidents can be any key relationship or circumstance or event that has had significant influence in our shaping. Perhaps it was a gift given, a promise broken, a skill imparted, an experience on the job, the loving attention of an adult, a trip to another part of the world, and on and on. These events can be both positive and negative. God is sovereign, creative and utterly good. He is able to form and reform our lives even out of the most unlikely and painful circumstances and events we experience. Paying attention to some of these processing events in our lives opens us to a deeper discovery of God's good workmanship in and through us (Eph 2:10).

(T) God's development over **time.** We can learn so much from the narratives of others who sought to faithfully serve the Lord over the long haul. God's wise and timely faithfulness is far clearer in retrospect. One thing that jumps off the pages of people's lives is that God's shaping is *a lifelong process.* To fail to take this into account limits us to a very shallow understanding of who we are and who we might become. We too often become impatient, ignoring or minimizing the critical element of time in God's shaping work and in our response to God's shaping. Any sort of development as persons and leaders is a process over time.

(R) A person's **response** *to God's shaping.* We are not simply passive recipients of God's shaping in our lives. We have a critical role to play. The apostle Paul tells the believers in Philippi, "Work out your own salvation with fear and trembling; for it is God who is at work in you, enabling you both to will and to work for his good pleasure" (Phil 2:12-13). God does not impose his formation upon us. Our formation is a deeply shared process in which we play a responsive role. *Have we re-*

sponded faithfully to God's faithful working in and through us or have we for various reasons not recognized or even ignored God's shaping action over time? Reflecting on our narratives can uncover patterns of response to God's shaping action. Such discoveries from our past will prayerfully prepare us for the growth challenges we will face down the road.

THREE CRITICAL FORMATIONS

Clinton's research also led him to discover that there were three types of formation critical to a Christian leader's development: *character formation, skill formation* and *strategic formation*. Each of these formations holds a particular timing and purpose along the developmental process.

Character formation. Character formation relates to our spiritual maturation, which is concerned with the ongoing dynamics and qualities of our inner life or heart. The formation of godly character is absolutely essential to those of us who seek to influence this world in Jesus' name. Our ability to lead others fruitfully is inextricably linked with the maturing of godly character. Of the three formations, character formation is lacking significantly in the development of emerging leaders. It is the neglect of character formation early in our formation, as well as during those times when we are faced with significant challenges or transitions, that can precipitate barriers preventing us from finishing well.[19] *How are we giving attention to the shaping of the person?*

Skill formation. Skill formation is concerned with the skills, knowledge and practice related to the work of leadership. As a person develops there is a tendency to need development in the understanding of leadership dynamics related to the leader, the follower and the situation, as well as organizational development, influence means, giftedness development and motivational dynamics for those being led.[20] There is a tendency to move from a time of exploration, or a sort of trial-and-error approach to discovering certain capacities, to a time of

---

[19]See appendix 1, "Lessons from Those Who Have Come Before Us," for a more complete description of various barriers that have prevented those in leadership from finishing well.

[20]There are four cyclical patterns that repeat in each new ministry situation. These four patterns show a progression in skill formation: (1) entry, (2) training, (3) relational learning, and (4) discernment (J. Robert Clinton, *Leadership Emergence Theory* [Altadena, Calif.: Barnabas Resources, 1989], p. 395).

learning where skills are enhanced, to a time of practice where certain competencies are matured. *What is involved in the work of leadership?*

Strategic formation. Strategic formation looks at the development of a coherent ministry philosophy of values, which serves to steer the person toward a more effective, focused and purposeful life and ministry. Paying attention to strategic formation in the mid to latter chapters of one's development brings a movement toward the desire to deepen one's inner life, while at the same time invest more particularly in the leadership formation of others. In other words, as a leader matures, greater concern emerges for the development of other leaders who will either carry on with the given work of the kingdom or be empowered to do uniquely what God has called them to do. *How do I deepen my own inner life, while at the same time investing in the formation of others?*

A TIMELINE PERSPECTIVE

Clinton's research also reveals that leaders go through some similar chapters or phases in their development. He explains:

> A development phase is a unit of time in a person's life. We identify different units by the nature of the development or the means for development in a leader's life. . . . Development phases are not absolutes. They are helpful, however, because they force one to analyze what God was doing during a given time in a person's life.[21]

Generally speaking, these chapters reflect a developmental movement toward maturity and a perceived fulfillment of God's purposes for their lives. These phases can be best portrayed through the use of a timeline. A timeline perspective brings with it certain limitations. The most obvious one being that life does not consist of clear divisions along a straight line, but is made up of twists and turns and lessons along the journey that may prove to be more cyclical in nature. However, as limiting as a timeline may appear, it provides a very helpful way of thinking about various seasons and transitions along the journey.

Clinton's theory can be useful for providing a general *description* of one's development in comparison with the journey of those who have finished

---

[21]J. Robert Clinton, *The Making of a Leader* (Colorado Springs: NavPress, 1988), p. 44.

well. As we will discover in part 2 of this book, there are certain developmental cues we can listen for and begin to notice as we walk alongside others in their formation. Being cognizant of some of the more significant times of development and then describing those places along the journey for others can provide them significant hope. Understanding the timeline perspective can also be useful for *predicting* what others might encounter in their development. And finally, the theory can be helpful in carefully *prescribing* what might be needed next for one's ongoing maturity (see fig. 2.2).

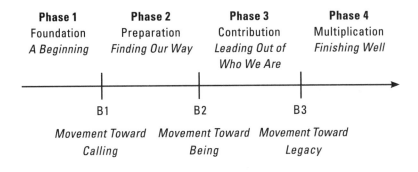

Figure 2.2. Timeline perspective

Phase 1. Foundation. Generally this is the time of growing up as a person: childhood, early and late adolescence, and young adulthood. It is the time when our "defaults," or habits of managing life, become instilled within an individual. Various factors shape our personality for the journey ahead. Family of origin, other social influences and the historical context within which the person lives all give shape to who the person becomes. The early formation of basic skills needed for leadership may also be fostered, as well as possible hints of personal destiny. God's sovereign shaping always remains in the background of this growing up process. For some this will remain a difficult presence to discover and trust because these years were deeply painful. For others who look back it is a confirmation of who God is, who they are, and what God has called them to do.

Phase 2. Preparation. It is through an extended period of preparation lasting anywhere from ten to twenty-five years that God's work *in* us seems to be paramount in his development *of* us. A person initially establishes a maturing commitment to God, evidenced by the continued development and testing of character growth in holiness. Along the way an individual develops an experiential understanding of the body of Christ. During this time a person is also given increased responsibility, and in conjunction with this he or she (1) becomes more deeply aware of his or her giftedness and (2) seeks to develop skills that enhance that set of gifts. Although we are learning competencies and developing proficiencies during this time, we are still maturing toward the good work God has prepared for us. God is more concerned in the preparation phase with who we are becoming than our ability to do.

Phase 3. Contribution. Phase 3 is a person's most highly productive and effective period of service and influence. Through the Spirit's shaping, the person comes to terms with the reality that his or her service is inextricably linked to identity in Christ. That is, we serve out of who we are. This realization aids in the development of a mature, biblical way of life and service grounded in obedience and intimacy with God. The person thereby increasingly influences others with spiritual authority. And God's sovereign shaping moves the person toward a contribution of work that provides a greater *focus* of service and greater *fit* with the person's being, calling, passion, giftedness and style.

Phase 4. Multiplication. The final phase of development invites us toward deeper growth and maturity in following the Lord, while at the same time stewarding what God has given us to do. However, in the multiplication phase a deeper concern grows within us for the investment and development of others. We are at a time in the journey when we hold the benefit of wisdom and experience to pass on to others. And we also develop a growing desire to recognize others and call them out to be mentored, deepened and empowered for the good work God desires to do through them. Developing others for kingdom influence becomes the focal point of our efforts. *We learn to lead strategically by tending to the deep work within us while at the same time tending much more intentionally to the development of others.*

A NOTE ON TRANSITIONS (BOUNDARY TIMES)

You will notice on the timeline (see fig. 2.2) lines of demarcation signifying a change from one major season of growth to another. These changes represent transitional movements referred to as boundaries. Clinton defines a boundary time as "an identified period of time embracing the transition a leader goes through in moving from one developmental phase or sub-phase to another."[22]

There are three major transitional movements that take place in the life of a Christian leader. The first is a *movement toward calling (B1)*, where the events of one's life culminate to stir within the person a desire to surrender all of one's life to follow and serve wherever God may lead. The second is a *movement toward being (B2)*, where a person comes to discover through a radical paradigm shift that the work and *service* of leadership must flow out of who we are—our being. And the third major transition can be referred to as a *movement toward legacy (B3)*, where the driving concerns for the person becomes how one will continue to deepen their own inner life, while at the same time invest more intentionally in the formation of others.

These major transitional movements become heightened times of learning for those going through them. Guiding the leadership formation of people during boundary times requires a careful approach in order to partner with the work of the Spirit as well as seize the teachable moments that will emerge.

EDITING OUR LIVES

It is critical that we remember all are unique persons. Clinton's general timeline is not meant to pigeonhole or force our life experience into these four chapters whether they fit or not. Life is far too complex for such a simple application of this theory. Rather figure 2.2 offers a helpful point of view from which we can prayerfully consider what God has been doing in our life or in the life of another. It offers *perspective* on where we have come from, where we are currently and where we might be heading.

Few recent books have helped communicate the transforming power of understanding our lives as a story better than Donald Miller's *A Million Miles in a Thousand Years: What I Learned While Editing My Life*. While working on the movie adaptation of his previous memoir-like book *Blue Like Jazz*, Miller discovered the possibility that what makes for a compelling story is the same thing that makes for a compelling life. *A Million*

---

[22]Ibid., p. 236.

Miles in a Thousand Years is an exploration of his discoveries along the way of editing his life. He begins the book with this short scenario:

> If you watched a movie about a guy who wanted a Volvo and worked for years to get it, you wouldn't cry at the end when he drove off the lot, testing the windshield wipers. You wouldn't tell your friends you saw a beautiful movie or go home and put a record on to think about the story you'd seen. The truth is, you wouldn't remember that movie a week later, except you'd feel robbed and want your money back. Nobody cries at the end of a movie about a guy who wants a Volvo.
>
> But we spend years actually living those stories, and expect our lives to feel meaningful. The truth is, if what we choose to do with our lives won't make a story meaningful, it won't make a life meaningful.[23]

In essence, he confronts the reader with the question, Are we living a good story or have we settled for something far less? According to Miller the central reality of a good and meaningful story is *character transformation*. The character in the story faces all sorts of challenges, tests and conflicts along the way, but he or she is able to courageously face them and thereby change and grow through them. Out of conversation with a friend, Miller wonders whether we weren't primarily "designed to live through something rather than to attain something, and the thing we were meant to live through was designed to change us. The point of the story is the character arc, the change."[24] Sure there are deadlines to meet and goals to achieve, but perhaps the greatest thing in our development is who we are becoming along the way. And somehow God then delights in using who we are along the way to accomplish "greater things than these" (Jn 1:50).

It is the subtitle of Miller's book that lingers with us as we consider the slow and deep work of developing others—*what I learned while editing my life*. What can we learn from looking back on our life? What can we do to help others learn as they edit their lives? Guiding others involves walking *with* them and inviting them to see and accept their story as God's curriculum for their transformation. And this requires great courage and loyal friendship.

---

[23]Donald Miller, *A Million Miles in a Thousand Years: What I Learned While Editing My Life* (Nashville: Thomas Nelson, 2009), p. xiii.
[24]Ibid., p. 70.

Both Megan and Gary reflected deeply on their faith narratives in the company of some fellow believers at their church. A task for each participant in the group was to develop a timeline and then write a spiritual narrative of their lives. The goal of this effort was to help them seriously, honestly and courageously seek God's active and gracious presence within the story of their lives. For everyone in the group it was an absolutely eye-opening experience.

As Megan investigated God's activity in her story, she painfully discovered how much hidden shame she had lived with throughout her life. The grace and truth of the gospel was now reaching into deep parts of her inner person as a fifty-one-year-old woman. The more she reflected on her life in the context of Paul's words "We are God's handiwork, created in Christ Jesus to do good works, which God prepared in advance for us to do" (Eph 2:10) the more she recognized the Spirit's gracious invitation to turn from her false ways of seeing herself.

In the context of this group Gary discovered how little he had reflected on his life for the past twenty-five years of adulthood. He had drifted in and out of church for decades and never really thought seriously about what God had been up to in his life or in the world for that matter. By prayerfully reflecting on his life in the context of this loving small group, he experienced what he would term a wake-up call. After decades of holding a steady job and trying to raise a family, Gary began to sense that God had been preparing him—creating and shaping him for a long time—for something more both at home and within his vocational direction. He was just beginning to grasp the reality of God's loving character and way in his life.

Our journey throughout the next several chapters will entail learning how to faithfully pay attention *with* others (like Megan and Gary) to their stories so that we might discover together the Spirit's already present work. We can discover much if we take time to edit our lives.

In part 2 we will enter more deeply into the dynamics of each of these major phases of development from the timeline (fig. 2.2) in order to better recognize God's shaping activity in the lives of others. We will also discuss the significance of each of the transitional movements, as well as unpack what takes place more particularly during these important times of boundary. In part 3 we will then discuss how to become more effective guides and learn to cultivate the conditions for the leadership formation of others.

Paying attention to the stories of others invites us into our own. Clinton's discoveries will provide perspective on our own development. The lessons learned from the lives of others invite learning in our own lives, in the hope that somehow we might recollect our own experiences and relationships and circumstances and make sense of them from a kingdom perspective. In sum, Clinton's research provides us a rutter with which we travel as we pay attention to what God is doing in our lives and the lives of others.

REFLECT ON YOUR LIFE

- When was the first time you thought of your life as a story? From your perspective, what are the benefits of seeing each other's lives in a story framework?

- Think back on a time in your life when you were going through a significant transition or boundary. What did you learn during that time? Who walked alongside you during that time?

REFLECT ON YOUR CONTEXT

- What would it look like for your organization or church to become more developmental in its dealings with others? In other words, what would it look like for your community to really care about both the formation of its people and getting the job done?

- Robert Thomas says, "We need to find ways to leverage the critical formative and transformative experiences that men and women have in their own lives that can reveal to them who they are and where they stand."[25] What do you think Thomas means here? How would you create learning opportunities in your setting for this to take place in people's lives?

---

[25]Robert J. Thomas, *Crucibles of Leadership: How to Learn from Experience to Become a Great Leader* (Boston: Harvard Business Press, 2008), p. xii.

Part Two

Learning from Those Who Have Come Before Us

3

FOUNDATION
A Beginning

Our life is a faint tracing on the surface of mystery,
like the idle, curved tunnels of leaf miners on the face of a leaf.
We must somehow take a wider view, look at the whole landscape,
really see it, and describe what's going on here. Then we can
at least wail the right question into the swaddling band of
darkness, or, if it comes to that, choir the proper praise.

—ANNIE DILLARD, *PILGRIM AT TINKER CREEK*

God providentially works through family, contextual
background, and historical events including the timing of the
birth of each leader. Personality characteristics are formed. These
later will be reflected in the leadership style of the leader. Early
skills are learned. Early lessons of life are learned. Values
are inculcated. All of these will effect later leadership.
God is sovereignly working in this period of time.

—J. ROBERT CLINTON, *LEADERSHIP EMERGENCE THEORY*

Overview

Foundation Phase—Generally this is the time of growing up as a person: childhood, early and late adolescence and young adulthood. It is the time when our "defaults," or habits of managing life, become instilled within us. Various factors shape our personality for the journey ahead. Family of origin, other social influences and the historical context within which the person lives all give shape to who the person becomes. The early formation of basic skills needed for leadership may also be fostered, as well as possible hints of personal destiny. God's sovereign shaping always remains in the background of this growing up process. For some, this will remain a difficult presence to discover and trust because these years were deeply painful. For others who look back it is a confirmation of who God is, who they are, and what God has called them to do.

WHAT SORT OF TALE HAVE WE FALLEN INTO?

J. R. R. Tolkien's enchanted vision of Middle Earth has been one of the big cultural stories in recent years. In many parts of the world children and parents alike sat and read through this great tale, and people flocked to the cinema to see the movies. Both on paper and on the big screen *The Lord of the Rings* has stretched our imagination and challenged our convictions of what it means to live in the world. In offering an alternative world, a fantasy world, Tolkien confronts our world with questions of good and evil, of friendship and loyalty, of beauty and darkness, of power and hope. The characters are held together by an adventure of grand scale, perhaps grander than even the wisest of them imagine.

The hope of Middle Earth rests on the efforts of two hobbits who are on a quest to return a powerful and evil ring to the mountain in which it was forged. Frodo, as ring bearer, and Sam, his servant companion on the journey, go to Mount Doom to destroy the ring. In a world of elves and dwarves and orcs and eagles and men and wraiths and wizards, these hobbits, or halflings as they appear (when full grown they are the size of a child), are the most unlikely of adventurers, the most unlikely of heroes.

Let's listen in on one conversation between Sam and Frodo. At this point in the story they have already faced tremendous danger and have refused to turn back even though they doubt they can complete their task. Now exhausted and despairing, they rest, eat a small meal and talk together in the shadow of great evil. The darkest and most dangerous part of the journey is right in front of them and they sense it. Sam speaks,

> And we shouldn't be here at all, if we'd known more about it before we started. But I suppose it's often that way. The brave things in the old tales and songs, Mr. Frodo: adventures, as I used to call them. I used to think that they were things the wonderful folk of the stories went out and looked for . . . because they were exciting and life was a bit dull. . . . But that's not the way of it with the tales that really mattered, or the ones that stay in the mind. Folk seem to have just landed in them, usually—their paths were laid that way, as you put it. But I expect they had lots of chances, like us, of turning back, only they didn't. And if they had, we shouldn't know, because they'd have been forgotten. We hear about those as just went on—and not all to a good end, mind you; at least not to what folk inside a story and not outside it call a good end. You know, coming home, and finding things all right, though not quite the same—like Mr. Bilbo. But those aren't always the best tales to hear, though they may be the best tales to get landed in! I wonder what sort of tale we've fallen into?[1]

Sam's question is a good one to consider for ourselves as well as those in our settings: "I wonder what sort of tale we've fallen into?" Certainly there are relentless and subtle pressures in the modern culture that cause us to see our lives as less than what they are. When it comes down to it, we have a difficult time imagining anything grander than life as we have come to know it. *What sort of tale have we fallen into?* We have grown blind to the possibility of any larger tale. For many, even the Christian life is increasingly misunderstood, defined individually in terms of virtue, morality, knowledge and a few emotional experiences. But the sort of adventure of faith, hope and love in Christ, of which the apostle Paul speaks, is difficult to imagine, particularly in our own ordinary set of circumstances.

---

[1]J. R. R. Tolkien, *The Two Towers*, 2nd ed. (Boston: Houghton Mifflin, 1982), pp. 320-21.

It is a wonderful moment when we can help others realize God's Spirit has entered their particular story. Amid the circumstances of life—work and family, neighborhood and nation—when they pause and turn around they realize that God has been lovingly present and active all along. An even greater moment occurs when we guide others to discover that not only is God part of their story but they are part of God's story. The great tales never end—and "we're in the same tale still." The tale of Abram leaving his home and going where God leads, the tale of Moses returning to Egypt and leading the Israelites out of slavery, the tale of God disclosing himself so vulnerably and compassionately in the person and work of Jesus Christ, the tale of Jesus' promised return. These stories and much more compose God's story of reconciling this world to himself. And we have fallen into this same tale—this work of faith, hope and love.

One of the greatest dangers we face today is the failure to see our lives as part of this grand tale. We settle on living what we imagine to be a much smaller life. We understand the plot line of God entering our story, but we fail to realize we have entered God's story. Our stories are too small. And consequently our God is too small. Such ignorance is the enemy's great strategy in this age. *What sort of tale have we fallen into?*

Inviting others to return to the early chapters of their own story can be extremely helpful, for within them lie intimations of God's already-present and good work. We can then walk with them through their stories, helping them notice how God has been at work deepening their character in order to ready them for those "good works" he has prepared for them to do. It is interesting to note that if there is a neglect of "returning to the beginning," there will be fault lines that appear later on in one's life and leadership. We will come to learn that the leadership we provide essentially flows out of who we are. And if we have not come to honest terms with who we are, eventually that will show itself when the work of leadership becomes more stressful and challenging. It is hopeful to know that the forging process in our lives has been taking place along the way—if we only have eyes to notice.

WHY REMEMBER THE EARLY YEARS?

Steven Covey points out, "The Chinese bamboo tree is planted after the earth is prepared, and for the first four years, all the growth is underground. The only thing visible above the ground is a little bulb and a small shoot coming out of it. Then, in the fifth year, the bamboo tree grows up to eighty feet."[2] In the same way, much of God's early preparation in our lives goes on below the surface, so to speak, and the ultimate results are often not apparent until much later. The psalmist says,

> For it was you who formed my inward parts;
>> you knit me together in my mother's womb.
> I praise you, for I am fearfully and wonderfully made.
>> Wonderful are your works;
> that I know very well.
>> My frame was not hidden from you,
> when I was being made in secret,
>> intricately woven in the depths of the earth.
> Your eyes beheld my unformed substance.
> In your book were written
>> all the days that were formed for me,
>> when none of them as yet existed. (Ps 139:13-16)

God's formation of our lives is mostly invisible to us at first. When talking with Nicodemus, Jesus compares the Spirit's work to the wind. "The wind blows where it chooses, and you hear the sound of it, but you do not know where it comes from or where it goes. So it is with everyone who is born of the Spirit" (Jn 3:8). *It is an invisible personal work with visible personal effects.*

For many of us our growing up into Christ has been stunted because we have failed to recognize and appreciate God's shaping hand throughout our whole story. We tend to restrict our God attention to only certain parts of our lives that fit comfortably with our definitions of growth. We look for God where we expect God to be—church, weddings, funerals and the like. It is difficult to imagine that God could be present with us in time of failure or questioning, in moments

---

[2]Steven Covey, *First Things First* (New York: Free Press, 1996), p. 263.

of hurt or rebellion. But God uses the entire landscape of our lives to craft and mature us—the good, the bad and the ugly of our stories. It is with this entire landscape in mind that we want to briefly summarize three particular reasons for why it is important in our development to explore these early years.

Remembering these early years challenges us to live an examined life. Socrates said, "The unexamined life is not worth living." If we go through life without ever trying to make sense of where we've come from, where we are and where we'd like to go in the future, we will experience our lives very superficially or devoid of meaning altogether. It is unimaginable that this is the sort of life Jesus is inviting us to. The promise of the gospel requires an engaged and thoughtful consideration of our lives. Jesus says in John 10:10, "The thief comes only to steal and kill and destroy. I came that they may have life, and have it abundantly." Luke 9:25 records Jesus asking his followers, "What does it profit them if they gain the whole world, but lose or forfeit themselves?"

The Bible is full of admonitions for us to take regular stock of our relationships with God and others. Jeremiah pleads with his people in Lamentations 3:37-40,

> Who can command and have it done,
> > if the Lord has not ordained it?
> Is it not from the mouth of the Most High
> > that good and bad come?
> Why should any who draw breath complain
> > about the punishment of their sins?
> Let us test and examine our ways,
> > and return to the LORD.

As we mentioned earlier, Paul encourages the young pastor Timothy with these words in 1 Timothy 4:16, "Pay close attention to yourself and to your teaching; continue in these things, for in doing this you will save both yourselves and your hearers." The Scriptures urge us to invite those in our midst to be listeners, to examine themselves as an opportunity to turn back to God. Inviting others to live an examined life will help them cultivate good soil for what needs to grow.

Remembering these early years helps us to notice the significant role they have played in the unique shaping of who we have become. The ways we tend to respond to life were formed very early in our development. Looking back on our past allows us to pay attention to the habitual ways we tend to make sense of the world. These ways are descriptive of our personalities. The critical incidents of our pasts have contributed in so many ways to how we respond to the events, relationships and challenges of the present.

There are many psychometrics available today to help us better understand ourselves, but when used without an understanding of God's character and purposes, these tools often can lead to excessive excuse or shame ("I responded that way because it's my personality type," or "I'm no good because I have this sort of personality"), or unthinking acceptance ("I am who I am and people just need to accept that"). We need God's help in making sense of who we are and who we might become.

In our adult years we begin to recognize that some of the ways we learned to habitually see and respond to the world are actually ways of living and surviving without trusting God. Consequently, a deeper understanding of who we have become will clarify some of our unique waywardness and rebellion from God as well as our need for God. Looking back on these formative years can help us experience a greater sense of inner freedom and faithfulness as we realize our need for the Spirit's reforming work in our personalities and characters.

Remembering these early years challenges us to see and embrace the already present action and love of God in our lives. When we take the time to patiently examine our lives, we discover that God has been there all along. And it is this simple discovery that offers a providential awareness and hope to our lives. It is the simple recognition of the hand of God that moves us from randomness to order, from confusion to perseverance, and, in time, from unawareness to gratitude. In his essay "A Room Called Remember" Buechner writes:

> "Remember the wonderful works that he has done," goes David's song—remember what he has done in the life of each of us, and beyond that remember what he has done in the life of the world; remember above all what he has done in Christ—remember those moments in our

own lives when with only the dullest understanding but with the sharpest longing we have glimpsed that Christ's kind of life is the only life that matters and that all our other kinds of life are riddled with death; remember those moments in our lives when Christ came to us in countless disguises through people who one way or another strengthened us, comforted us, healed us, judged us, by the power of Christ alive within them. All that is past. All that is what there is to remember. And because that is the past, because we remember, we have this high and holy hope: that what he has done, he will continue to do, that what he has begun in us and our world, he will in some unimaginable ways bring to fullness and fruition. . . . Remember and hope.[3]

Inviting others to this sort of remembering will certainly not uncover what every detail of their lives means, nor will every "Why did this happen to me?" be satisfactorily answered. But exploring the past will *provide perspective* for the particular work God has been doing all along—the Spirit's shaping work in our hearts. It will also *renew a hope* in God's deep and gracious love for his children. That is, discovering God's work in the past will foster a confidence that God's Spirit continues to do his loving work in and among us for the present and the future.

EARLY SHAPING EXPERIENCES

Anne Lamott looks back at her journey and compares the many different incidents of her life path to lily pads that brought her step by step closer to the verdant pad of faith.

> My coming to faith did not start with a leap but rather a series of staggers from what seemed like one safe place to another. Like lily pads, round and green, these places summoned and then held me up while I grew. Each prepared me for the next leaf on which I would land and in this way I moved across the swamp of doubt and fear. When I look back at some of these early resting places . . . I can see how flimsy and indirect a path they made. Yet each step brought me closer to the verdant pad of faith on which I somehow stay afloat today.[4]

---

[3]Frederick Buechner, *A Room Called Remember* (New York: HarperCollins, 1984), pp. 11-12.
[4]Anne Lamott, *Traveling Mercies: Some Thoughts on Faith* (New York: Anchor Books, 1999), p. 3.

What are some of the lily pads in your story or in the story of the person you are walking with?

We each need help and courage in seeing God's grace at work in our lives and our communities. For sometimes it is found in the most unlikely of places, as David cries out to God,

> Even the darkness is not dark to you;
>> the night is as bright as the day,
>> for darkness is as light to you. (Ps 139:12 ESV)

God is an immensely creative being who weaves together all the stuff of our lives into a holy and human shape. Our early years are foundational in our development. Paying attention to the different critical incidents of these early years is in many ways a hard and fearful work, but it can also be very freeing and healing when joined with a personal yearning to recognize and trust God's Spirit at work in our lives. Four lenses in particular can help us recognize important aspects of our early formation: (1) our cultural and historical context, (2) our family history, (3) our social base, and (4) the story behind our spiritual background.[5] If we grow are to mature in our capacity to be "detectives of divinity" then we will attentive with these four lenses to others' lives.

LENS 1: *Cultural and Historical Context*

What might be the significance behind the where and when of my life story?
Warren Bennis and Robert Thomas write in their book *Geeks and Geezers:*

> All of us come of age in a particular place and time—an era—that shapes us in large and small ways. Although we are rarely aware of this influence from day to day, our era determines choices both mundane and profound, from the music we prefer to the things that we long for, the things we take for granted, and much of the emotional coloration of our lives.[6]

---

[5]The process items, response patterns and other dynamics associated with leadership emergence theory used throughout the book and in particular within part 2 have been used with permission from J. Robert Clinton, and taken primarily from three of his basal resources: *Leadership Emergence Theory* (Altadena, Calif.: Barnabas, 1989); *Strategic Concepts That Clarify a Focused Life* (Altadena, Calif.: Barnabas, 1995); *Leadership Development Theory* (Ph.D. diss, Fuller Theological Seminary, 1988).
[6]Warren Bennis and Robert Thomas, *Geeks and Geezers: How Era, Values, and Defining Moments*

Our cultural and historical contexts have given shape to how we see and live in the world. Culture acts in many ways like a template shaping the way we see the world. It is not until well into our formation that we realize the nature of this template we have been given. For example, anyone growing up in North America in the past two hundred years has been formed in a very individualistic way. Cultural contexts are most often taken for granted and go unnoticed until we have an encounter with a different cultural template. When North Americans come into contact with a culture that offers a more collective and communal way of seeing the world, they then bump into some of the individualistic perspectives they have on the world.

Even within the same country there can be significant cultural differences that have a shaping effect. For example, consider the different perspective of one who grew up in a rural context with someone who was raised in a suburban or urban context. Or consider how someone who was raised in the subculture of a church community sees the world differently from the person whose first experience with the church comes in adulthood. Each of these examples reflects a difference of perspective and preparation due to time and place.

Historical events can also have a shaping effect in preparing a person for adulthood. For example, persons who grew up experiencing the Great Depression of the 1930s have vastly different perspectives on life, affluence and security from those who never knew such dire economic straits. The experience of the Great Depression pervaded a person's whole outlook for the rest of his or her life. Similarly, many in more recent years have a hard time imagining not having ready access to what they want when they want it. This too shapes how we approach people, opportunities and challenges that come our way.

God places people into particular places and particular times. Often the significance of these incidents may not come to light in a person's life until long after they occurred. For instance in the biblical story, the importance of Esther losing her parents and living with her cousin Mordecai in the capital of Persia is not fully realized by Mordecai until

---

Shape Leaders (Boston: Harvard Business School Press, 2002), p. 2.

after her ascension to the throne as queen of Persia and the onset of Haman's threats. Mordecai reveals his depth of insight to Esther: "For if you keep silence at such a time as this, relief and deliverance will rise for the Jews from another quarter, but you and your father's family will perish. Who knows? Perhaps you have come to royal dignity for just such a time as this" (Esther 4:14). In coming alongside others we must not ignore these larger cultural elements that form the backdrop of our growing up.

LENS 2: *Family History*

What might be the significance of my particular family background and history? Much of our shaping as persons has taken place within the context of our family story. Often our default responses to people and situations comes from what has been learned and who helped us learn it. Our more difficult times in walking alongside others in their formation will come as a result of discovering a link to something from our family past. Paying attention to our family of origin will shed significant light on who we are and how we eventually give our hand to the work of leadership—both positively and negatively. And sometimes what first appears as negative and painful pieces to one's story becomes the very pieces that brings hope, perseverance, perspective and even confirmation of calling later in life. Listen to part of the early family story of Leighton Ford:

> I was chosen in love by my adoptive mother, Olive Ford, but I was twelve years old before I knew this. My mother took me for a walk in High Park in Toronto and told me, "We did not have to have you, we choose to have you." Although I was fairly old to be learning of my adoption, so far as I remember I felt neither hurt nor resentment. Instead I felt great love from her and my adoptive father, Charles.
>
> Shortly after I was born, my mother Ford held me in her arms and presented me for dedication to Dr. Henry Frost, a veteran missionary of the China Inland Mission. "Mrs. Ford," he told her, "I believe God has given you this child for a purpose." And she, who had herself wanted to be a missionary, agreed. In a very real sense my life trajectory was set then.

Much later I would realize that her love, like all human love, had its flaws, with an obsessive side to it. Yet I think back and ask: What was God's purpose, and how should I pay attention to it?[7]

As we consider our development, the influence of our family must not be underestimated. Families pass on to their children a way of seeing and being in the world. What we were not taught in the everydayness of our lives, we caught along the way. And it is not until well into our own stories that we realize, like Leighton, the particular blessings and hazards of what was passed on to us. Consider these stories:

Sandy's family seemed like such a peaceful place to those on the outside. But from Sandy's perspective it was painfully stifling to everyone. Any sort of overt conflict was completely unacceptable. Any serious disagreement was squelched immediately. Now a mother of three and serving in all sorts of leadership roles, Sandy continually is frustrated by her inability to confront others and is overwhelmed by any sort of criticism she receives. She is beginning to discover by God's grace that her growing up spiritually is going to involve as much unlearning as it is learning.

Okalo experienced rejection and embarrassment whenever he had to explain the uniqueness of his family. He was the son from his father's second wife in a polygamist family, at a time when war ravaged the Ugandan landscape. Okalo felt there seemed to never be a day of peace that he can recall from his early years at home, school or his community. And yet, what gave him hope that life could be different and that he could make it so, came through a dream he had as a nine-year-old boy. Eight years later while riding a bicycle to visit his dying brother he was overwhelmed with the love of Christ and believed God called him to offer hope, education and love to others in need. He followed and never looked back. The dream has become his reality.

Jim was well into his thirties before he recognized how detrimental his father's explosive anger was on his heart growing up. When he faced serious frustrations in his adult life he recognized the lurking anger and fear reminiscent of his father's rage. Instead of dealing with some

---

[7]Leighton Ford, *The Attentive Life: Discerning God's Presence in All Things* (Downers Grove, Ill.: InterVarsity Press, 2008), pp. 54-55.

painful past, Jim inadvertently chose to work harder, keeping the lid on tight so things would not boil over. His sharp responses eventually cost him his job and the trust of his wife and two young sons.

Sometimes we are confronted by parts of our story that we would just as well leave hidden. It's as if things get set in motion and we simply find ourselves bearing the brunt of the situation. Although we would never sign up for such encounters or find them on any leadership development curriculum, such moments can often confirm a deeper work within, bringing healing and empowering us for the journey ahead because God is in charge of the syllabus.

A number of years ago now I (Randy) was asked to be an interim pastor for the summer months in a small church in Ebenezer, Saskatchewan. It seemed both the right thing to do and a good learning opportunity as a seminary student, and so Susan and I packed the Jeep and headed north. One of my first duties was to go door to door in the community to introduce myself and let the folks know that I would be the new pastor over the summer, and that if they needed me I was there. The post office was one of my stops, and before entering I noticed an interesting sign posted above the door, "Postmaster: Floyd Reese." I found that very curious. I introduced myself to the gentleman behind the counter who I assumed to be Floyd. "Hello, I'm Randy Reese and I'll be the new pastor at the church down the block for the summer. You must be Floyd?" He didn't respond, just stared back with an inquisitive sort of look. "Forgive me," he said and then continued, "but it is amazing how much you look like my cousin." Politely, I responded, "Well Floyd, who is your cousin?" "Dennis Reese," he said rather hopefully.

Dennis Reese happens to be the name of my biological father, whom I had never met. Although Floyd may not have known it at the time, he rescued me from what seemed like a long, awkward sort of pause, and asked, "Would you like to meet your grandfather, who will be coming to town next week?" I was raised with the knowledge that although Dennis was a charming person, he was also unpredictable, involved in armed robberies and from time to time wanted to meet his kids—my sister and me. I was afraid of Dennis and somehow felt like his father must be just like him, able to do me harm if allowed the chance. Because you're not supposed to say no in such moments, I said "Sure, I would like to meet him."

The time came to go meet Alvin Reese, my grandfather. Susan and I went together. I found myself clutching her arm rather tightly as we rode up the elevator of the retirement home to meet Alvin and the brother he came to visit. Susan reassured me no one would take me away and that this would be good. I wasn't so sure. The elevator door opened and there to greet me was a ninety-year-old version of myself named Alvin. With a warm smile and warmer handshake he introduced himself to us and invited us in for tea.

After a few hours of exchanging stories and questions, I drummed up the courage to ask Alvin, "So, how is Dennis doing?" A quivery voice responded, "I haven't seen my son in the past twenty-five years. Not sure how he is doing, really." He then said something I will never forget, "I am sorry for the pain my son may have caused you." His words were like an ointment on an old wound. Then he stretched his arm across the table to give me a wrinkled envelope with a one hundred dollar Canadian bill. "I hope it can help," he said.

I'm not sure of all that went on that afternoon, but I know I left the meeting with my grandfather Alvin a changed person—somehow more complete, released from a plaguing fear and more confident and sure of who I was.

Leighton Ford asked himself, "What was God's purpose, and how should I pay attention to it?" There are significant situations and events we have experienced and people we have encountered in our family life that have marked our character, perspectives, abilities and habits. Paying attention to these family incidents is important because they may be playing a significant role in how we respond, positively or negatively, to God's intentions for our development as people of integrity and influence.

LENS 3: *Social Base*

What might be the significance of the habits I learned for managing my life?
Social base refers to our habits of personal life management. These

include habits of how finances were dealt with, how basic needs were met, how emotional needs were met, and how we were encouraged to make decisions for direction in life. Obviously there is some overlap between social base and one's family history.

In general, we are interested in helping others consider the following questions: (1) How have we over time come to order and manage our everyday lives? (2) What habits and patterns related to our life management could have the potential to trip us up in the future? It is often well into our life journey that unaddressed social-base issues surface—like fissures noticed in a foundation—causing problems amid the pressures of life and leadership. The unfortunate reality is that many people pretend all is well, while continuing to neglect the deeper work that needs to take place. These habits develop largely through the kinds of support we received and observed around us in our formative years.

Economic support. We have developed habits for saving, spending and managing our financial resources along the way. Those habits have been formed by our own experiences and observations of how finances were handled by those around us. The sum total of these experiences will have a lot to do with the way we tend to approach money management, our possessions, being able to give resources, receive resources or even how we may need to ask for money for various purposes.

Social support. Social support relates to how our basic needs were met growing up. Were our families willing or even able to feed and clothe us? Was our education provided for and prioritized as a child? Did we come to see the world as a trustworthy place or a place of hardship? These sorts of social dynamics inform our present ability to trust others and move toward others with freedom and vitality. These dynamics also affect whether we feel free to provide appropriate self-care in our lives when needed (issues of health, pace, caring for family, etc.) Those involved in Christian leadership are often neglectful of the needs within their own families, only to have devastating effects.

Emotional support. Emotional support includes the relational dynamics of intimacy, freedom and friendship, to name a few. Did home provide a definite sense of belonging or did we find that belonging somewhere else? With whom was it safe to share honestly when we were growing up? Did our opinions matter or were we told in so many words to keep our opinions to ourselves? Did others respect our emotional lives? Past emotional support will have a lot to say about our abilities and tendencies to enter into intimate friendships and to create healthy boundaries with others.

Strategic support. Some of us move through major decision-making processes very logically, while others of us are much more intuitive. Some of us are very impulsive while others are deliberate. We learned these approaches from our experiences and observations from our family context. This is pertinent especially to how we were encouraged to make decisions for our own growth and development, and who helped us think through such issues. For some, it was appropriate to seek out sponsors, teachers or heroes in order to get their opinions on what we should do with our lives. Others would never consider doing such a thing, but find their own ways to inform their decisions.

Too many leaders have been sidelined because of a failure to take seriously one or more of these four social-base issues. The stories are often tragic and painful for everyone involved. The downfall is rarely caused because these leaders failed to do their job well. In fact, their ambition often drives them to be very accomplished and successful people. However, not too far below the surface of their polished lives lay fault lines with the potential to cause devastating damage. *If we are walking closely with others, we must not be fooled by the success we see.* One of the great gifts we can offer others is to invest the time and muster the courage to ask honest questions about what we are noticing in their lives. Chances are that we would hear a response that is deeply connected to one or more of these social base issues.

LENS 4: *Spiritual Background Patterns*

What might be the significance of the story behind our spiritual background? The lessons from those Christian leaders who have come before us reflect patterns along the journey. The recognition of these patterns can be helpful in providing appropriate and timely input, feedback, evaluation and presence for those with whom we are walking. Our stories have in many ways seeded dynamics of how we respond to God's shaping activity over time. For example, in the early years there tend to be five patterns behind our spiritual background, that is, when we first took God's calling seriously. Clinton encourages us to pay attention to these patterns. He writes,

> Leaders usually emerge out of one of five foundational patterns or a modified version of them. Each of the foundational patterns carries with it some inherent advantages and disadvantages. But each leader is unique and will reflect more or less the advantages or disadvantages of the pattern accordingly. It is helpful to recognize these patterns and implications of them in order to make decisions for training or concerning experiences, which will build on the advantages and minimize disadvantages.[8]

The *heritage pattern* emerges when a person comes from a Christian (or at least a nominal Christian) background and is more or less imbued with Christian values through the home or church life. This pattern carries with it the advantage of an early Christian foundation, a foundation that will likely provide good background for later influence. These people are more familiar with the biblical stories and aware of how things work within various Christian subcultures. Disadvantages inherent in this background include the tendency to take faith and relationship with God for granted, which brings with it a plateauing in both their spiritual life and leadership. There may also be a tendency to wait until all of the pieces are in place before trusting God to move forward with the task or opportunity at hand. Although they possess a rich heritage, they may lack an intimate connection to the love and power of God as their own.

The *radical commitment pattern* develops when a person makes a radical decision to follow Christ, which involves a significant life change or redirection in his or her values and life goals. Advantages inherent in this pattern include a strong commitment to serve and influence others, combined with a fresh perspective or lens on what it means to follow God in service into "impossible" opportunities. People who relate to this pattern can do so because they have experienced how

---

[8]Clinton, *Leadership Emergence Theory*, p. 342.

God changed the impossibilities of their lives. They know firsthand nothing is impossible for God. Potential roadblocks for this person can be a lack of biblical background and the presence of emotional, spiritual and relational challenges that could weigh down forward developmental and practical progress.

The *accelerated pattern* is often associated with a person who comes from a Christian background that stretches back several generations and responds positively and rapidly to a call to serve. This offers the advantages of both a solid Christian background and early advanced leadership opportunities stemming from being well-connected in the Christian community. However, those who identify with this background should watch their ego and its tendencies for self-deception. Overconfidence can mask a need for continued development. The recognition that further training is required can aid in combating this potential disadvantage.

The *delayed pattern* might develop when a person comes from a Christian background that stretches back several generations but who turns away from their heritage initially, only later making a deep recommitment to Christ. Persons that display this sort of background bring valuable life experiences—experiences that can help them show compassion toward and give direction to those who are attempting to move away from unhealthy environments into healthier ones. They often reflect high levels of responsibility and tend to be quick learners, bringing with them certain street smarts. Potential disadvantages inherent in this background include carrying guilt because of missed opportunities and the neglect of their spiritual heritage. They may also be resistant to ongoing learning, including formal educational opportunities because of a perception they are too old to go back to school.

The *destiny pattern* can emerge among people who display a strong sense of internal drive or instinct to make a commitment to a life of service early in life. Persons with this sort of pattern tend to be very focused in their service. Their focus and drive provide great motivation to those who follow them. They tend to see clearly a need worth addressing and how to do so, even if they have to start something from nothing in order to meet the need. They have an undying and tireless determination. However, they must be careful not to become a prisoner to personal vision. In such cases they can become isolated and lose perspective that comes from participating in a relational network of mentors and peers. In their drive to succeed they either alienate or neglect others. And although they may accomplish great things for God, they can fall prey to pride, believing that the gig really does depend on them.

Having even a small awareness of these early shaping patterns can help us understand why people may behave or respond as they do under certain circumstances. Paying attention to the stories that prompted their decisions to take God seriously will be helpful in discerning what sort of learning and guidance to suggest for their development.

LEARNING TO NOTICE

It is disheartening when we learn of people who have settled for less than who they could have become, or who have driven themselves through success to destruction, or who have lived in the trap of approval, or who didn't finish well because of a string of small but poor choices, or who didn't really believe *their* story mattered. Learning to pay attention to those around us can make a considerable difference in our communities. A hopeful note is that one of the common denominators apparent among those who lived well, led well and finished well was that they had people—mentors, teachers, advisers, counselors, guides, friends—who had the love, patience and courage to walk alongside them through various seasons along the journey. They were the ones who noticed, not from a distance but up close, in order to see what was really taking place, to ask a timely question, to offer perspective, to bless with a word of hope.

We have come to see how certain processes are used early in the journey to help shape our character. If we trust that God is intimately concerned with who we are and who we are becoming, then we can have tremendous hope that the foundational chapters of our lives, as well as those to come, are intended for our maturity. We can come to reinterpret our experiences and relationships in the light of the reality of a good and loving God at work amid our story and our community. Our horizon is Christlikeness.

We have been granted an astounding opportunity to participate with the Spirit in deepening and empowering God's servants within our own context. Our work can be lightened considerably as we learn from those who have come before us. We will pick up on things if we pay attention carefully and prayerfully. Here are some helpful recommendations to keep in mind as you invest deeply in the lives of those in your setting:

- *Trust the already-present action of God.* We can develop a measure of confidence in the work of guiding the leadership formation of others when we recognize that the primary work belongs to the Spirit of God. Our role is secondary. It is to notice, discern and guide persons toward a cooperation with God's good work within and through them.

- *Honor the person before you.* We begin the process of walking alongside another by honoring who he or she is, and cherishing the gift of time we have been granted to walk together. The people we are with are not a riddle to be solved. They are not necessarily persons to be categorized or "typed." But rather, they are particular—like no other.

- *Invite discovery through reflection.* We can lead people into significant discovery and learning as we invite them to reflect upon the particulars of their unique history. Reflection is a powerful yet delicate tool of a teacher. It will enhance our ability to help people discover the mystery that their story is lovingly and purposefully connected to God's story.

- *Pay attention to the early years.* Our foundation has been shaped in the early years. Our place and time in history, the uniqueness of our family background, the habits of life management we've learned along the way, and our spiritual background have all contributed toward how we see and function in the world. If explored with care and respect, we can help others become astonished at who God is, who they are and what God has given them to do. We will also help them recognize places in the foundation that need some attention if they are to be counted among those who finish well. It's all there waiting to be discovered.

- *What sort of tale have we fallen into?* The story becomes more complete and whole when we explore how it began. And after returning to the beginning, we may even wonder how we could have missed something so obvious and necessary for the rest of the story to take its proper shape. And so the story continues from its beginnings into a time of testing, exploration, discovery, confirmation, alignment and change. It is a time of finding our way in the light of God's character and development in our lives.

REFLECT ON YOUR LIFE

- What are some of the more significant events or relationships in your growing-up years that seem to impact your life and ministry today?

- In what ways could you benefit from learning from those who have come before you?

- What would it look like for you to become more intentional in your context with the leadership formation of others? What might need to change personally?

A NARRATIVE EXERCISE FOR YOUR CONTEXT (PART 1)

Brainstorming one's life. Developing a personal timeline can be a simple yet extremely beneficial process in helping others (1) recognize the significance of their life story and (2) discover how certain people, events, circumstances have been used to shape them. Consider using the following exercise with those in your context. We hope that it will invite them into a deeper sense of gratitude for God's faithfulness, an examination of some areas for further growth, as well as a fuller hope for their future.

Preparation. From your setting consider people you would like to invest in. At this point we are interested in helping people to develop a personal timeline. At a later point you will consider having your participants share significant lessons from their timeline, as well as a fuller description of their life story from a written narrative. This exercise is best done together at a table where each person has adequate space. Provide each participant with

- a white poster board (22" x 14")
- 75-100 small yellow Post-it notes
- 35-40 small pink Post-it notes
- 5-10 small blue Post-it notes

Step 1 (15 minutes). Brainstorm as many critical incidents you can recall of your life. Put each incident on a yellow Post-it note and place them on the poster board. Don't dwell on their significance; just remember and list incidents. Brainstorm!

Step 2 (10-15 minutes). Transfer the painful or negative incidents from the yellow Post-it notes onto pink Post-it notes. Continue brainstorming, adding incidents on yellow or pink Post-it notes to the poster board as they come to mind.

Step 3 (10-15 minutes). Lay the yellow and pink Post-it notes out in a rough chronological order across

> A *critical incident* can be any key relationship, event or circumstance that has had significant influence in shaping your life, whether that incident was positive or negative. What have been some central images, stories, events, people in your life? What comes to mind? Be patient and prayerful as you recall these memories.

the top of the poster board, leaving the top two inches blank. Events occurring around the same time can be layered down the poster board. Continue brainstorming, adding incidents to the poster board as they come to mind.

Step 4 (10-15 minutes). Look for natural breaks in the flow of incidents. Break them into chapters that correspond to the breaks. We may recognize four or five phases of development. Give a title to each of the chapters in order to represent a significant theme for that particular phase. Put that chapter title on the top of the poster board (develop 4-6 chapters). Continue brainstorming, adding incidents to the poster board as they come to mind.

Step 5 (10 minutes). Stop brainstorming. Begin to reflect on the lessons learned from each chapter. Record initial lessons on blue Post-it notes and put these at the bottom of the chapter. This is just some initial reflection and interpretation.

Step 6 (15-20 minutes). Share some initial overall thoughts with one another that stick out to you as you reflect on this exercise and your life. Some may choose to share a blue note or two from their poster board. Remember to honor and respect each other as you go through this exercise. This process will often surface an awareness of the holiness that comes with each person's story.

4

PREPARATION
Finding Our Way

*God's Spirit is continually challenging, changing,
and maturing us. Although we may be able to point to a
single and decisive conversion experience, remaining faithful
always involves a journey of continual conversion. It can never
be said in our lifetime that we have "arrived." The spiritual life
invites a process of transformation in the life of a believer. It is a process
of growing in gratitude, trust, obedience, humility, compassion,
service, joy. As we deepen our relationship with God, we
begin to choose God's ways and purposes as our own. . . .
Spiritual growth is essentially a work of divine
grace with which we are called to cooperate.*

—MARJORIE J. THOMPSON, *SOUL FEAST*

*During [this time] God is primarily working in the leader and not
through him or her. Though there may be much ministry activity and
even fruitfulness, the major work is that which God is doing to and in
the leader, not through him or her. Most often emerging leaders don't
recognize this. They are constantly evaluating productivity, activities,
or fruitfulness. But God is quietly, often in unusual ways, trying to
get the emerging leader to see that a leader basically ministers out
of what he/she is. He is concerned with what the leader is in
terms of being (character), more than doing (productivity).*

—J. ROBERT CLINTON, *LEADERSHIP EMERGENCE THEORY*

Overview

Preparation Phase—Through an extended period of preparation lasting anywhere from ten to twenty-five years, *God's work* in *us* seems to be paramount. A person initially establishes a maturing commitment to God, evidenced by the continued development and testing of character growth in holiness. Along the way a person develops an experiential understanding of the body of Christ. During this time a person is also given increased responsibility, and in conjunction with this he or she (1) becomes more deeply aware of his or her giftedness, and (2) seeks to develop skills that enhance that set of gifts. Although we are learning competencies and developing proficiencies during this time, we are still maturing toward *the good work God has prepared for us.* God is more concerned in the preparation phase with who we are becoming, more than are our ability to do.

A NOTE ON CALLING

The testimony of Scripture is very clear: *God is up to something good in this world, in our communities and in our unique lives.* The primary burden of our lives is not to persuade or coax or cajole God to do something good, as if he was disinterested or reluctant. Rather, it is to pay prayerful attention to the good work God is already doing. And as we pay attention to God's gracious, renewing work we begin to sense an invitation not just to be *spectators* of this work but *participants.* God wants us to patiently align our whole lives around this good work (Rom 12:1). Consequently, God's Spirit invites us to step out of the stands and get onto the playing field or the stage of this ongoing grand drama in which he is so intimately involved.

Being called by God, and all that it involves, both generally and specifically, means we are being personally invited to participate with the whole of our lives in God's good work. And in so participating, we become more of who we have been created to be (Mt 16:25; 1 Tim 6:19). Gordon T. Smith's *Courage and Calling: Embracing Your God-Given Potential* unpacks three different dimensions of being called by

God.[1] He suggests that we are a called people in that (1) God calls us to himself in love, to follow Jesus, to love God and neighbor (general/ primary calling); (2) God invites us to live and serve out of who we are, a vocation or way of life unique to who we have been created and are being redeemed to be (specific calling); (3) God invites us to be responsible with the present demands and tasks of our lives (immediate calling).

Exploring our sense of calling seeks to encourage a growing awareness of and responsiveness to how God desires to express his life through the unique set of gifts, capacities, experiences and circumstances that make up who we are as individuals. This awareness will take time, prayer and friendship, and will come in varying forms. Debra Rienstra, an English professor at Calvin College, articulates how this awareness can be expressed differently in each person:

> Some people's passions are obvious, and God leads them through those passions into a single path of service. Mother Teresa, for example, or the lifelong kindergarten teacher, or the musician who offers his skillful playing every day for God's glory and other people's joy. Others, like me, have less obvious passions: what gives them energy develops over time or remains partially hidden or blooms suddenly in response to new situations. As a result such people offer an assortment of odds and ends as service: a regular job done with integrity, some volunteer work, a career decision that seeks service over money and prestige, kindness to neighbors, maybe a late-life passion for going on mission trips or teaching teenagers appliance repair. Their lives may not have the clean simplicity of vocation, but at the center of everything they do is a deep love for God—and that is everyone's true vocation.
>
> I've learned that God treasures the lives made of a single piece of cloth, cut in the shape of service. But God also values the lives that look more like a bag of fabric scraps, some big pieces, some tiny pieces, different colors and weaves. At each stage in my life, with each piece of it, I try to ask God, "How can I offer this to you?" I have to trust that if I offer all the odds and ends of my life, God will stitch together the pieces in some lovely pattern and receive it as my gift.[2]

---

[1]Gordon T. Smith, *Courage and Calling: Embracing Your God-Given Potential* (Downers Grove, Ill.: InterVarsity Press, 1999), p. 10.
[2]Debra Rienstra, *So Much More: An Invitation to Christian Spirituality* (San Francisco: Jossey-Bass, 2005), pp. 221-22.

We are each hooked up differently, in terms of capacities and perspective and passions, and our journey in discovering God's calling in
our lives will reflect these differences. Sadly, we can too often lump this
category of calling into a "For Special Christians Only" box. Many do
not seriously ponder that their lives could really be lived as a response
to God's voice or God's leading. Missionaries and pastors are not the
only ones who must wrestle with this notion of a calling in their life.
All Christians must patiently grow to see their lives with this sort of
lens and possibility. Our hope is that Rienstra's question—*How can I
offer this life of mine to you?*—will both grab us and free us to be who
God has created us to be (Eph 2:10).

For Jill this discovery involved a series of events that centered around
a trip to Eastern Europe. She had graduated from college three years
earlier and now was working in an accounting firm. She and some
friends decided to take a two-and-a-half-week trip to Europe. During
that time she encountered some Romanian believers who were working
in an orphanage. Their lives expressed a mixture of joy, endurance and
service that cracked something in her well-scripted life. By the time she
returned home, Jill had a keen sense that God was stirring her soul,
inviting her to something different, something more. The various compartments of her life began to collapse and she was grabbed by this
question: "How am I to be faithful to God with my whole life?" On the
surface of life one did not notice a lot of major differences with Jill. She
would continue to work in the accounting firm and live in the same
neighborhood, but those who spent any extended time with Jill were
immediately struck by her deep concern and conviction that somehow
her life was wrapped up in God's larger story. She was becoming increasingly open and responsive to God's presence and work in her life
and her community.

Sam was in his early fifties when he came to the gracious discovery
that everything in his life matters to God. Significant disappointments
at work coupled with some health concerns for one of his children confronted him and forced him to recognize how much he was gripping to
stay in control of his own life. He had been a very involved member at
his church for years, but it would take this season of real disorientation

and questioning for him to realize that God was lovingly inviting him to trust at another level. For Sam this period in his life provided the conditions for him to encounter God more intimately, to experience God as being both present and involved in his life and the life of his community. Sam described these discoveries as "a new beginning" that would resonate through the whole of his life and decisions.

For Gonxha Agnes Bojaxhiu it was at age twelve that she knew she wanted to become a missionary to those in poverty. At age eighteen she left her home, Skopje, Macedonia, to join the Loreto Sisters in Ireland. The parting words to Gonxha from her mother before she left for Ireland were, "Put your hand in His [Jesus'] hand, and walk alone with Him. Walk ahead, because if you look back you will go back."[3] These parting words were fitting words describing the lifelong faithful service of Gonxha—that is, Mother Teresa. Eighteen years later almost to the day Mother Teresa had an experience (one which we will call a *destiny moment*) that captured both her imagination and her heart, and set a new trajectory of service. While on a train ride to a retreat center near Darjeeling for some rest from teaching at a girls' school at a Loreto convent in Calcutta she had an encounter with God. She wrote of this moment,

> It was a call within my vocation. It was a second calling. It was a vo-
> cation to give up even Loreto where I was very happy and to go out in
> the streets to serve the poorest of the poor. It was in that train, I heard
> the call to give up all and follow Him into the slums—to serve Him in
> the poorest of the poor. . . . I knew it was His will and that I had to
> follow Him. There was no doubt that it was going to be His work.[4]

Mother Teresa's obedience and trust to follow in that moment on the train led over time to a movement that would span the globe. God's love for her fueled the leadership she provided for Missionaries of Charity, even during the times when God felt distant. It was a relational trust with God nurtured over decades that shaped who she was and in turn, how she led. There were many lessons she learned over the years—

[3]Brian Kolodiejchuk, *Mother Teresa: Come Be My Light* (New York: DoubleDay, 2007), p. 13.
[4]Ibid., pp. 39-40.

cultivating her devotion to God, trusting a call, caring for those with severe needs, recruiting others to join her cause, establishing intentional training processes, guarding ongoing spiritual formation for herself and those served through the Missionaries of Charity, knowing how and when to gain direction and permission from those in authority, being strategic with establishing dozens of Missionaries of Charity chapters in other countries while maintaining the same vision and ethos. She was faithful to her Lord and his calling in what she called the "little things," and consequently she led with remarkable spiritual authority.[5]

There are many Sams and Jills, and even a couple Mother Teresas, out there whom God is inviting and calling. We have a tremendous need today for wise and caring people to provide encouragement, challenge and support for those who need to remember what God has done and is doing in their life. How is God's Spirit prompting and calling them to serve? How can we learn to notice them more particularly in order to help them find their way toward their unfolding story of service and impact?

The many leaders who have come before us will continue to be instructive. How did they begin to recognize and embrace the possibility that God wanted to use them for certain purposes? Clinton's research reflected that though they may have accomplished much during this particular season of growth, the primary concern within their formation had more to do with their own preparation—their own growing up—than it did with how well they were able to provide leadership or make an impact. Our hope then from these lessons is to see how we can learn to more effectively guide the leadership formation of others in a timely developmental manner.

SIGNS OF GOD'S PREPARATORY WORK

We must all go through a season of preparation—a time of cultivation which raises our awareness that "something is going on" or that "God is up to something good" with us. When we respond to God's call to follow, the Spirit stirs our hearts and minds to greater faithfulness and spiritual

---

[5]Louise Slavicek, *Mother Teresa* (New York: Infobase, 2007), pp. 90-91.

hunger. We would do well to pay attention to some of the dynamics of this preparatory work in our lives or in the lives of others. These dynamics are sure clues or signs of God's forming and calling work in our lives.

An increased yearning for intimacy with God. Sometime early in our adult Christian formation we begin to recognize that living faithfully is less a matter of duty and more a matter of relationship with God. Many of us leave our foundational years with notions of God as somehow less than a person, more like a great mysterious force of nature that balances the universe, kind of like a moral force of gravity, which corrects us when we contradict it. But as we grow up and pay attention, the biblical portrait of God, expressed most fully in Jesus, confronts our impersonal notions of God.

We read the Scriptures, we observe mentors and other influential lives of faith, we pray, and in time we begin to be let in on the possibility of God's wonderful fellowship with us. Deep in our hearts, the Holy Spirit expresses the possibility of the Christian life, a fully human life, found in personal communion with God. Our Christian lives become more and more relational in their orientation and we find ourselves yearning for deeper intimacy with God.

A growing recognition of the importance of holiness. Godly character is foundational to godly service. Over the history of the church this has been referred to as growth in holiness. The apostle Peter calls his readers to holy living by echoing a challenge from the book of Leviticus (Lev 11:44-45; 19:2; 20:7). Peter writes:

> Therefore, prepare your minds for action; discipline yourselves; set all your hope on the grace that Jesus Christ will bring you when he is revealed. Like obedient children, do not be conformed to the desires that you formerly had in ignorance. Instead, as he who called you is holy, be holy yourselves in all your conduct; for it is written, "You shall be holy, for I am holy." (1 Pet 1:13-16)

The apostle Paul appeals to his readers, "by the mercies of God, to present your bodies as a living sacrifice, holy and acceptable to God" (Rom 12:1). The person who finishes well realizes early in his or her development that holy living is not peripheral to all the responsibilities and challenges of service. Holiness is central to Christian service. *We serve and lead out of who we are.*

Desiring relationships with seasoned believers. Those who flourish over the long haul recognize early in their development the importance of having models, men and women who are farther down the road in their life and leadership. Wisdom is most often caught rather than taught. The subtleties of faithfulness slip through the cracks of good principles and formulas, and can only be given proper expression in authentic relationships. Timothy Jones observed, "Sometimes we need to see the Christian life lived out; we need to stand in the presence of the genuine article, not just be told about it."[6] There is a growing desire to seek such men and women with whom they might share their lives and from whom they might have the opportunity to learn. There is much inspiration that comes from being noticed by someone we admire. Such recognition by another instills tremendous hope that we too might be able to become and achieve what their lives have shown us.

A growing awareness of leadership as a work of service. Positions of authority can seduce us with the promises of secure identity and great influence, and hide their challenges, dangers and humiliations. There is a certain romance and glory to leadership that appeals to many of our deep insecurities. The people who thrive for the long haul recognize early the illusory nature of these glories. They begin to learn in the nitty-gritty of their lives that Jesus' images of slave and servant (Lk 22:24-27) begin to conflict with their romantic notions of what leadership is all about.

There are many times when the work of leadership is hard and anything but a glorified work. Our maturity requires a sober self-honesty with regard to how authority and influence tempt us. John the Baptist's words capture the journey: "He must increase, and I must decrease" (Jn 3:30). God prepares those who flourish over the long haul, not through the images of glory but by the alternative and eccentric image of a humble servant, a servant of God, a servant of others. They thereby begin to grapple early on in their development with Jesus' words "but not so with you" within the challenges of their faith and service.

---

[6]Timothy Jones, *Finding a Spiritual Friend: How Friendships and Mentors Can Make Your Faith Grow* (Nashville: Upper Room Books, 1998), p. 36.

A growing awareness of a sense of destiny. Clinton has noted from his observations that those who finished well often viewed their lives as having a sense of destiny. Now within our contemporary culture, popular notions of fate (determined to some future) or romance (destined for another person) characterize many people's conception of destiny. However, destiny can also describe something far deeper than fate or romance; it can be a concept more closely linked with notions of calling or vocation. Clinton defined this sense of destiny as "an inner conviction arising from an experience or series of experiences that God has his hand on [them] in a special way for special purposes."[7]

Awareness of a sense of destiny grows from a retrospective look at these experiences. *Destiny moments are such experiences that when looked back on confirm God has his hand on us for something special.* There are four common types of destiny moments:

- *Awe-inspiring moments* are times when God intervenes in a clear and unmistakable way in your life. Examples of awe-inspiring moments include Paul on the Damascus road, Jacob wrestling with the angel, a conversion experience, a realization of a specific calling, a significant relational encounter and a significant event where God's interaction was very real.

- *Indirect influences* are experiences in which some aspect of destiny is linked to a person other than you and is done indirectly for you; you must simply receive its implications. Hannah's contract with the Lord for the service of her son Samuel, Moses having his life saved by his parents, and a blessing given by a parent or grandparent for some special purpose or service.

- *Providential reflections* are retrospective glances at key circumstances woven together by God that give strong indication of God's sense of destiny for a person. Joseph being ditched by his brothers, Paul's historical and cultural background, the timing of unique circumstances, events, opportunities or relationships.

---

[7]J. Robert Clinton, *Leadership Emergence Theory: A Self Study Manual for Analyzing the Development of a Christian Leader* (Altadena, Calif.: Barnabas, 1989), p. 101.

- *Unusual blessings* occur when the powerful presence or blessing of God is displayed in a person's life and service. Others often recognize these unusual blessings. Joseph's unusual level of influence, the unusual respect given to Daniel, the extraordinary moments of influence, effectiveness or blessing, times when "it" went so well there was no way you could have done it on your own, in a sense proving that a power much greater than your own was somehow involved.

When walking alongside others we must pay attention to these sorts of experiences because these destiny moments foreshadow future points of significance in our lives. They are moments of promise and blessing in our stories. These incidents may include significant relationships we have developed with certain people, circumstances in our stories that have displayed God's providence or just some of our own everyday decisions which, when viewed in retrospect, add firmness to a sense of life purpose and confirm God's guidance in our lives.

GROWING TOWARD DEPENDABILITY

In Luke 16:10 Jesus says, "Whoever is faithful in a very little is faithful also in much; and whoever is dishonest in a very little is dishonest also in much."

"How are you becoming a person of integrity?" may be the primary question of our formation during this season of growth. It is a shaping of our person—our character that becomes a foundation for the rest of our life story and service. If we are to lead in Jesus' name, then part of our curriculum needs to include processes that invite us to become truthful and honest with ourselves. Dan Allender puts it this way,

> The actual word in the Greek— *charakter*—originally was used in connection with tools designed for engraving. And character is indeed a tool that marks us—that in one sense cuts us, shapes us, and engraves us. We are image-bearers who are intended by God to make him known in a fashion that no one else on the earth can do in the same way.
>
> Our marking is as unique as a snowflake. . . . Our character is a complex interaction between God's writing of our body and background, the contributions others make to our life, and our unique

participation in cowriting our story with God. The totality is our character, how our "marking" appears to others.[8]

Jillian and Steve had always looked up to Sandy. Ever since they had graduated from college and started attending the church, they had been struck by Sandy's wise and generous spirit. This had become evident to them when a few years back they started conversing with Sandy after a Sunday service. Jillian and Steve found themselves trying to sit near her every week after that, and so began their friendship with this older wise woman at church. Sandy showed genuine concern and asked such good questions of their lives as young professionals.

The week before last she had made a comment about God being up to good things in Steve's life after he had dumped on her some of the tensions he had experienced at work the week before. But then the conversation got interrupted and she didn't get to elaborate on what she meant. Both Jillian and Steve wanted to understand what Sandy was seeing in them. They had been having a difficult time seeing God up to anything particular in their lives over the past year. How and where was God up to something good in their lives? So two weeks later they took Sandy to Sunday brunch.

"Steve, you just seem to be becoming a person of integrity." And so the brunch conversation with Sandy began. Jillian had asked her, "What did you see in Steve a few weeks back when you said that God was up to something good in his life?" Sandy recounted the work challenges Steve had spoken of. From Sandy's perspective it seemed that he was being pressured to compromise on what he knew to be true and right. What stood out to her was the way he was striving to be a person of good, honest character despite the seeming lack of support from his coworkers, even his supervisor. For Sandy this was a clue or marker of the Spirit's deep work in Steve's life.

Sandy went on to explain that God wants to form us into people he can trust. He wants to know that he can rely on us. So consequently he will prepare us, even lovingly test us, through the different circumstances and events of our lives. He will show us the areas where we may

---

[8]Dan Allender, *Leading Character* (Grand Rapids: Zondervan, 2008), p. 20.

need to grow. He will affirm our faithful responses amid challenging situations. And over time, sometimes through painful periods of failure and forgiveness, when we prove ourselves faithful and dependable, God invites us into places of greater influence and responsibility.

Sandy's intuitions of God's movement in Steve's life reflect more than simply her personal experience. Proverbs 17:3 puts it this way:

> The crucible is for silver, and the furnace for gold,
> but the Lord tests the heart.

In the lives of many there seems to be a preparatory process of testing, a person's response to the testing, and consequent expansion of influence and responsibility (depending on the faithful response of the person) that takes place early in their development. These sorts of processes, also called *checks*, reflect God's shaping activity amidst the everydayness of our lives.[9]

- *Integrity check.* An integrity check is an experience in which our character or heart intent is revealed through the congruence or incongruence of our inner convictions and our outward actions. Examples include Joseph fleeing from seduction by Potiphar's wife (Gen 39), and when Daniel refused to adapt to the unclean dietary customs of his Babylonian captors (Dan 1). *Will we remain consistent to our inner convictions of what we know to be true and right even when it is not immediately rewarded?*

- *Obedience check.* An obedience check is an experience that tests our ability to hear and respond to God's prompting. The classic biblical example is Abraham's remarkable willingness to obey God's command to sacrifice his young son Isaac (Gen 22). His act of faithful obedience to God transcended any reasonable course of action. He obeyed God in spite of all conceivable reservations he had. It was his great act of faith that was honored. Obedience checks are often invitations for us to commit our lives and work to follow wherever God may lead, even when it does not make logical sense. *Where are we being invited to follow?*

---

[9]Clinton, *Leadership Emergence Theory*, p. 143.

- *Word check.* A word check is an experience that tests our ability and willingness to hear God speak through Scripture, to understand and receive God's truth, and then act on it. When we respond faithfully, we experience a heightened view of the authority of God's truth. Word checks are often found in combination with obedience or integrity checks. *How are we growing in our respect and dependency upon Scripture to guide the way we chose to live life?*

- *Faith check.* A faith check is an experience that challenges us regarding some issue in which God's reality and faithfulness can be tested and seen to be true, and which forms a confidence builder for trusting God with bigger issues. God prepared David to stand up in confidence against the giant warrior Goliath through earlier challenges of lions and bears in which the young shepherd David learned trust in God in the face of great threat (1 Sam 17:34-37). *Where are you being invited to trust that God will "show up"?*

Do we really know what to look for when we are searching for those who reflect the potential to do the work of leadership in our context? Our propensity may be to look for those gifted people who can really make it happen, or those who have a larger than average dose of charisma, or those who are the brightest and the best, or even those who can influence others to follow. But we would suggest that we ought to begin by paying attention for those men and women in our contexts who are experiencing these sorts of checks in their faith journey. For these challenges seem to consistently reflect God's preparatory shaping in a person's life. These people may not exhibit characteristics we typically assign to leadership, but God is behind the scenes nonetheless doing a deeper work within.

We must grow increasingly sensitive to these sorts of processes in people's lives. When we help them notice God's shaping work it can instill a confidence that God has their best interest in mind and that he will tailor the circumstances of their lives in order to help them become persons of integrity with an appropriate gifting, so that over time they might bear the weight of God's work and blessing on their lives. We would certainly not choose the set of circumstances we often find ourselves in the midst of, we may even question God's tailoring at the time, and yet, as we submit to the Spirit's shaping work, we can become more true to our created design.

GROWING THROUGH CHALLENGES

There were lessons that continued along the journey of those Christian leaders who have come before us—lessons deepening them as persons, lessons helping them become proficient at certain skills, lessons reminding them of their need for a community of others and lessons reminding them of their dependent need for God. The learning was not something that came overnight but took place over a span of several years, even decades. Although a significant focus of the learning during this phase had to do with various leadership skills, the undercurrent was concerning itself with the question, What sort of person am I becoming? There are five categories of learning challenges that we want to pay attention to in this phase of development:

Paying attention to submission to authority. For many of us the word *submission* conjures up more negative than positive experiences. Working for someone who was an ineffective leader, choosing to remain silent while others talked about the boss, enduring menial tasks when you felt you had more to offer, knowing there was a better way, doing what you were ordered to do by someone for whom you have little respect or receiving the word that you did not get the position because they felt you were not ready yet. These situations and many others create for us "surprise quizzes" on how we respond to those in authority. And they also provide an invitation to learn how we might exercise authority ourselves when the time comes.

The Scriptures are emphatic on this topic when it comes to authority. Here are just a few highlights of submission found within the New Testament.

> You who are younger must accept the authority of the elders. And all of you must clothe yourselves with humility in your dealings with one another, for
> "God opposes the proud,
>   but gives grace to the humble."

Humble yourselves therefore under the mighty hand of God, so that he may exalt you in due time. (1 Pet 5:5-6)

Be subject to one another out of reverence for Christ. (Eph 5:21)

Obey your leaders and submit to them, for they are keeping watch over your souls and will give an account. Let them do this with joy and not with sighing—for that would be harmful to you. (Heb 13:17)

Everything that the Father gives me will come to me, and anyone who comes to me I will never drive away, for I have come down from heaven, not to do my own will, but the will of him who sent me. (Jn 6:37-38)

There is a clear invitation for us to ponder the apostles' words and perhaps marvel at Jesus relationship to his Father as expressed most beautifully in John's Gospel. What is it that they all knew about submission that we do not know today?

An attitude of submission seems hardwired into a faithful life. However, submission to God or others can be a difficult learning process. While growing up we have received so much encouragement and modeling in learning how to be right and how to distrust authority that by the time we are in our early adulthood it is quite a challenge to learn to follow another's lead. Yet this learning is so critical to our character formation, that is, who we are becoming by God's grace. Clinton's research reflects that the early critical lessons of submission became precursors to learning the more important lesson of submission to God. In other words, people who have learned to submit appropriately to human authority figures in their lives also seem to reflect a consistency with submitting to the work and direction of God in their own lives. Moreover, the research always shows that those who had difficulty following authority seemed to struggle with exercising authority well when given roles or positions of leadership.

So if we are going to walk closely with women and men who are early in their leadership development, then their giftedness or insight must not fool us. We must recognize that their character is key over the long haul. In this regard we must pay attention to how they are responding to supervision or correction. Do they undermine or question authority at every turn? In response to other's leadership or ideas are they competitive or dismissive? All of these things reflect where the Spirit may be trying to get their attention. We must learn to be a truthful and gentle voice in their lives when necessary, to graciously mirror to them the ways their character may be more self centered and willful and in need of further shaping by God.

Paying attention to giftedness and style. We lead from who we are and we discover much of who we are when we put our hand to the plow. We begin to notice that we are more effective when we exercise certain skills over others and see types of fruit being produced from our efforts. We also become keenly aware of a style that begins to form from the leadership we provide, and so we move into situations with a marked wisdom and approach.

Spiritual gifts, natural abilities and *acquired skills* contribute to a more holistic awareness of how God shapes us over time so that we might become effective in what we do.[10] According to Scripture we have received from the Spirit certain gifts. Romans 12:6-8, 1 Corinthians 12:4-11 and Ephesians 4:11-14 are three places in the New Testament where we are provided lists of spiritual gifts. These gifts reflect various functions that work together toward the building up of the body of Christ (the church) in love and the eventual accomplishment of God's mission. Because God is concerned with the whole of our formation, we can be confident that any natural abilities we may have been given or acquired skills we may have learned along the way can also be considered part of a broader notion of giftedness.

The process of discovering this giftedness takes place over time within the company of a local body of believers. What seems apparent from Clinton's research is that as developing leaders are faithful to the tasks and responsibilities before them, they grow more aware of their gifts and increasingly utilize those particular gifts, which in turn results in more responsibility in line with who they are. One type of giftedness discovery process took place as a result of being thrust into a

---

[10]For a fuller understanding of the notion of giftedness and a more detailed analysis of spiritual gifts, see J. Robert Clinton and Richard Clinton, *Unlocking Your Giftedness: What Leaders Need to Know to Develop Themselves and Others* (Altadena, Calif.: Barnabas, 1993).

role that forced certain things to come forth from the person. A second type of discovery took place as a person transitioned from one set of responsibilities to another. Through feedback from others and reflection on what took place, the discovery of giftedness became apparent. And sometimes a third type of discovery took place as a person was attracted to how another person did things. This type of discovery brought with it the question, What if I could do what they do? What is important to note is that no matter how the giftedness was discovered, there was both the exercise of the gifts and an affirmation of the gifts from a mentor or the larger community, which confirmed the work of the Spirit in and through the person.

As we learn to exercise our giftedness we also become more aware of the need to adapt our approaches, given the uniqueness of various situation. The ways that a person influences people constitute his or her *leadership style*. For one person it is his bellowing visionary enthusiasm that sways people toward his ideas for the community. For another, her expertise and problem solving are fundamental to her recognized leadership style within her community. And for yet another it is his steady, collaborative approach that builds trust and loyalty from his team that most distinguishes his style.

Over the last few decades many researchers in the fields of leadership and management have been in search of a "best style" of leadership. All sorts of helpful insights, categories and descriptions have been developed through this research. But in the end their research has led them to the conclusion that there is no single, all-purpose leadership style. Effective and successful leaders are those who can adapt their leadership activity to meet the demands of unique situations, circumstances and people. We would recommend exploring Paul Hersey's *The Situational Leader* or J. Robert Clinton's *Conclusions on Leadership Style* for further exploration of leadership style.[11] Both of these resources can be highly instructive for learning how to read and navigate the many dynamics that emerge in understanding another's leadership styles.

[11]Paul Hersey, *The Situational Leader* (Escondido, Calif.: Center for Leadership Studies, 1992); J. Robert Clinton, *Conclusions on Leadership Style* (Altadena, Calif.: Barnabas, 1992).

Leadership is a complex matter involving far more than just providing a clear vision and big inspiration. In walking with others in this preparation phase it is important to provide space for others to share what they are discovering about themselves amid the many experiences they have and situations they find themselves in.

Paying attention to an expansion of influence. A third category of growing and learning during this season of development has to do with *influence*. Influence is the act of shaping or altering the way another person thinks, feels or acts. Aubrey Malphurs suggests, "Influence involves moving people to change their thinking and ultimately their behavior."[12] In this sense, influence is something we do. We can either intentionally or unintentionally influence others. Pause for a moment and consider your own story: *Why is it that you have followed certain people in your life? Why is it that people have followed you at different times?* We grant authority to others for many different reasons. For example, the reason we followed a parent's guidance in elementary school may be very different from the reason we followed a teacher's guidance in high school. Or the reason we gave a close friend such authority over our lives last year is most likely drastically different than the reason we grant our supervisor authority at work. And sometimes we grant authority to the same person but for different reasons, depending on the situation.

In his study Clinton observed that a person's influence in a community was derived from different sources or *power bases*. A power base "refers to the source of credibility, power differentials, or resources which enables a leader to have authority to exercise influence on a follower."[13] He goes onto to describe three different kinds of power bases—*positional, personal* and *spiritual*. And many times a person operates out of a combination of power bases at the same time.

Positional power is influence exercised because of one's position in an organization and the degree of power delegated by the organization for

---

[12]Aubrey Malphurs, *Being Leaders: The Nature of Authentic Christian Leadership* (Grand Rapids: Baker, 2003), p. 92.

[13]J. Robert Clinton, *Clinton's Biblical Leadership Commentary Series,* Commentary CD vol. 2 (Altadena, Calif.: Barnabas, 2001), p. 439.

that position. A leader influences followers because he or she has been granted authority by those with even greater authority. And in turn, he or she may use reward or discipline as ways to exert influence over followers. Strictly speaking, when a person is using power based on a positional power base, the followers do not grant the leader permission to influence them but rather submit to the person's leadership due to the hierarchal nature of the organization.

Personal power is influence exercised through a person's mix of personality, character, skills and behavior. The source of the authority is somehow intrinsic to the person as opposed to the position, which is extrinsic to the person. Those being led follow because of the leader's expertise, skillfulness, access to information or charisma. This kind of power depends on the confidence and trust a person generates from the people he or she is attempting to lead.

Spiritual power is influence exercised because of the perception of the person's *spiritual authority*. The followers recognize evidence of a close relationship with God and see the leader as credible and trustworthy because of his or her apparent close relationship with God. Jesus speaks of this type of power in John 15:5: "I am the vine; you are the branches. Those who abide in me and I in them bear much fruit, because apart from me you can do nothing." There is a deep dependency on God that characterizes the leader's life.

One of the critical leadership development lessons learned from those who have come before us is that *effective Christian leaders value spiritual authority as a primary power base*. And this spiritual authority flows out of a deep concern for and commitment to intimacy with God and a life lived with integrity. Their influence does not exclude personal or positional authority, but these power bases become secondary. Over time, their communities increasingly recognize their lives as characterized by spiritual power and authority.

Some of us can immediately think of men and women who seem to live and work out of something greater than their own personality, skills or position. They are not coercive or authoritarian. They do not manipulate followers or use guilt to motivate them. But their lives and words are compelling in a deep and authentic way. We might say that

God has anointed them with unusual power and influence. Such authority is not achieved by promotion, education or performance. In fact, one wonders whether such influencers are even aware of the gravity of their life and words upon others. Their eyes are not focused on acquiring or exercising such authority, but rather are set in a different direction. They are looking to Jesus.

Spiritual authority develops over time as a person gains a deeper knowledge and personal trust of God amid the ongoing challenges of his or her life and work. The authority is not sought after as the end or the goal. Clinton writes,

> Spiritual authority is not a goal but rather a byproduct. It is a delegated authority that comes from God. It is the major power base of a leader who has learned God's lessons during maturity processing. Leaders have various power bases that give credence to their ability. Spiritual authority comes out of experience with God. A leader does not seek spiritual authority; a leader seeks to know God. Maturity processing enhances this desire to know God. Spiritual authority results from a leader's experience with God.[14]

In the second century Clement of Alexandria described prayer as "keeping company with God." In this sense spiritual authority develops from a prayer-full life. There is a fellowship with God that must be constantly cultivated as followers of Jesus. Any number of practices or disciplines can help deepen our awareness and responsiveness to God.[15] These practices—such as meditating on Scripture, extended times of solitude and prayer, and spiritual mentoring—provide the conditions for learning to "keep company with God."

Amid this companionship with Jesus we encounter all sorts of challenges that prepare us further to influence out of a spiritual authority. For example, maturing leaders can find themselves tested by periods of conflict and leadership backlash when followers seemingly turn their backs on them. Other leaders have found themselves struggling to serve well

---

[14]Ibid., p. 167.

[15]For an extensive overview of spiritual practices and disciplines see Adele Ahlberg Calhoun, *Spiritual Disciplines Handbook: Practices That Transform Us* (Downers Grove, Ill.: InterVarsity Press, 2005).

and stay healthy within a dysfunctional organizational culture. We should not be surprised by hard and puzzling times in another person's development, or our own development for that matter. Rather, we should look a little deeper as to how God might be using this set of circumstances to draw us into a more intimate relationship with himself. These sorts of experiences have a way of calling out from us gifts, abilities, passions and sensitivities that may have been dormant in our earlier development. What a privilege to help others discover how God is creatively shaping them and inviting them into a deeper friendship with Jesus for his kingdom's sake.

Paying attention to an expansion of faith. Finding our way eventually brings us to lessons that have a more pronounced way of stretching our faith in God. This same faith, which accompanied us when we initially began to follow and serve God seriously, now faces challenges that invite a renewed discernment and trust of the voice of God for our lives and leadership. Brian says yes to a new level of responsibility he knows is way over his head and prays fervently that God will use him as a source of hope and positive change for the company. Henrietta steps out believing God will provide an impossible amount of finances to purchase a retreat center. Mario leaves the security of his organization, sells it all in order to begin an orphanage in Sudan. Sarah, in very unfamiliar territory, prays a prayer of release and protection for a high school girl riddled with evil spirits, and the girl is set free. We may have thought such faith lessons learned back in the beginning of our followership would have made us "good to go" for a lifetime, but it seems as though the opposite is true. Newer invitations, tougher situations and kingdom-sized missions all bring us to the place of renewed dependency on God.

The writer of Hebrews puts it this way, "Without faith it is impossible to please God, for whoever would approach him must believe that he exists and that he rewards those who seek him" (Heb 11:6). We move from experience to experience, from situation to situation applying ourselves and wondering if we would ever be able to get the job done. And thankfully we have discovered over time that God does show up and empower us to get it done. However, the work of leadership brings with it a peculiar temptation. As we grow in our competencies, we begin to see that we can be quite effective at doing certain things. The more we practice our competencies, as we certainly should do, we gain confidence in our ability to make things happen. Soon we begin to realize how vital our role has become in bringing things about, and how dependent our community is on our important role. And therein lies the field for deception to take root. A deception that settles in, developing into an overconfidence in our doing, a reliance on our competencies to make things happen, and worse yet, a shifting of dependency from the love and power of God to our own competencies.

God is concerned with nurturing us toward a maturity that is well beyond what we think to be possible. In doing so, the opportunities to serve become the classroom for expanded dependency on God. What is required of us reaches well beyond what our current competencies or charisma can muster. We find ourselves moving toward a way of prayer that is more foundational to our work. We are reminded that the work we have been given to do in Jesus' name is a spiritual work, one not without opposition. This season of growth brings with it a realization that conflict or challenge may be the result of a spiritual attack from Satan and the forces of evil. And try as we might to utilize well-thought-through strategies and plans, we are rekindled in the conviction of our utter reliance on the power of God for the situation at hand. Clinton says it this way: "Leadership issues are more than what appears on the surface. An expanding leader will be processed in discernment in order to better assess ordinary and super-ordinary causes."[16]

We are all inspired by the stories of those who have ventured well beyond their competencies to move toward the power of God that was made evident in their doing. As they discerned God's way among them they acted in obedience toward that which seemed sometimes illogical, leaving behind tales of adventure, miracle, hope, accomplishment, celebration and worship. These stories can energize our communities to press through toward a similar empowerment to take place in their situation. In developing others we must pay close attention to how God may be stretching those we walk with to a greater trust and faith in his ways among us.

---

[16]Clinton, *Leadership Emergence Theory*, p. 237.

Paying attention to our social base. Our journey through the pressures that often accompany life and leadership may reveal stress fractures in our person, and if left unaddressed they could become our undoing. We referred to these things in chapter three as *our social base.* In adulthood we often bump into the reality that not everyone sees and relates to the world in the same way we do. Others have divergent ideas, values and ways of managing their lives, in large part because their early life experiences were different from ours. Consequently, tensions will come as we work with others, disagreements will occur, and inner and outer conflicts will confront us. For example, a coworker will procrastinate year after year to the frustration of everyone around her, a spouse will periodically make impulsive and costly purchases that threaten the whole family's financial well-being, an elder will explode in anger amid a church board meeting, or a friend will repeatedly refuse others' help and insight in discovering life direction.

These behaviors are often puzzling, but they are examples of how our ways of managing life can come to be truly destructive to us personally, as well as to those we live and work with. These behaviors do not emerge out of a vacuum. They most often stem from our own family history. And whether they are dynamics of our early emotional, economic, decision making or social support, they all have given shape to the way we currently influence and interact with others. What is critically important for our growth is our willingness to admit how we have come to manage our lives and where we need help. The people who are self-ignorant in this regard persist in stubborn and reactionary behavior, either running over others or being run over by others. Humility and self-honesty will be required if we are to mature and learn.

During this preparation phase it is critical to take inventory of these four components of our social base.[17] *Who can help me process what is going on emotionally within me? What are the financial ramifications of what I am about to step into? Who can help me think through whether this opportunity fits who I am and the direction of my life? Given this opportunity, how will I take care of the basic needs of my family and myself?* The

---

[17]Ibid., p. 118.

questions are simple yet have the potential to help us take care of significant concerns that will emerge along the way of our service.

LEARNING TO NOTICE

During this season of growth we move from (1) a preparatory work in which we learn to trust in and depend on God's inward work in our lives, (2) through a time of exploration and discovery of how we can contribute to making things happen, (3) toward a time of deeper dependency on God for what may be required of us. As we learn to pay attention to God's shaping activity during this preparation phase we can participate more effectively in the formation of others. Here are some helpful recommendations to keep in mind as you consider investing in the lives of those in your setting:

- *The good work begun is being brought to completion.* The apostle Paul's encouraging words to the Philippians reflect an important promise for us to pass on to others—that God desires to see us mature to our capacity and is responsible for ultimately guiding that process (Phil 1:6). As we watch for signs of God's preparatory work in peoples lives we can offer timely words of encouragement and expectation.

- *In pursuit of holiness.* The foundation of character is integrity, which means our development must include lessons to help forge within us what it means to be truthful, honest and dependable. We desire holiness because we have seen the importance of our dependency on God for all we are and do. *What are the stories behind the development of integrity in the lives of those in your setting?*

- *An attitude of submission.* We have seen how there seems to be a relationship between those who learned to submit to authority and their ability to exercise authority faithfully. They became more discerning of situations where authority became abusive or simply false. Learning to submit to God and others is a precursor to serving out of spiritual authority. *How are the people we are walking alongside becoming teachable in attitude and action?*

- *Trial and error.* This is an important time for people to explore options of service in order to discover where they may be gifted, what might ignite their imagination and passion, and what might be appropriate contexts for them to flourish. This process may take several years before a sense of fit becomes apparent. *How are we cultivating learning environments for people to explore and discover?*

- *Enhancing the learning.* This is also a season to explore more advanced learning in a given area or discipline. For some this takes the form of formal educational programs to prepare them for the service they feel called to pursue. For some it means connecting with certain types of mentors to provide challenge and support. And for others it may mean entering nonformal types of learning (workshops or seminars) to improve upon a particular type of learning. *How can we become aware of what people need to enhance their learning and how to link them with the proper resources to meet their learning need?*

- *A deepened dependency.* As people continue to develop certain competencies there is a move toward becoming proficient. In the work of leadership there exists an inherent temptation to believe that "It's up to us to make something happen." And, after all, it is to a certain extent. However, because God seems interested in bringing the good work begun in us to completion, we encounter learning that takes us beyond our competencies toward a deepened dependency on the love and power of God. *How is God at work disrupting those in your setting to move beyond their competencies and successes?*

- *An attention to social base.* We hear and are surprised at the stories of those who seemed to be at the top of their game only to crash due burnout, moral failure or a bizarre decision they made that seemed incongruent with who we had hoped them to be. Somewhere along the way a slow erosion was taking place, which caused an eventual undoing. *How can we help people in the business of life and service develop habits where they take inventory of how they themselves and those closest to them are doing?*

As guides alongside others we have a privileged role in helping people claim their *chosen-ness by God* for purposes that may have yet to be discovered. What is important to help people recognize during this time is that God is deeply concerned with who they are becoming—in their being and in their doing. If this present season can be characterized as a time of preparation, the next season along the journey may well be characterized as a time of contribution.

REFLECT ON YOUR LIFE

- What did you notice about your own formation as you read through this chapter?
- Revisit your poster board or timeline.

The perspectives and questions presented in this preparation chapter may have surfaced additional stories, lessons or relationships from your own life. Take some time to return to the poster board you developed from the "Brainstorming One's Life" exercise of chapter 3. What new insights are standing out to you?

- What do you look for when identifying those who may be ready to participate in the work of leadership?

A NARRATIVE EXERCISE FOR YOUR CONTEXT (PART 2)

Begin composing a spiritual narrative. Looking at your life from a timeline perspective can reveal some significant moments of discovery and learning. What we want to invite you to do now is to begin to convert your timeline/poster board into a written narrative of your own life story. Composing a written narrative sharpens our focus and yearning toward that which is central in our development—toward those essential themes, happenings and people—and move us away from what we deem to be peripheral to our lives and God's gracious work. This is difficult, fearful and rewarding work.

Develop an outline. Use your timeline or poster board to provide the initial structure. Begin to select what you want to highlight within each chapter. What are the things—critical incidents, themes, relationships, impressions, lessons learned—that you want to share in order to communicate what is central to your development and God's activity within your narrative? Take some notes as you think through these things. Some pieces of to your outline may need reordering once you see them together as a whole.

Start writing. Just begin writing. It may not even be at the beginning. You may begin with a particular incident or person. Take some of the things you have selected as part of your outline and start describing and identifying what happened. Let go of any pressure to do this well. Just start writing. It is often as we try to write things down that we make new discoveries. Don't feel locked in to telling your story in chronological order. You may discover a creative way to tell your tale. For some the writing process will be cathartic and healing. It may be helpful to limit the length of this particular exercise to a range of five to ten pages (single spaced). Ideally, it is good to get a rough draft written and then go back to revise. In chapter 5 we will encourage you to complete your narrative and then read it out loud in the company of trusted friends.

Remember the big picture. Our objective in composing our spiritual narrative is not to figure out our lives or to write a riveting narrative, but rather to seriously, honestly and courageously seek God's gracious and active presence in the story of our lives.

5

CONTRIBUTION
Leading Out of Who We Are

You stir us to take pleasure in praising you, because we have been made for yourself, and our heart is restless until it rests in you.

—AUGUSTINE OF HIPPO, *CONFESSIONS*

The more self-reliant we become, priding ourselves in our skills and abilities, the easier it is to practice atheism.

—JAMES M. HOUSTON, *THE TRANSFORMING POWER OF PRAYER*

We really trust in God when we come to the end of our own resources.

—J. ROBERT CLINTON, *INTERVIEW WITH THE AUTHOR*

Overview

Contribution Phase—This is a person's most highly productive and effective period of service and influence. Through the Spirit's shaping the person comes to terms with the reality that his or her service is inextricably linked to identity in Christ. That is, we serve out of who we are. This realization aids in the development of a mature, biblical way of life and service that is grounded in obedience and intimacy with God. The person thereby increasingly influences others with spiritual authority. And God's sovereign shaping moves the person toward a contribution of work that provides a greater *focus* of service and greater *fit* with the person's being, calling, passion, giftedness, and style.

Our leadership formation consists of both long, slow stretches of continuity and more sudden turns of discontinuity. These sudden turns in our stories offer such significant possibilities for how we learn, who we are and how we serve others in Jesus' name. A new event, circumstance or person in our life can precipitate a whole new way of seeing, believing and living. And if we are walking alongside people who are maturing into this contribution phase of development we must pay particular attention to these periods of *confrontation* and *discontinuity* in their lives; for these seasons often prove to be heightened times of learning and growth.

In 1977 Oscar was born in Panama to a loving mother and an absent father. At the age of five he moved to the inner city region of Miami. Oscar never knew his biological father, was physically abused by his second father, and felt most secure around his third father, who was a voodoo high priest in the syncretistic religion Santeria. He spent most of his teen years looking for love in all the wrong places and found he was gifted in winning people over to do what he wanted—which at the time usually produced the fruit of violence, drug abuse and a promiscuous lifestyle. Oscar knew how to make things happen his way.

His travels took him to places where he began to explore world religions, trying to squelch the growing noise in his life. By now Oscar had become a religious young man in the Islamic faith. In his senior year of high school he was recruited to play football at Trinity University in the greater Chicago area. In time it was the attention from a professor and a small group of Christian students that eventually encouraged Oscar to surrender his allegiance to Jesus. And so he did. There was a phrase in the song "Knowing You, Jesus" that held special meaning to Oscar because of the drastic turn in his life:

> Knowing you, Jesus, knowing you.
> There is no greater thing.[1]

A number of years later, I (Randy) met up with Oscar at a very successful time in his pastoral ministry. His zeal for ministry was evident in the things he was able to accomplish within his newly planted Latino congregation. He had the gift of getting people to do what he felt they

---

[1]Graham Kendrick, "Knowing You, Jesus." Words and music by Graham Kendrick, 1993.

could do, and together they produced much fruit in the life of the church community. Some people were discovering a relationship with God for the first time, while others were invited into a deeper way of life with Jesus. New ministries were started and organized as people were empowered to serve in the places that seemed to fit. Oscar was a central figure in the church—instrumental in igniting people for ministry and service, and capable of making a lot of things happen. And many good things did.

As the ministry grew, so did Oscar's concern to get it all done. How could he invest more deeply in the lives of others when his own life felt like it was growing out of control and moving toward a dull kind of hollowness? How could he continue to love these people when he felt in his more honest moments a growing critical spirit toward all of the demands? If this was still the place and the people he was to serve, why did he feel like he was becoming more toxic the more he served? At this same time, Oscar's family was dealt some major health blows that resulted in Oscar and his wife providing care for two of their parents going through cancer treatment.

As I (Randy) listened to this confluence of circumstances in Oscar's life, it became clear that God was inviting him into a new way of living and leading in the world. Amidst all that was going on in his life, a timely and honest question was beginning to surface—*"What sort of person am I actually becoming?"* The words to the song "Knowing You, Jesus," which held such rich definition for Oscar's life once-upon-a-time, returned and became for him a curriculum for the journey ahead. Most of us, like Oscar, would never dream of signing up for this set of events, but in time we too can come to discover God's nurturing and shaping curriculum for our lives within such disorienting circumstances. For amid the discontinuities God is often at work deepening our relationship with him, refining our character and empowering us for what is yet to come.

ACHIEVEMENT AND PRODUCTIVITY VERSUS IDENTITY AND CHARACTER

Oscar's question—*What sort of person am I becoming?*—anticipates a central concern for what takes place during this contribution phase. We must encounter a profoundly significant lesson at this point along the journey—God is more concerned with our identity and character than with our achievement and productivity. This lesson is hard for some to swallow because of the importance they have placed on their ability to "crank it out" for Jesus. But it brings with it a radical invitation to change how we see, believe and live. All our achievements and capacities and reputations will not adequately define and ground us; rather it is God's creative and reconciling love that must define us. We grow into a freeing awareness that *we lead and serve out of who we are in Christ.* Eugene Peterson, who stretches many of our contemporary notions of Christian leadership, puts it this way:

> Leaders influence followers far more by the context out of which they live—body language, personal values, social relationships, dress, consumer choices, chosen companions—than the text they articulate. Leadership is not primarily a skill, although it employs skills. Leadership is a way of living that suffuses everything we do and are. Leadership is a way of being in the family and marriage, a way of being among friends, a way of going to work, a way of climbing mountains; most basically, a way of following Jesus. And so in a culture in which there is an enormous attention to leadership, it is essential that we take a long hard look at what is previous and foundational to leadership, namely, "followership"—following Jesus (Mark 1:17).
>
> Followership gets us moving obediently in a way of life that is visible and audible in Jesus, a way of speaking, thinking, imagining, and praying that is congruent with immediate realities of "kingdom" living. . . . For those of us who are in positions of leadership—as parents, teachers, pastors, employers, physicians, lawyers, homemakers, students, farmers, writers—our following skills take priority over our leadership skills. Leadership that is not well grounded in followership—following Jesus—is dangerous to both the church and the world.[2]

During this contribution phase we move into a way of life derived from a deepened character, a renewed sense of the power of the Spirit, and a more focused fit between our calling, giftedness, responsibility and an honoring our context of service. And thereby we mature into a place of contribution

---

[2]Eugene Peterson, "Follow the Leader," *Fuller Focus*, Fall 2001, p. 31.

and influence more befitting to *who* we really are and *whose* we really are. We delight yet again that we are loved deeply and particularly by God. God *calls out our true name*, asks us to trust and follow, and grants us the love and power to do what we knew all along was beyond our reach.

For most of us, however, this movement into a new way of living and leading doesn't come without some inner struggle or resistance. We find ourselves wanting to follow Jesus, but if truth be told, mostly on our own terms. Sometimes our resistance develops into a fearful refusal of a new way of life, like the Israelites in the wilderness who cried and groaned to return to the familiarity of Egypt and captivity (Num 11). Our "groaning to return" can take the form of plateaued spiritual growth, hanging on to resentment and pride, believing that what we are able to accomplish for God is far more significant than anything or anyone else (even our own soul). Other times this groaning and resistance to a new way precipitates an indiscretion of some sort due to the pressures of work and home life, or due simply to the pleasures of this life becoming more attractive than faithfully following Jesus.

In all of this, leaders must be vigilant to guard their hearts so that doing good things for Jesus doesn't get in the way of loving Jesus. Or as Peter Scazzero puts it, "We were gaining the whole world by doing a great work for God while at the same time losing our souls."[3] There are subtle dangers of self-reliance that come along with growing proficient and skillful in the work of ministry. In this regard, James Houston argues for the priority of prayer in the face of such self-reliant leading. He writes,

> Prayer is the greatest antidote to professionalism, because it expresses our friendship with God as Father, Son and Holy Spirit. Yet the more the experts take over, the less incentive there is for prayer. Why pray if the experts can solve the problem for us? The more self-reliant we become, priding ourselves in our skills and abilities, the easier it is to practice atheism.[4]

---

[3]Peter Scazzero, *The Emotionally Healthy Church: A Strategy for Discipleship That Actually Changes Lives* (Grand Rapids: Zondervan, 2003), p. 25.
[4]James M. Houston, *The Transforming Power of Prayer: Deepening Your Friendship with God* (Colorado Springs: NavPress, 1996), p. 274.

Ruth Haley Barton offers a similar warning of the dangers of self-reliance. She likens our experience to that of Moses as he led the Israelites through the wilderness:

> Although we may feel invincible (based on our earlier triumphs), God knows that we are not. He knows that if we were to experience any real dangers, toils and snares, we wouldn't be ready for them. One of the main lessons we learn during this stage of the spiritual journey is that God is not in any particular hurry to get us to the Promised Land. He is much more concerned about the transforming work he is doing *in us* to prepare us for greater responsibilities of freedom living. Onlookers may observe our journey and, like Pharaoh, think we are just wandering around aimlessly, but God knows what he is doing; he is concerned about strengthening our faith so that we are prepared when there are real challenges to be faced.[5]

Although most would never say such a thing out loud, for some it is hard to fathom the possibility that God may be more concerned with our transformation personally (who we are becoming) than with all the things we have been able to accomplish for the kingdom (what we do). Is it any wonder that a good number of congregations in many parts of the world today have people longing spiritually for something more than the spiritual capacity of those leading them can provide? A central thrust in our walking alongside those persons moving toward this season of contribution is to invite a fresh awareness of Jesus' words in John 15:4-5:

> Abide in me as I abide in you. Just as the branch cannot bear fruit by itself unless it abides in the vine, neither can you unless you abide in me. I am the vine, you are the branches. Those who abide in me and I in them bear much fruit, because apart from me you can do nothing.

UNDERSTANDING THIS BOUNDARY TIME

Clinton found that for most on the leadership journey (like Oscar) this mature awareness—that they live and lead in the reality of who God designed and shaped them to be—grew out of a significant boundary time, a transitional period of disorientation, brokenness and refinement

---

[5]Ruth Haley Barton, *Strengthening the Soul of Your Leadership: Seeking God in the Crucible of Ministry* (Downers Grove, Ill.: InterVarsity Press, 2008), p. 94.

in their story. At the end of chapter 2 we called this boundary time a *movement toward being* in which a person comes to discover through a radical paradigm shift that the work of leadership must flow out of who we are—our being.

Understanding this boundary time, and how to help someone process through it, is of primary concern in our mentoring of Christian leaders. Many Christian leaders get stuck, refusing to learn what God wants them to learn through this trying and disruptive season in their journey. They spend years and sometimes decades leading out of their own ego strength, managing and measuring their service in terms of achievement and productivity, which can fit rather well with a warped pursuit of the Great Commission—what could be more noble than following hard after leading others to Jesus, even if it means that I sacrifice becoming more like Jesus. In many ways it is Jesus' inviting words that echo through this transitional mid-season in a leader's life, "Those who want to save their life will lose it, and those who lose their life for my sake will find it" (Mt 16:24). One can hardly overestimate the importance today of helping such men and women make better sense of their life and leadership in the light of God's invitation in this boundary time.

So let's get a better grasp of what might be going on in this difficult boundary time. To begin with, the larger leadership development literature can be instructive in elaborating on the disorienting dynamics of the boundary time. In particular, Robert Thomas refers to such life-shaping situations or transitions as *crucibles*. He defines a crucible as "a transformative experience from which a person extracts his or her 'gold': a new or an altered sense of identity."[6] Thomas writes that leaders typically enter into such crucibles in one of three ways: (1) by "walking off the map" into some *new territory*, (2) by "getting our legs knocked out from under us" in some sort of *reversal*, or (3) by "being placed in a holding pattern" of reflection and waiting, which he calls a time of *suspension*. These crucibles, according to Thomas, each operate like trials or tests that corner individuals and force them to answer questions about who they are and what is really important to them.

---

[6]Robert J. Thomas, *Crucibles of Leadership: How to Learn from Experience to Become a Great Leader* (Boston: Harvard Business Press, 2008), p. 5.

Clinton discovered a similar developmental process in the life stories he researched. *Conflict, crisis* and *isolation* were all used to deepen one's relationship with God, to gain a clearer sense of personal identity and to become empowered for the types of service and leadership they entered into.[7] For some, all three elements were present; for others it was just one or two that were used to forge their person. *Conflict* can be described as a clash, disagreement or severe frustration resulting from a given task or context that interrupts positive and harmonious relationship with another or others. The conflict may play itself out between relationships at home, within a given community or in a work environment. *Crisis* can be described as a more immediate and oftentimes surprising hardship caused by natural disaster, finances, political tensions, death, an indiscretion, a disease or any situation that creates a sense of emergency. *Isolation* can be described as a time of being set aside from the regular routine and familiarity of life and ministry. Shelley Trebesch likens a time of isolation to that of a desert experience. She writes,

> A person in a desert time may not feel the presence of God, and it may seem that he/she is alone in a dark and foreign land. One cannot rely on what used to be familiar. The person consequently walks through a breaking or stripping process after which his/her character becomes transformed.[8]

Although extremely painful while going through such experiences, on the other side of good processing of the boundary lay descriptions like, "I'm not sure anything else would have got my attention from the busyness of my life," or "I needed to be stripped of my arrogant ways," or "I never thought I would be doing what I am now doing with such conviction and confidence," or "It feels like I've fallen in love with Jesus again," or "I needed to learn to how to discern God's guidance of my life before I could discern where God wanted to lead this organization,"

---

[7]J. Robert Clinton, *Leadership Emergence Theory* (Altadena, Calif.: Barnabas, 1989), pp. 273-79.
[8]Shelley Trebesch, *Isolation: A Place of Transformation in the Life of a Leader* (Altadena, Calif.: Barnabas, 1997), p. 9. Trebesch further describes two types of isolation experiences: (1) *involuntary*, where something unexpected takes place that precipitates the isolation (sickness, wars, disasters, organizational changes or discipline), and (2) *voluntary*, where the person is the catalyst for causing the isolation experience (personal renewal, educational leave, taking care of one's personal life needs).

or "It feels like I've heard my name for the first time and I now know who I really am."

In Thomas's crucible study, the person's capacity to learn in and from the situation is the key to whether the experience is in fact transforming for their life and leadership. And in this regard the transition from preparation to contribution works very similarly to a crucible in our leadership journey. Many people can walk into this boundary time and seemingly end up only bitter, resentful and even stuck in the conflict or the personal crisis for decades, while others seem to learn and grow and walk through the painful and perplexing season in a way the frees them up and empowers their ministry over the long haul.

Consider the story of Jordan. In his twenties he was voted "most likely to succeed" at whatever he might put his hand to. Jordan could converse with others in a way that left them feeling like they mattered, and that they had something very important to contribute. Jordan's ideas were usually plentiful and focused on how things could be better within the student development division on the university campus he had come to love. At national conferences Jordan was seen as a rising star and soon won the attention of another university campus across the country who was looking for a gifted leader who knew how to develop both people and a struggling student life department. Jordan was hired.

In his usual manner Jordan was able to quickly earn the trust of those in his newly inherited department, and he helped them see how they had timely contributions to make for the overhaul of their service to the campus community. Within three years Jordan and his team had not only put a new face to the department but had gained the attention of the senior administration for the new hope they had fostered, which was now leaking out into other areas of the campus community.

However, as good as things had seemed to be for Jordan after three years, things began to unravel in his fourth year. He discovered one of his trusted associates was "going over his head" to file various complaints about how he was handling various concerns within the department. Hearing after hearing took place where Jordan's integrity and ways of handling things were called into question. The institution had also fallen on hard times financially, which resulted in several positions needing to be eliminated, including positions within Jordan's department. Jordan had the unfortunate privilege of telling good and faithful people their service was no longer needed at the school. The final turn came when Jordan's supervisor stopped by Jordan's office for a visit to let him know that he too was being let go from the institution. Jordan was devastated.

In the months that followed, Jordan strained to figure out how this could have happened. Although there are two sides to every story, those who knew Jordan well were also perplexed about how this could have happened to someone like him. The questions and the scenarios all seemed to lead to the same place—nowhere. Days, weeks and months ticked by and Jordan found his questions turning from an analysis of what took place toward honest frustration with God. This turning would become a two-year period when Jordan wrestled, prayed and listened to God. People who knew and loved him well came alongside to help process what the Lord might be up to. After many tears, prayers and conversations, Jordan began to find peace with the way things were. He realized that trying to get to the bottom of why he was disrespected and then dismissed by those he trusted was not what was most important.

In the *space* that Jordan was given he came to realize how addicted he was to making something become successful. Through trusted soul mates who had the courage to be honest with him, Jordan came to see that although he knew how to gain the loyalty of those he served, he had a driving need to prove something to his superiors—even if it meant pointing out what they could do to lead more effectively. At the time Jordon thought he was doing them a favor. But after two years of thinking and praying about these things, he discovered what a selfish and dishonoring person he had become. Moving into a space where his abilities and drive to create a winner were of no use, Jordon became *still* enough and *open* enough to encounter a love that felt both familiar and new at the same time. His same friends would listen to Jordan talk about knowing the love of God as if for the very first time. He used Jesus' name in the descriptions of how he was doing more than he had for some time, and he didn't seem to need to prove anything. Jordan's disposition reflected a deep-set and grounding love.

Soon after this painful and illuminating season of suspension (to borrow Thomas's language), an acquaintance of Jordan's contacted him and invited him to consider a new opportunity. The mission was outside his familiar university environment, but it provided Jordan an opportunity to help develop resources that would foster learning among teachers, plumbers, engineers, homemakers, pastors and retired folks. Somehow the opportunity felt right "on time" and opened up for Jordan a pathway for the next few decades of service.

A NOTE ON CHARACTER AND IDENTITY

God's transforming work within us must always precede the transforming work God desires to do through us. If this were not the case, Dallas Willard suggests we would crumble and disintegrate under the weight of God's blessing and work. Why? Because our character and person could not hold up to what God wants to give us.[9] The most critical formation in the life of those who desire to finish faithfully and well is the cultivation of godly character. God is persistently concerned with shaping our lives at the deepest layers of our soul. Clinton has defined this spiritual or character formation process as "the development of the inner life of a person of God so that the person (1) experiences more of God, (2) reflects more God-like characteristics in personality and everyday relationships, and (3) increasingly knows the power and presence of God in ministry."[10]

In this regard, claiming, embracing and resting in our identity as beloved sons and daughters of God is a fundamental development we return to repeatedly. Henri Nouwen suggests that we learn to identify ourselves in our culture—or put another way, we live out the question Who am I?—in one of three ways: *I am what I do* (competency, achievements, etc.), *I am what others say about me* (popularity, reputation, etc.), and *I am what I have* (power, family, skills, possessions, etc.).[11] Throughout our lives much personal energy is expended proving our

---

[9]Dallas Willard, *Leadership and Spirituality* (Vancouver: Regent College Audio, 2008).

[10]J. Robert Clinton, *The Making of A Leader* (Colorado Springs: NavPress, 1988), p. 255.

[11]Henri J. M. Nouwen, *Life of the Beloved* (New York: Crossroad, 1992). The described framework for the question Who am I? is discussed throughout Nouwen's book.

worth, trying to find love and significance, answering this question Who am I? in one of those three ways. That said, nothing is intrinsically wrong with *what I do* or *what others say about me* or *what I have*. Achievement, reputation and influence have their good and proper place in our lives. But when any of these occupy the core of our identity, our lives are perched on some rickety scaffolding. Why? Because these are not who we are at the core! All of these ways prove insufficient in defining ourselves. They provide no true *rest*. God has a much more intimate and personally involving definition in mind. We are, by God's creative and gracious design, his beloved children (Eph 1:3-5). God created and established us in love, and God patiently matures us in love by the Holy Spirit.

A dangerous exchange takes place when Christian leaders substitute other peripheral, parts of our identity for the core of their identity as children of God. It is so easy to exchange or resist this true identity, which God has intended us to be, for a pale imitation in today's world. There are so many defining voices seducing us into a misunderstanding of who we are. This is especially true in the work of leadership.[12] We need much help from our brothers and sisters in Christ reminding us who we really are. Faithfulness to whom God has made us, and is making us to be, reforming our character and inner life, is not a task for lone-ranger Christians.

PROCESSING THIS BOUNDARY TIME

As we mentioned earlier in this chapter, understanding this boundary time and how to help someone process through it is of primary concern in our mentoring of Christian leaders. We recognize that timely and significant development takes place all along the journey. However, this boundary (movement toward being) described earlier holds out to us the possibility of profoundly altering the trajectory and focus of a leader's life direction. It is a *heightened time of learning*. And if we are at all grabbed by a desire to invest more deeply in people's lives, then we must become adept in this boundary time. Development from one

---

[12]Henri Nouwen's *In the Name of Jesus: Reflections on Christian Leadership* (New York: Crossroad, 1992) is an excellent set of reflections on this dynamic.

phase to another is not like hopping on the train and assuming we will get to the next stop. Not everyone develops and learns. There must be greater intentionality if a person is going to grow. Figure 5.1 suggests a general learning process that we can pay attention to in helping people walk in and through their boundary time.

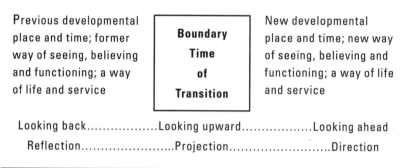

Previous developmental place and time; former way of seeing, believing and functioning; a way of life and service

Boundary
Time
of
Transition

New developmental place and time; new way of seeing, believing and functioning; a way of life and service

Looking back..................Looking upward..................Looking ahead

Reflection.......................Projection...........................Direction

Figure 5.1. General learning process

Moving into and through a boundary time of transition may be for most a gradual thing that won't always have an exact date and time attached to its beginning and ending. But there is little doubt as to when someone is immersed in one. People know they have entered a focused time of learning when they are invited to reflect more deeply and critically on the meaning of their lives in light of the disruptive and disorienting set of circumstances they find themselves in. Moving through these times faithfully with others will require *looking back, looking upward* and *looking ahead.*

Looking back is a time of processing critical questions that can help people face and embrace more honestly the past that they have just left behind. *Why did these things or events happen to me? How might God use me given my past hurts and dreams? Why do I feel so alone after all I have invested in others? Is this as good as it gets? How will I utilize my time and energies in a more focused manner?* Looking back is also an important grieving time when people find themselves in the midst of conflicts or life crises that are painful and disillusioning. Without proper grieving they will carry their pain, frustrations and unresolved anger into the next chapter of their life and service. As we help people reflect back on "what just happened," they often find themselves experiencing a mixture of regret, anxiety, frustration, anger, fear, anticipation, wondering, disillusionment and a sense of loss. Having a trusted mentor, counselor or friend is critical to helping leaders see what they cannot see on our own. We all need someone who has the love and courage and patience to travel with us through this disruptive time.

Looking upward is the time in the boundary when people prayerfully seek God's guidance, not only to make sense of the past but to surrender what has been in order to embrace what is and what is yet to come. Looking upward brings with it the opportunity for greater transparency before God—honestly bringing to the table what they have discovered within themselves. This becomes the time when we *listen* with them for God's direction through the Scriptures, through life circumstances, through the stirrings of their heart and through the wisdom of our community. Looking upward is a time for discernment, in which the company of a spiritual mentor can help a person trust and envision the Spirit's work within. This also becomes a time when he or she begins to *project* what the future may hold, consider the options available and imagine once again how God might use him or her within his larger story.[13]

It is only after they have honestly looked back and prayerfully surrendered themselves before the Lord that they are ready to enter the third stage of a boundary time of transition, *looking ahead.* Too many people transition from present situations or places in life only asking the question, What should I do for my next job or ministry? This is a premature question unless an honest looking back and surrendering before God precede it. Looking ahead brings with it the anticipation of a new chapter of life and the ability to make decisions about the direction toward the future with a greater sense of clarity and purpose. And their ability to make a wise decision is helped and confirmed from the understanding, wisdom and guidance of those who walk alongside us.

What makes boundary times, in general, so difficult for all of us is that we are leaving what we can see and moving toward what we cannot see. It can get very dark along the way. Like Abram's departure from Ur

---

[13]Terry B. Walling offers a helpful process for those in leadership positions who may be going through difficult boundary times of transition. See his resource *Stuck: Navigating the Transitions of Life and Leadership* (St. Charles, Ill.: ChurchSmart Resources, 2008).

for "the land I will show you," we are invited to make a risky move from the familiar to the unfamiliar (Gen 12:1-4). Richard Rohr offers a helpful perspective in this regard by elaborating on what he refers to as living in this "liminal space." He writes,

> "Limina" is the Latin word for threshold, the space betwixt and between. Liminal space, therefore, is a unique spiritual position where human beings hate to be but where the biblical God is always leading them. It is when you have left the "tried and true" but have not yet been able to replace it with anything else. It is when you are finally out of the way. It is when you are in between your old comfort zone and any possible new answer. It is no fun. Think of Israel in the desert, Joseph in the pit, Jonah in the belly, the three Marys tending the tomb.
>
> IF YOU ARE NOT trained in how to hold anxiety, how to live with ambiguity, how to entrust and wait, you will run, or more likely you will "explain." Not necessarily a true explanation, but any explanation is better than scary liminal space. Anything to flee from this terrible "cloud of unknowing." Those of a more fear-based nature will run back to the old explanations. Those who love risk or hate thought will often quickly construct a new explanation where they can feel special and again in control. Few of us know how to stay on the threshold.[14]

The place of "unknowing" is a place we find very unsettling, but it is often the place from which the Spirit of God leads us. Boundary times require learned postures of "holding anxiety" and "living with ambiguity" and "entrusting and waiting" as Rohr put it. Such places and postures reflect the experience and testimony of the psalms. And if we are to walk well with others we would do well to be schooled by the prayerfulness of the psalms. For they offer language for living the whole of our lives before God honestly and hopefully. They are chock full of complaint and lament, on one hand, and thanksgiving and celebration, on the other hand. These psalms become our mentors in prayerfulness as they teach us and invite us to connect our everyday reality with their bold language and living before God.[15]

---

[14]Richard Rohr, "Grieving as Sacred Space," *John Mark Ministries*, January 3, 2003, http://jmm .aaa.net.au/articles/1266.htm.

[15]Walter Brueggemann's *The Psalms: The Life of Faith* (Minneapolis: Fortress, 1995) can be very instructive as to these dynamics in the psalms.

During this boundary time leaders will also bump into poignant reminders of their own frailty, fallenness and limits. By God's good and patient grace (*his steadfast love* as Psalms put it) they encounter twists and turns in their stories that bring them to places of *brokenness*. The central issue in dealing with brokenness is a painful confrontation with our egos, a time in our formation when, as Clinton describes it, we come to the end of ourselves.

> A leader has come to the end of his/her personal resources before this deepened level of trust can be appropriated. Strong leaders will operate out of ego strength until they encounter processing which leads to brokenness before God. The results of such brokenness are usually a paradigm shift of viewing success in ministry in terms of one's relationship with God, rather than in one's accomplishments for God.[16]

The scorecard for ministry begins to change during these times. We must help others revisit Jesus' invitation to his first followers to die to themselves and their way of life. As we mentioned earlier, facing one's brokenness is a process of losing one's life in order to find it again (Mt 10:39). Or as Jesus spoke of his own journey, "Very truly, I tell you, unless a grain of wheat falls into the earth and dies, it remains just a single grain; but if it dies, it bears much fruit" (Jn 12:24). They must not be fooled but always remember that the practice of leadership is filled with traps and temptations for their egos. And as John of the Cross understood this, "To come to be what you are not you must go by a way in which you are not."[17]

If our concern is the development and formation of others, then we must come to see this boundary time as a major opportunity for growth and learning. But we mentors must guard against the propensity to envision these difficult times in others' lives as stepping stones for advancing to something greater and better, and so try too quickly to rush through it, or worse yet, try to get around it. Such thoughts may be evidence that we still need to work through a few things. Clinton has mentioned on many occasions that we must never be in a hurry to get through

---

[16]Clinton, *Leadership Emergence Theory*, p. 390.
[17]Kieran Kavanaugh, ed., *John of the Cross: Selected Writings* (New York: Paulist, 1987), p. 78.

these boundary times. We must learn what God has for us to learn in his timing. This boundary or invitation toward being acts like a hinge toward a deeper processing of our lives in order to experience and serve God out of a renewed love, holiness and empowerment by the Spirit.

LEARNING TO NOTICE

The curricular pieces of our formation during this important transitional time emerge from concrete experiences in our life stories: a nagging sense that we really should be doing something different with our life, personal or organizational crisis, promotions or demotions, moving to a new location or country, health concerns, isolation, conflict, empty nests, burnout, an encounter with someone who could have only been a divine appointment, a new job challenge, a failure in the marriage, a whisper in your heart. In other words, God seems to creatively shape and reshape us toward growth, development and fitting opportunities through the everyday stuff of our lives.

Our lives, and the lives of those persons with whom we journey, take some significant twists and turns in this *movement toward being*. And on the other side of the turns we often find rich perspectives and discoveries: a renewing of faith and dependency on God, being let go from a job was absolutely necessary in order to face internally what I needed to be faced, a celebration of our true identity as a person, assisted in strategic decision making for next chapter in life, reignited the imagination for what could be down the road, a grateful disbelief that a place of life and service could seem so right even amid new sufferings, and becoming more intentional in the investment of others. On the "other side" are often testimonies of renewed hope reflective of Hebrews 11:1, "Now faith is the assurance of things hoped for, the conviction of things not seen." The learning has been seared with the truth that "without faith it is impossible to please God" (Heb 11:6).

The following are some suggestions to consider as you invest in the formation of those who may find themselves in the good struggle of learning more truly who they are and the implications then for how they go about ministry and leadership:

- *Affirm growth toward proficiency.* We can encourage people to exercise their giftedness, competencies and strengths so they develop a measure of excellence in those areas. This is a season of growth development where we want people to become proficient at the things for which we have a passion. Perhaps for some they will need to consider ongoing education of various types and forms in order to be taken to a "next level" in their ability to do well.

- *Invite an inventory of the mystery of weakness.* We can also affirm an honest look at the perceived weaknesses of those whom we walk along side. For it may be through our weaknesses where God may decide to show up in a way of strength (2 Cor 12:7-10). We hold this in good tension with the perceived need in this day to be doing most everything we do out of a focused exercising of our strengths.

- *Don't be fooled by success.* We would do well to be excited for the achievements and successes of those we walk alongside, but not enamored by them. Whether it be ourselves, or someone whom we might recommend, we need to encourage a form of guidance that can honesty and delicately "walk in someone's soul," to help them listen and notice the ongoing work of the Spirit within. Spiritual direction or mentoring is needed not only when we feel we have lost our way, but during those times when we are surrounded by successes.

- *Prescribe time of solitude and silence.* It may be time for the person we are walking alongside to take a sabbatical of sorts from the regular routine in order to take inventory of questions like: Am I making priority time for the care and investment in the members of my family or friendships? How am I doing with financial matters? Are there personal needs that are going unmet? Where am I experiencing conflict or crisis? Am I thinking about my successes or level of ambition to accomplish more?

- *Reinvest in friendship.* Oftentimes people involved in significant responsibilities struggle with friendships and the ability to have fun. It may be time to challenge those you walk alongside to reinvest in past friendships or to make new ones. It may also be timely to recommend taking some time off to have some play, fun or develop a new hobby. Some people need to fast from their hyper-responsibility.

• *Be patient in the boundary time.* If you find someone going through a transitional time of boundary it may be helpful to lead them through a process over a period of time where they could process the three stages of a boundary (*looking back, looking upward, looking ahead*). J. Robert Clinton would often tell his students, "Never try to get out of a boundary until you learn in the boundary all that God has for you to learn from the boundary."

In the early 1990s Henri Nouwen was asked to speak on the future of Christian leadership at the Center for Human Development in Washington, D.C. Having just lived through a significant boundary in his own story, Nouwen struggled to believe that he had something worthwhile to offer, but he began by saying, "Somehow I have to trust that God is at work in me and that the way I am being moved to new inner and outer places is part of a larger movement of which I am only a very small part."[18] He offered these words when describing what sort of person will be needed to offer leadership "in Jesus' name" in the future:

> The central question is, Are the leaders of the future truly men and women of God, people with an ardent desire to dwell in God's presence, to listen to God's voice, to look at God's beauty, to touch God's incarnate Word and to taste fully God's infinite goodness?
>
> The original meaning of the word "theology" was "union with God in prayer." Today theology has become one academic discipline alongside many others, and often theologians are finding it hard to pray. But for the future of Christian leadership it is of vital importance to reclaim the mystical aspect of theology so that every word spoken, every advice given, and every strategy developed can come from a heart that knows God intimately.[19]

May these words provide us a horizon for what Jesus may be inviting us to be and do in the world.

---

[18]Nouwen, *In the Name of Jesus*, p. 9.
[19]Ibid., pp. 29-30.

REFLECT ON YOUR LIFE

- Think back on your own story to a time when you experienced *confrontation* or *discontinuity*. How were they significant for your formation? What did you learn as a result?

- Boundary times are times of *heightened learning*. Trying to make sense of why things happened as they did, entering prayerful seasons where we are brought to a deepened dependency on God, and being brought to a fresh vantage point in order to make a confident decision about tomorrow are all important as we move toward maturity. Consider a boundary time you have gone through. What did you learn as a result of going through that boundary time of transition?

- Revisit your poster board or timeline.

The perspectives and questions presented in this contribution chapter may have surfaced additional stories, lessons or relationships from your own life. Take some time to return to the poster board or narrative you have been developing in the previous chapters. What do you need to add to your timeline? Any new questions emerging?

A NARRATIVE EXERCISE FOR YOUR CONTEXT (PART 3)

Completing your spiritual narrative. In chapter 3, "Foundation: A Beginning," you were invited to have a group of people from your setting complete a timeline of their life story. Then in chapter 4, "Preparation: Finding Our Way," you were invited to have the same group of people develop a written narrative of their life story from their timeline. Now we would like to invite you to consider having those same people share their written narratives with one another over a shared meal.

Sharing a meal together. Good things happen when people gather together around a table with good food and drink. Remember the people in your life (parents, grandparents, that special couple or person from church, uncles and aunts) who had a way of showing hospitality. Oftentimes such people have a way of making leisurely space around good food, good conversation and good care.

Think of such people as you make preparations for your group to come together to share their narratives. How can you be hospitable in providing good food, conversation and care for one another? It may be a great experience to make the meal together as a way of relaxing and being together before you share your narratives.

Sharing your narratives. You will want to give some attention to thinking through a few details of the sharing time. For example it may be good to complete your meal together and then over dessert begin to share the narratives. Also think through how much time each person should be allotted to share, as well as how you will bring a sense of closure after each person shares.

People often feel vulnerable talking about themselves, so whatever instructions you can provide before you begin will help. This is also a holy time, so you will want to encourage an *honoring* of the person sharing by having others in the group lend their attention, and to prayerfully listen to their brother or sister share their story.

After each person has shared from their narrative, it would be good to allow others in the group to respond with words of encouragement and affirmation. And then together as a group *pray* for the person who shared. This is not the time to offer advice on what the person may need for their development, but a time of *honoring*, *listening* and *praying* for one another.

6

MULTIPLICATION
Finishing Well

*Keep on doing the things that you have learned and received and
heard and seen in me, and the God of peace will be with you.*

—PHILIPPIANS 4:9

*When Christ calls leaders to Christian ministry He intends to
develop them to their full potential. Each of us in leadership
is responsible to continue developing in accordance with
God's processing all our life. . . . Unless we experience
God's ongoing development we will not be able to
help others develop their leadership capacity.*

—J. ROBERT CLINTON, *THE MAKING OF A LEADER*

Overview

Multiplication Phase—*The final phase invites us toward deeper
grow*th and maturity as we follow the Lord, while at the same time
stewarding what God has given us to do. However, in the multiplication phase a deeper concern grows within us for the investment
and development of others. We are at a time in the journey when
we hold the benefit of wisdom and experience to pass on to others.
*And we also develop a growing desire to recognize others and call them
out to be mentored, deepened and empowered for the good work God
desires to do through them.* Developing others for kingdom influence

becomes the focal point of our efforts. *We learn to lead strategically by tending to the deep work within us while at the same time tending much more intentionally to the development of others.*

The movement toward finishing well brings with it its own timely set of discoveries and questions, which cannot be fully understood until we get there. Terry Nyhuis describes this third-third of life as a time when significant contribution is still likely but can only come when we are fully present in that particular stage of life. Rather than hoping to get by with what we already know, we must be open to God's unfolding lessons in these new chapters. Nyhuis shares a story about encountering one such person in her third-third of life.

> Twelve years before writing this dissertation, I was pastoring a church in Holland, Michigan. One of my favorite mornings was when I led a Tuesday morning Bible study for women who were well into their Third-Third. There I encountered many of the sages, mystics, and seers embedded in that congregation.
>
> One Tuesday morning I described to these women something I had recently learned and said, "I wish I wasn't so slow to learn. If only I'd learned this lesson ten years ago, it would have helped me and the church so much."
>
> One of the women slowly and laboriously pulled herself up by her walker and shuffled over to me. She patted me on the head affectionately and said, "Oh, Pastor, you couldn't possibly learn a fifty-year-old lesson when you are only forty years old. You have to be fifty to learn a fifty-year-old lesson. Someday when you are sixty you will learn sixty-year-old lessons. Just wait until you are ninety like me. Pastor, you are hardly half way through your lessons. The best lessons are still to come for you."[1]

Why does it seem like such a rare find when we discover someone who keeps on growing and learning all the way to the finish line? And yet, thankfully, there are saints among us who continue to go the distance, who model a wise and spiritually attractive way of life.

---

[1]Terry Nyhuis, "A Developmental Approach to the Third-Third of Life," unpublished Doctor of Ministry paper, George Fox University, 2010, p. 16.

Cultivating careful reflective thinking has been such a critical part of a leader's life all along the way. This is no less the case as a person matures into his or her later chapters. We find in these later years yet another shift reflected in the lives of those leaders who have come before us and sought to be faithful to Jesus' way. They began to see the need to step back and take inventory of who they had become and what they had given their hand to over the past number of years. They found themselves wondering what an "ending to the story" might look like, which caused them to raise familiar but timely questions of stewardship. When we fail to look back, look up, look ahead, we uncritically adopt the horizons of our cultural expectations. In contrast to this, John Piper recalls hearing J. Oswald Sanders's passionate prayer at the age of eighty-nine:

> O God, don't let me waste my final years! Don't let me buy the American dream of retirement—month after month of leisure and play and hobbies and putzing around in the garage and rearranging the furniture and golfing and fishing and sitting and watching television. Lord, please have mercy on me. Spare me this curse.[2]

Helping others practice a more reflective way amid the busyness and demands of life is a hard sell but a necessary step as we walk alongside those who may find themselves in this fruitful season of life. Our formational concerns during this *multiplication phase* become more strategic in nature: What is the deepest nature of what we are to be about? What should become areas of focus if we are to finish well? Our processing leads us to think more clearly about the manner in which we must approach our work from here-on-out.

A unique group of people gathered in April 2011 to celebrate Dr. Clinton's legacy and influence in their lives. The group was composed of pastors, professors, missionaries and parachurch folks, men and women experienced in applying and implementing leadership emergence theory in their settings. During this occasion Clinton addressed the group with a talk titled "Finishing Well or Testing My Legacy." He returned to some themes and observations very familiar to the group.

---

[2]John Piper and Justin Taylor, eds., *Stand: A Call for the Endurance of the Saints* (Wheaton, Ill.: Crossway, 2008), p. 48.

Leadership is difficult. Very few leaders finish their race well—that is, with a maturity, commitment, faithfulness, humility and zeal for Jesus. God's enabling presence is the *essential* ingredient for successful leadership. *Spiritual* leadership can make a real difference.

As Clinton reflected on those who had finished well he underscored the importance of "passing on values to insure a legacy." The lesson he drew out of his study was that modeling and sharing values is the strongest way a leader can pass on his or her values to the next generation. He then unpacked for the group six personal values, that is, underlying assumptions about how he perceives leadership and practices it:

- *Value 1.* A leader must seek intimacy with God, for ministry flows out of who we are in relationship to God.

- *Value 2.* A leader should have a developmental mindset, for God is a God who develops people.

- *Value 3.* A leader must continually be developing in terms of his or her grasp of God's Word, for God's Word is his foundational revelation of himself and his purposes.

- *Value 4.* Over a lifetime, a leader must walk in obedience to God, for obedience is the key to knowing God's will for a life.

- *Value 5.* Over a lifetime a leader must be transformed into the image of Christ by the power of the Holy Spirit, for a major goal of the developing God is transformation of an individual toward Christ-likeness in terms of the leader's uniqueness.

- *Value 6.* A leader should minister with gifted power, for the essential ingredient of leadership is the powerful presence of the Holy Spirit in the life and ministry of the leader.[3]

Each of these six values have been scattered throughout part 2 of this book, albeit expressed in different ways at times. They get to the crux of the matter in this slow and deep work. But it is Clinton's emphasis on a leader's *developmental mindset* that seems particularly pertinent to us at this point. In his notes for this talk Clinton elaborated on this value:

---

[3]Unpublished notes from J. Robert Clinton's "Finishing Well or Testing My Legacy" (Pasadena, Calif.: Fuller Seminary, April 2011).

God is a developmental God. He intends to develop each of his children over their lifetimes so that they become and achieve his purposes for them. None of us are finished products. We are all in process. The more we recognize and identify the processes in our own and others' lives the more we will participate with God in the development of self and others.[4]

What Clinton expressed in terms of a personal value, he also found to be true among those who finished well: they have come to adopt a developmental mindset in regard to themselves and to others.

We have come to highlight and express this developmental mindset by asking leaders to steward two critical questions on their journey: *How will I continue to cultivate a growing interior life with God? How can I move toward an entrusting way with others?* The movement toward finishing well requires that we pay particular attention to the ongoing deepening of our life with God and at the same time become increasingly more intentional in the formation of other Christian leaders. None of us are finished products and none of us walk alongside finished products.

A DEVELOPMENTAL MINDSET

Question 1. How will I continue to cultivate a growing interior life with God? I (Rob) was home in Philadelphia several summers back when the decision was being made about what to do with the back porch off the living room. It was beginning to become an eyesore. After fifteen years of use, the porch looked worn. Its dark stain color was gone and its wood had weakened. Bees' nests and weather had rotted it a bit. It was on its last legs. The choice: do we load on some new stain or do we tear it down and rebuild? From an appearance standpoint there would be little discernible difference between a new porch and a newly stained porch. After all, no one really sat on this porch. We had a screened-in porch off the family room and kitchen that got all the use. Additionally, the cost to rebuild would be much more, the labor would be considerable and the expertise of construction would be beyond the Loane's skill set. (We never have been real handy with a hammer and nails or nuts and bolts or anything that reads "assembly required," for that matter.) From both an

---

[4]Ibid.

appearance perspective and cost perspective, staining was a very tempting choice. In the end however, we concluded that more radical measures were required—the porch came down and a new one was constructed. On more than one occasion since that summer the condition of my character and person has reminded me of the condition of that back porch. When I am frustrated by my inability to love God and others deeply and authentically, I grab for some sort of behavior or strategy that works quickly on my character like stain on the porch.

Any person who intends to serve faithfully over the long haul will face this persistent temptation. We prefer dealing with outward appearances rather than dealing with our heart. The demands of meeting the expectations and responsibilities of leadership overshadow the necessity of cultivating a whole person. The question we must then continue to answer throughout our life story is, *Are the ways we are nurturing an inward life adequate to the outward demands of leading in Jesus' way?* An honest reflection on this question will require a necessary groundwork—an ongoing foundational sort of work necessary for both our followership and our leadership over the long haul. There are three recommendations for the ongoing groundwork of cultivating growing interior life with God: (1) cultivating a love of God, (2) cultivating a desire to learn, and (3) cultivating a life together.

Cultivating a love of God. Ezekiel 34:1-16 records one of the most scathing critiques of leadership in the Scriptures. The shepherds or leaders of Israel were not paying attention to their sheep because they were too preoccupied with "feeding" and "clothing" themselves, "slaughtering the fatling" for themselves and neglecting the well-being of their sheep. Their self-serving way resulted in a rule of neglect and harshness. In the end, the self-serving shepherds lost their sheep and the sheep were scattered. We wonder whether the leaders of Ezekiel's day were conscious of just how self-serving their leadership had become. Or were they blindsided by Ezekiel's message from God? In either case, the picture was clear. This was not the sort of leadership God was wanting.

Ezekiel 34 demonstrates so poignantly that the primary temptation of leadership has always been to serve oneself instead of serving others or God. Cultivating a love of God will help guard our hearts and actions from being dominated by this self-serving way. Much could be said about this movement toward love of God in our lives. In some ways this is descriptive of the whole of the Christian journey. A. B. Simpson wrote,

> From many standpoints the Bible looks at our spiritual life. Sometimes it is as a life of faith, again as a life of holiness, evermore as a life of service, deepest of all as a life of patience and victorious suffering; but the highest and divinest view of it is a life of love. Nor is it love in any ordinary sense, but the tenderest and most intimate forms, and the most exquisite figures of human affection and friendship are used to describe the unspeakable bond which links the heart of God with the souls He calls to be His own.[5]

We are emphasizing the necessity of this ongoing movement toward love of God even during this season of our formation. How is it that we are not going to be dominated over the long haul by a self-serving way of life and leadership? How is it that we are able to live, from our center, Jesus' vision of kingdom authority? Such willingness freely grows in the good soil of loving God. This said, we must remember there is a deeper soil than our love of God. It is God's love of us. The apostle John put it very simply: "We love because he first loved us" (1 Jn 4:19). The importance of cultivating a love of God rests on the prior reality that God loves us and loves us first. Loving God will grow in our awareness of being loved by God. Prayer, meditation on Scripture, and worship remain some of the central practices that help us deepen our awareness of God's love in our life.

Cultivating a desire to learn. Cultivating a desire to learn will help guard our minds and actions from plateauing in our growth. Consider Robert Greenleaf, who was, among many other things, a learner. He was an executive for AT&T from the 1920s until the 1960s. After an early retirement he did a fair amount of business/leadership consulting. The men and women he influenced—scholars and writers, educators and business people, familiar names like Ken Blanchard, Warren Bennis, Stephen Covey, Margaret Wheatley, Peter Drucker, Parker Palmer, to name just a few—all point to Greenleaf's radical thoughts on leadership and influence captured in his articulation of the servant-leader.

Greenleaf's ideas and convictions did not emerge out of some pie-in-

---

[5]A. B. Simpson, *The Love Life of the Lord* (Harrisburg, Penn.: Christian Publications, 1900), p. 3.

the-sky speculation, nor were they a thought out experiment prompted by Jesus' words in the Gospels. His convictions stemmed from his experiences, intuitions and observations of those who thrived and flourished in the growing institutional world of business, education, government and religion. For Greenleaf the influence of such men and women could not be reduced to qualifications of competency and personality. He recognized something more at work, something more human—the impulse to serve. As we become acquainted with him through his writings and others' writings of him, we cannot help but recognize the thread, woven through his whole life, of Greenleaf-as-learner. Integral to the many dynamics and expressions of a servant as leader is the reality of this learning disposition. Study and service are some of the central disciplines that cultivate lifelong learning.

Cultivating a life together. Cultivating a life together will help guard us from predominantly taking a lone-ranger approach life and leadership. Spiritual growth is just too hard to maintain alone. David Benner tells the following story.

> A friend who was unhappy with the church had an interesting reply when I recently asked him why he continued to attend, even if intermittently. He answered that he was afraid that he would stop growing if he dropped out of church. He went on: "Even if I get nothing out of the sermon and even if I have trouble encountering God in the rest of the service, church keeps me in touch with others on the spiritual journey. Spiritual growth is just too hard to maintain alone."[6]

Benner goes on:

> The Christian spiritual journey is a journey we take with others. Each of us must take our own journey, and for each of us that journey will be unique. But none of us is intended to make that journey alone. The myth of the solitary Christian making his or her own way alone flies in the face of everything the Bible teaches about the church as the body of Christ (1 Corinthians 12:12-31). . . . We cannot make the journey apart from spiritual companions and community.[7]

---

[6]David Benner, *Sacred Companions: The Gift of Spiritual Friendship and Direction* (Downers Grove, Ill.: InterVarsity Press, 2002), pp. 39-40.
[7]Ibid., p. 40.

Nowhere in the Christian community is the need to hear these words greater than in the lives of men and women who are in leadership. The myth of a solitary Christian is a most tempting story for the person who seeks to lead others. If we are to exercise Jesus' sort of kingdom authority, it will be done in the company of others. *A servant way of life is nurtured in the soil of a shared way of life.* Living truthfully and faithfully in this world while serving others is a difficult and lonely task. Due to the pressures of performance and the subtle struggles for power in so many local settings, surviving and succeeding are the challenges of the day. Ministry competency and political maneuvering are the skills required—yet underneath this, many long to simply be heard and recognized as persons with unique stories and questions and contributions to make. It seems that by an expression of God's Spirit today there is a deep yearning to be recognized and to be heard—that someone would acknowledge the isolation that accompanies leadership. God seems to be reshaping so many lives into more of a shared way of seeing and being in the world. The disciplines of solitude and spiritual mentoring and service have a way of moving us from an "I consciousness" to a "we consciousness" in Jesus' name.

Question 2. How can I move toward an entrusting way with others? This second question critical to a developmental mindset concerns how we are investing more particularly in the formation of others. In some respects this entire book is devoted to this question. I (Randy) had gifted moments when people modeled for me what I later had come to value and practice. It was happening long before I had words to describe or understand what was taking place. In my early life as a Jesus follower I encountered a small band of believers, an odd mixture of folks who cared deeply about my life. Some hilarious, pointed, caring and even tear-filled conversations took place over many pots of coffee and home-cooked meals. Good company and good conversation happened when we—Linda, Warren, Kevin, Mary Jean, Terry, Wendy, Donna, Allan, Deb, Lavern and Marv—got together. We were not sophisticated enough to try to work around each others' schedules; we just made it happen by showing up on each other's doorsteps. And it never felt intrusive.

Ebenezer Baptist Church was a unique congregation in the village of Ebenezer, Saskatchewan. On a busy day, the village boasted just under about one thousand people; on a busy Sunday morning, the church knew its place at about seventy-five. My early coffee conversations did not consist of those who were only in my age range but also those younger and much older. Those were the conversations that seemed to pull me closer to the table.

Two senior saints, Connie and Alvin Bohn, were in their seventies at the time. Both had the gift of laughter and hospitality—two exceptional qualities of sainthood. One of my favorite questions I loved to hear them ask was "Are you comin' over?" It was the question that led to all others and was usually asked on the spur of the moment, hardly ever planned too far in advance. My life was both ignited and shaped in the Bohn home by the questions they asked, the company they provided and the encouragement they offered. They were kind enough to share with me what they noticed in me, and from time to time they offered suggestions on what I might need to do to get there. We usually ended our visits with either or both Bohns praying for me and giving thanks for our time together.

Back then I didn't read a brochure to know if Ebenezer Baptist Church could meet my needs or provide a well thought through discipleship process. It just happened, and as a result I grew with the company I trusted and kept—a people who deepened my life and helped give it direction. I'm not sure they could have told you back then or even now what they actually did, but they certainly had everything they needed to be the church for me. Maybe it was a place before its time, or a place that hung onto those practices which should never be lost over time.

This Ebenezer Baptist experience has become a template for my own thinking, writing, teaching, pastoring, consulting, mentoring, hosting and coffeeing with others about this whole conversation of developing others as persons and leaders. It was how it happened with me, and oddly enough it is what I find written about in some of the latest books that talk about the "best practices" in dealing with the deepening and empowering of others.

The apostle John once said, "I have no greater joy than this, to hear that my children are walking in the truth" (3 Jn 4). John discovered a great joy that came from seeing others empowered. His joy allows us to peek into a window of leadership maturity—to become concerned with the growth and maturity of others, to move from leading others to developing others as leaders. This move finds itself in the broader wake of giving away what we have received as those who have been blessed and changed by the processes and relationships associated with our own development.

We can learn a few things from someone who has come this way before. Paul the apostle, in his first letter to Timothy, writes to his young friend providing advice and encouragement on how to address problems that have arisen in a local church of Ephesus. (*What was it about Paul that allowed him to give such responsibility to such a young leader for such a young movement? Could we do the same with those important responsibilities we keep telling ourselves only we can do?*) Later, in what appears to be his final days, Paul writes another letter to Timothy. The words are rich with things Timothy can cling to in order to help mature the church, to grow toward maturity himself, and eventually to move toward finishing well in a manner similar to his friend and mentor. In the first two verses of 2 Timothy 2, Paul reflects on what seems to be the punch line of what he had been saying up to that point in chapter 1: "You then, my child, be strong in the grace that is in Christ Jesus; and what you have heard from me through many witnesses entrust to faithful people who will be able to teach others as well."

Paul exhorts Timothy in three ways that we must also prayerfully echo in our formation efforts. (1) *Be strong in the grace that is in Christ Jesus:* We need to rely on the renewing and dynamic work of the grace of God. Life calls forth from us an honest recognition of our own limitations and invites us to delve deeper into the living Spirit of Jesus who has graced our lives. (2) *What you have heard from me through many witnesses:* We need to pay attention to the influence of the Pauls in our lives—those who have entrusted to us what has been entrusted to them along the way. (3) *Entrust to faithful people who will be able to teach others:* We ourselves need to pass on what has been given to us by entrusting others who will also pass it on. We must not hoard what we have been given. Paul underscores the generativity of this spiritual ministry. In an interview Paul Leavenworth discusses the important shift a leader must take toward this entrusting way of which the apostle Paul speaks:

> In order to be effective in the training of others as leaders, we will have to allow God to do a major re-orientation in us. We will have to move in our thinking and behaving to another level of application of the transition from "doing" to "being." This time we will have to move from "doing" to "being" to "being entrusting."
>
> The Greek word translated "entrust" is *paratithēmi* which has also been translated into the word "commit." The word literally means "to put near" and suggests a relational involvement that is committed to one's change. Entrusting involves the changing of beliefs, values, perception and lifestyle out of relationship with another who models these realities and helps facilitate like changes.[8]

Seeking to develop others like this is very challenging. It is not for those who have something to prove, or those who have a persistent need to be applauded, or those who hunger to be the powerful one at the top. It is for those who have a desire to become increasingly like Jesus in person and mission. It is for those who have the heart and vision to see their person and work as a gift entrusted to them and, in turn, grow ready and eager to wisely extend this gift to others. Such a person becomes a compelling and infectious witness to God's life and work in this world—imitated by those who have eyes to see and ears to hear.

Rivalry and envy, comparison and competition remain some of the central barriers to a developmental mindset. Just as tensions arose two thousand years ago when the disciples quarreled over who was greatest, so today such sentiments continue to lurk under the surface of our lives and communities. For us to finish well we must be open to discovering the foolishness of the competition and comparison between those who are found in Christ Jesus. So much anxiety, discontent and isolation stem from a misunderstanding and a refusal to be who we are. We swing back and forth perpetually between poles of contempt and self-

---

[8]Interview with Paul Leavenworth on the maturation process related to Christian leadership development, Omaha, Nebraska, September 2006.

loathing, or as one person puts it, between "Thank God I am not like so-and-so" and "Poor me. I wish I were more like so-and-so." So long as we measure ourselves against others we will fail to pay attention developmentally to others and to ourselves. We must allow the Spirit of God to enlighten us as to this our basic denial—our uniqueness is in Jesus Christ, found by God's mercy and grace. As with so many other things, this developmental mindset with respect to ourselves and to others—integral to finishing well as leaders—grows in the soil of God's grace.

OUR INVITATION TOWARD FOCUS AND LEGACY

There is a story told of Alfred Nobel, the man who established the Nobel Peace Prize in 1901. He was a Swedish industrialist who invented dynamite. When his brother died, the newspaper accidentally confused the two brothers and printed an obituary for Alfred. He read his own obituary and was horrified by its emphasis on dynamite and destruction. As the story goes, when his friends gathered together, he asked them what they thought was the opposite of destruction. Their answer was peace. From that moment forward Alfred changed the direction of his life, and in time he would be remembered for peace, not destruction. The Nobel Peace Prize he established goes to "the person who shall have done the most or the best work for fraternity between nations, for the abolition or reduction of standing armies and for the holding and promotion of peace congresses."

It is a rare opportunity to see one's future the way Alfred Nobel did. He got an opportunity to hear what people remembered him for before he even died. And the perspective shifted the focus and legacy of his whole life. This is the power of envisioning the future. Larry Crabb wrote, "A vision we give to others of who and what they could become has power when it echoes what the spirit has already spoken into their souls."[9]

Going through an examination process related to legacy is not only for the benefit of those fifty-five or older. We can too quickly assume that the developmental cues that follow are reserved for those closer to the finish line. There is a tremendous benefit for exposing younger and

---

[9]Larry Crabb, quoted in Andy Stanley, *Visioneering* (Sisters, Ore.: Multnomah, 1999), p. 109.

mid-career leaders to the questions associated with this final season of boundary. Clinton has often said to his students, "Remember, being forewarned is becoming fore-armed," and "Well begun is half done."[10]

For our purposes here, we have condensed a significant amount of process items and response patterns typical of this multiplication phase into four general categories or themes, and framed them into questions for your consideration:

- How do I see my life purpose now?

- What do I do best?

- What role would I love to have?

- How would I like to be remembered?

These four questions are an adaptation of Clinton's four focal elements of a leader who is moving with greater intention toward a focused life.[11] We would do well to become familiar with these developmental questions in order to hear them when they appear in the lives of those in this particular season. However, we also want to become familiar with these cues in order that we might effectively prepare people to finish well. There are significant lessons younger leaders can learn from those in the later stages of development.

What's my life purpose now? The question of life purpose is not new to us, but when we sink into it at this place along the journey, we find it has a weight we may not have felt until now. *What do we find ourselves really caring about now?* It is one thing to chase after life purpose when we are in our twenties, thirties and forties, it is another to receive what it offers us in our fifties, sixties and beyond. Anne Morrow Lindbergh offers us some hopeful words on the "second half." She writes,

---

[10]J. Robert Clinton, "Lifelong Development Class" (Pasadena, Calif.: Fuller Seminary, Fall 1995).

[11]J. Robert Clinton, *Strategic Concepts That Clarify a Focused Life* (Altadena, Calif.: Barnabas, 1995). Clinton defines a focused life as "a life dedicated to exclusively carrying out God's effective purposes through it, by identifying the focal issues, that is, the life purpose, effective methodology, major role, or ultimate contribution which allows an increasing prioritization of life's activities around the focal issues, and results in a satisfying life of being and doing" (ibid., p. 3). We have utilized Clinton's framework to describe the four questions or developmental cues apparent as one moves toward the invitation of legacy. We would encourage pastors in particular to read through *Strategic Concepts* as a way to enhance their own strategic formation.

For is it not possible that middle age can be looked upon as a period of second flowering, second growth, even as a kind of second adolescence? It is true that society in general does not help one accept this interpretation of the second half of life. And therefore, this period of expanding is often tragically misunderstood. Many people never climb above the plateau of forty-to-fifty. The signs that presage growth, so similar, it seems to me, to those in early adolescence: discontent, restlessness, doubt, despair, longing, are interpreted falsely as signs of decay. In youth one does not as often misinterpret the signs; one accepts them, quite rightly, as growing pains. . . .

But in middle age, because of the false assumption that it is a period of decline, one interprets these life-signs, paradoxically, as signs of approaching death. Instead of facing them, one runs away; one escapes— into depressions, nervous breakdowns, drink, love affairs, or frantic, thoughtless, fruitless overwork. Anything, rather than face them. Anything, rather than stand still and learn from them. One tries to cure the signs of growth, to exorcise them, as if they were devils, when really they might be angels of annunciation.

Angels of annunciation of what? Of a new stage in living when, having shed many of the physical struggles, the worldly ambitions, the material encumbrances of active life, one might be free to fulfill the neglected side of one's self.[12]

In John 2 we have a story of Jesus, Mary his mother and his disciples at a wedding ceremony in Cana of Galilee. As this celebration progresses, the hosts discover that they have underestimated the amount of wine consumed and will face an embarrassing situation if they run out. Jesus' time comes to perform an unusual miracle, which produces gallons of Cabernet. The guy doing the wine tasting that evening takes a mouthfull, and after some swishing and swallowing says to the groom, "Everyone serves the good wine first, and then the inferior wine after the guests have become drunk. But you have kept the good wine until now" (Jn 2:10). What if "the good wine" of your life has been kept until now? What if your time has come now, or as Lindbergh puts it, is "a new stage in living when . . . you *might be free to fulfill the neglected side of one's self?*"

---

[12]Anne Morrow Lindbergh, *Gift from the Sea* (New York: Pantheon, 1955), pp. 86-88.

Rick Warren's book *The Purpose Driven Life* has become one of the best selling books of all time because busy, spent, tired, bored, curious people are asking, What is the purpose of my life? Is there something more to my life than what I have been experiencing to this point? When we find ourselves at midlife having come through much and accomplished much, but yet we find ourselves restless, discontent and starving for more, could we be in a place where God may be inviting us to wrestle with issues of stewardship, how we will spend the rest of our lives in an obedient response to the movement of God in our lives? We are grateful for what has taken place along the way and yet we begin to wonder *if the good wine of our life has been kept until now?*

Clinton defines life purpose as "a burden-like calling, a task or driving force or achievement, which motivates a leader to fulfill something or to see something done."[13] Taking inventory of our life purpose in this particular place and time of development provides reaffirmation, confirmation and motivation to have the courage to be who God wants us to be and to spend the rest of our lives living for God's good pleasure and kingdom purposes.

This is also a time to give some careful thought and articulation to the *values* of our lives. Gaining a better understanding of one's most significant values can be a difficult process, requiring a willingness and determination to do some thorough self-examination. *What are those deeply held beliefs that consistently guide our decisions and actions?* Values act as guides for our decision making, steering us in our choices of how to do what we desire to do. Sometimes we are conscious of these beliefs and other times we are not. Jim Kouzes and Barry Posner write, "[Values] supply us with a moral compass by which to navigate the course of our lives. Clarity of values is essential to knowing which way, for each of us, is north, south, east, and west. . . . This kind of guidance is especially

---

[13]Clinton, *Strategic Concepts*, p. 35. In this resource Clinton does an analysis of the developmental concerns as leaders move toward finishing well, in particular the four elements he uses to describe a focused life, which he defines as, "a life dedicated to exclusively carrying out God's effective purposes through it, by identifying the focal issues, that is, the life purpose, effective methodology, major role, or ultimate contribution which allows an increasing prioritization of life's activities around the focal issues, and results in a satisfying life of being and doing" (p. 3).

needed in difficult and uncertain times."[14] As we face this juncture, it becomes increasingly important that we are conscious of our values.

We would also do well to take inventory of what scriptural passages or even whole books of the Bible have held a special place of importance in our formation. It is through faithful reading and reflection on the Scriptures that God forms and reforms us over the course of our lives. Through the stories, instructions, prayers and people of the Bible, the Spirit invites, challenges and guides us toward a greater understanding of who God is, who we are, and what God desires to do through our lives. What are those places in the Scriptures (verses or passages or whole books) that you would see as *core* or key to helping you understand your sense of purpose and calling? Particular biblical books, passages and verses typically hold a greater significance to us than other passages. We find ourselves returning to them during the significant turns in our stories. They repeatedly shape our soul, clarify our understanding and provide direction and motivation. These passages can serve as a sort of *biblical mandate* to help guide our lives in the present and toward the future as we think about our life purpose now.

In all of this reflection we need the help of others in processing our life purpose. Who are those trusted mentors and soul mates to whom we can go to ask for their attention? Or perhaps it is in assembling what Parker Palmer refers to as a "clearness committee," a group of friends who know you well and can come together to listen to your life, and then in an honoring way reflect back what thy hear and notice.[15] What does our community of friends see and hear in us at this important juncture of our lives? Honest, loving and prayerful feedback will be invaluable to an exploration of one's life purpose.

What do I do best? A second question of stewardship we face as we move toward finishing well has to do with the ways we serve that seem to bear consistent fruit. In other words, when we do things a certain way we notice that God seems to show up. In regard to these activities

---

[14]James M. Kouzes and Barry Posner, *The Leadership Challenge*, 3rd ed. (San Francisco: Jossey-Bass, 2002), p. 48.

[15]In order to learn more about clearness committees see chapter 8 of Parker Palmer's *A Hidden Wholeness: The Journey Toward an Undivided Life* (San Francisco: Jossey-Bass, 2004).

there is a distinctiveness to our approach that becomes a signature of how we do our work—others recognize it and God blesses it.

When we reflect on our experiences and get honest with how we have seen God work through us, can we begin to recognize what sorts of methods we tend to utilize more effectively than others? These are the means, methods or vehicles through which our life purpose is uniquely expressed. Evaluation becomes a very important element if we wish to steward well our resources of who we are and what we have to offer, however large or small we may perceive that to be.

I (Randy) take this question much more seriously as people in my community, church or workplace become more familiar with "what I can do well" amid the needs and opportunities that emerge in those contexts. I have come to appreciate the gift of time. My time is no more valuable than the next person's time, but I am becoming more aware of how I have to wisely discern how I use the time that I am given. Earlier in my development I used to think that every opportunity that came my way was meant for me to grab onto and help as I could. I now consider very carefully most of the opportunities and needs that come my way. One of my guiding questions has become, Is this an opportunity I must tend to, or is it a distraction from what I should really be doing? And a follow-up question is, Does this opportunity seem to line up with my life purpose and what I do well? Some choices require input from my own trusted community of guides who see my efforts much more clearly than I; other choices I am mature enough and comfortable enough in my skin to make on my own.

The longer we journey through life, the more we accumulate experiences that confirm what we do and don't do well. Taking inventory of these experiences can reveal certain breakthrough ways that have worked well for us in getting things done. When we have opportunity to walk alongside others during this season we must encourage them to decide and choose for future service based on their most effective ways of doing what they do, and to do so with a view toward accomplishing their life purpose. Some helpful questions to ask those we may walk alongside include:

- Where have you seen God show up in your leadership work?

- Describe some times when you received affirmation from others.

- How do others describe your style?

- Are there any "signatures" to your work that others point to?

- What opportunities do you find yourself drawn toward?

- What sorts of work cause you to become increasingly frustrated?

- What have been some significant mistakes you have made in your leadership?

What role would I love to have? The third question is closely related to the prior question of what I do best. When we come to these later chapters, we are more apt to lead out of our own values and convictions, but we may also be less tolerant of the positions, functions, tasks and jobs that may have frustrated us to some measure in the past. "*Whose job would I love to have at this stage in my life?*" Or, to ask the question another way, "*If I could wave my magic wand, what would I love to do?*"

Leading out of who we are will invariably bring some sort of transition with how we view and practice our work. We are willing to let go of a lot in order to focus on what is of utmost importance. And we find a new courage within ourselves to follow after the way we must, even if it means significant upheaval and transition. This may take the form of an alignment with a present job description, or it may even take the form of a complete change of job. Processing this question of role will confront our readiness and courage to take next steps of faith, steps which may not make logical sense, or ones which may pose significant job insecurity or financial risk, causing members of our family stress.

A helpful process to recommend for those wrestling through the question of role is to do an audit of their spiritual gifts, natural abilities, acquired skills, strengths and leadership style, and to then consider what sorts of roles or functions have allowed these things to be practiced most consistently. It is helpful to evaluate one's present or anticipated role in terms of what Clinton refers to as *base* and *function*.[16] The *base* com-

---

[16]Clinton, *Strategic Concepts*, p. 123.

ponent refers to the responsibilities associated with one's job description—those things that we are expected to do and get paid to do. The *function* component refers to those things a person really loves to do in his or her job, but are not necessarily a part of the job description. These are the things that cause us to love to get up in the morning to go to work because they add color or spice to our jobs. But even more importantly they confirm who God is calling us to be and what he is calling us to do in this season. The question related to base and function is, *"Can the base and function of my job actually affirm and allow me to play out my life purpose through the unique ways or means God tends to work through me?"* Some questions reflecting role exploration, which are timely for those moving toward finishing well, include the following:

- What were some of your favorite past jobs?
- Whose job would you love to have at this stage of your life?
- If you could write your ideal job description, what would it say?
- Are you allowed to be *you* in your present role?
- How do you think of your role in terms of *base* and *function*?
- How is your life purpose presently being played out?
- What might the Lord be requiring of you?

How would I like to be remembered? Future-perfect thinking is a phrase used to describe a person who is thinking and acting in the present as if it were the future. In other words, future-perfect thinking describes someone who seeks to live a life reflective of Hebrews 11:1: "Now faith is the assurance of things hoped for, the conviction of things not seen." As we imagine the future, what do we think might last long after we are gone from the scene? What might we leave behind in terms of *legacy*? How will we be remembered?

In an informal conversation I (Randy) had with James Houston, he mentioned how much he was learning in his eighties. His relationship with his grandchildren was providing one of his most significant lessons. In his slight Scottish brogue Houston remarked, "I have learned that I cannot strive with my grandchildren like I have in so many other areas of my life. My desire is to simply love them, and to give to them the very best that I can." In one of those rare moments an important lesson was given, a glimpse into a life well lived. Our present striving and struggling may simply be indicative of a few lessons we may have yet to learn.

It is in letting go, being fully present and simply loving that we experience the freedom that comes when we give ourselves away. It is a magical moment when we discover the truth behind Jesus' words, "Those who find their life will lose it, and those who lose their life for my sake will find it" (Mt 10:39). Something in us falls into place when we love and give and serve and lead in a way that empowers another, which at the same time confirms that which is also deepest within us. In the season of legacy there exists a freedom to give of ourselves, not for our own benefit but for the sake of the other.

Consider the story of coach Bob Young. Bob has become a legend to many, both for his ability to successfully coach a winning football team of college athletes at the University of Sioux Falls and for his ability to provide hope, challenge and encouragement as a mentor for many young men who played on his team, not to mention the other men and women he had as assistant coaches and trainers. There was no mistake about Bob's fierce coaching ability on the field. He was demanding and would accept nothing short of excellence from each of his players individually and collectively as a team.

After decades of coaching success, even a national championship, Coach Young still had the fire in his eye. But there was more to Bob than wins and losses. Although Bob loved winning at football, he loved investing in the lives of those around him even more, believing that what they learned on the football team might help them flourish and live more honorably the rest of their lives.

At his retirement banquet hundreds of people came from across the country, and even around the world, to honor Coach Bob Young. The program was strewn with story after story of how Coach Young was used to change their particular life. No one was surprised that when Bob gave his personal remarks at the banquet, he humbly expressed that it was his love for investing in others that made it all worthwhile. After the banquet was over, if you were in earshot, you could overhear Bob asking his former players more questions about how they were doing in life, letting them know how much they meant to him.

What if a banquet were held in your honor? Maybe even before you died. What would we honor in a program? Who would be invited to speak about you? What would they say? What would you say if you were invited to give some personal remarks?

Clinton suggests that there are certain types of legacies or contributions left behind by those who finished well. He divides these contributions into five general categories: (1) character, with a primary focus on issues of one's person; (2) ministry, with attention given to certain practices; (3) catalytic, having a focus toward starting new endeavors; (4) organizational, having systemic concerns as a focus; and (5) ideation, with a primary focus on the formation of new ideas and insights.[17]

In the following pages we will elaborate on each of these five categories of contributions. As you read and reflect upon them, ask yourself these two questions: *Which types of contributions tend to strike a deep chord within you? What prayerful thoughts are stirred in you as to how you might like to be remembered?*

Character-related contributions

- *Saint,* a model life, not a perfect one, but a life others want to emulate, a life reflecting the love, anointing and blessing of God

- *Stylistic practitioner,* a model of leadership that sets a pace for others and for which others seek to emulate

- *Family,* promotion of a God-fearing family, leaving behind children who walk with God carrying on a Godly heritage

Ministry-related contributions

- *Mentor,* a productive service investing in the formation of individuals and groups of people

- *Public rhetorician,* a productive service of public communication ministry with groups of people

---

[17]Ibid., p. 154.

Catalytic-related contributions

- *Pioneer*, a person who starts new ministries in order to meet specific needs, usually with a focus toward issues of leadership

- *Change person*, a person who rights wrongs and injustices in society and in the church, or generally facilitates positive change.

- *Artist*, a person who has creative breakthroughs in life and ministry and introduces innovation

Organizational-related contributions

- *Founder*, a person who starts a new organization to meet a need or capture the essence of some movement

- *Stabilizer*, a person who can help an organization to develop toward efficiency and effectiveness

Ideation-related contributions

- *Researcher*, a person who develops new ideation by studying various issues

- *Writer*, a person who captures ideas and reproduces them in written form to help and inform others

- *Promoter*, a person who effectively distributes new ideas or other related processes

LEARNING TO NOTICE

There are several places in Scripture where Jesus teaches us that unless something dies, it lacks an ability to produce more. "Very truly, I tell you, unless a grain of wheat falls into the earth and dies, it remains just a single grain; but if it dies, it bears much fruit" (Jn 12:24). The same can be said for us as we consider what it means to finish well. Such a season within our development brings us face-to-face with important questions of stewardship. It is good to remember that the "good wine of our life may be kept until now." And it is hopeful to know that as we move into the later chapters of our service and life, it may be then that we get to experience the fruit of our labor multiplied again and again. When we have opportunity to walk alongside persons in this multiplication phase, the following are some helpful things to notice and offer:

- *Keeping company with God.* As we move toward issues of focus and finishing well, the ongoing cultivation of their interior life with God must be a priority.

- *Taking steps of faith.* We intentionally invest in people who are in their fifties, sixties and beyond, encouraging them to consider taking another step of development in their faith journey, and in their service.

- *Provide learning communities.* We provide a caring and safe learning community where people can openly share their thoughts and feelings regarding this particular time of life.

- *Spiritual mentoring.* We encourage people to connect with a spiritual director or clearness committee who can listen, discern and provide perspective.

- *Historical mentors.* We encourage people in this time of development to read biographies and autobiographies of historical mentors. Much learning can take place vicariously (through the experience of others).

- *Pay attention to those in transition.* We sponsor others by way of encouragement and advocate for those making role transitions in this season of life.

- *Celebrate legacies.* Celebrate well those who accept the invitation to move toward legacy and those who finish well. Expose their stories to younger and mid-career leaders who need hope and inspiration.

Now that we have looked at the lessons we can learn from the life stories of those who have come before us, we must now turn our attention to the ways we can become more effective at guiding the leadership formation of others.

REFLECT ON YOUR LIFE

- What did you notice about your own formation as you read through this chapter?

- How are you currently paying regular attention to your interior life with God?

- Who is a person you believe has moved toward finishing well? As you think about him or her, what stands out to you? If possible, make contact with this person, inviting him or her for a meal or a cup of coffee and express how much your life has been impacted by his or hers.

EXERCISES FOR YOUR CONTEXT

Practice the daily examen. Examining one's life has been a prescription for development handed down to us through the centuries. Ignatius of Loyola introduced the practice of examen as part of his spiritual exercises. Practicing daily examen involves prayerfully reviewing the events of the day in order to discern the voice of God in one's heart, and where the Spirit might be at work—loving, affirming, convicting, revealing, instructing, guiding.

In their book, Dennis, Sheila and Matthew Linn invite the readers to practice "sleeping with bread," a daily examen.[18] Their process invites us to respond to two questions that get at the heart of the examined life: (1) Where was I most grateful today? (*what gave life*), and (2) Where was I least grateful today? (*what drained life*). The Linns's prescription of living an examined life is very much the order of the day as we move toward the later chapters in our life and service.

A day-long retreat. In this same spirit of examen, we would invite you to consider this retreat process for yourself, as well as for a group of people you may be walking alongside within your setting.

Find a quiet, comfortable place where you can be alone for an eight-hour period of time. You may certainly extend the time if you wish. You may also want to consider bringing some refreshments so that you will not have to leave your place of retreat for a lunch break, or you may also wish to use this time as a day of fasting from food and other refreshments.

[18]Dennis Linn, Sheila Fabricant Linn and Matthew Linn, *Sleeping with Bread: Holding What Gives You Life* (New York: Paulist, 1995), p. 1.

When you arrive at your retreat setting, take the first hour to quiet yourself before the Lord. Do what works best to help you gain a sense of peace, quiet and rest. Perhaps Scripture, music or simply sitting in silence will help you get centered.

Then for the next seven or more hours, focus your attention on the questions below. You may want to review this chapter as you ponder one or more of the questions. Be mindful of your time. We want to focus our thoughts and responses to the questions in order to see what surfaces within this one-day time frame. Don't get caught up in having to perfectly or conclusively answer these questions. Play and pray with them; be open to what you may discover.

1. *How do I see my life purpose now?* Reflect on your life. Your early sense of calling, destiny, values and key Scriptures. After a time of reflection, write a one-paragraph (two or three sentences) life purpose statement.

2. *What do I do best?* How has God tended to work uniquely through you? Think back on your various leadership experiences to see if you can identify times when God has shown up as you did what you did. After a time of reflection, write a one paragraph (two or three sentences) unique and effective methods statement.

3. *What role would I love to have?* If you could move toward your ideal role where your life purpose is played out through the unique ways you do what you do, what would that role look like. After a time of reflection, write a one-paragraph (two or three sentences) major role statement.

4. *How would I like to be remembered?* What sorts of things would you like to see continued after you leave the scene? How will you want to be remembered? What legacy do you want to pass on to others? After a time of reflection, write a one-paragraph (two or three sentences) legacy or ultimate contribution statement.

Be sure to arrange a time to share your discoveries with a close group of friends or staff members after the day-long retreat.

Part Three

Guiding the
Formation of Others

7

IMITATING JESUS' WAY WITH OTHERS

As you therefore have received Christ Jesus the Lord, continue to live your lives in him, rooted and built up in him and established in faith, just as you were taught, abounding in thanksgiving.

—COLOSSIANS 2:6-7

Ecologists remind us that a tree planted in a clearing of an old forest will grow more successfully than when it is planted in isolation in an open field. The roots of the new planting will follow more easily and more deeply the hidden pathways of old root systems. Likewise, human beings thrive best in following the paths of life already taken by others before them. None of us needs to reinvent the wheel or live as if no one has preceded us in the pathways of the wise.

—JAMES M. HOUSTON, *THE MENTORED LIFE*

A major function of all leadership is the selection of rising leadership. I don't mean picking young people to send off to Bible college or seminary, but rather observing those God is selecting and processing, and then finding ways to enhance their development.

—J. ROBERT CLINTON, *THE MAKING OF A LEADER*

There are a lot of Toms in my [Rob's] family. My father's name is
Tom, my pop-pop was a Tom, and even my middle name is Thomas. I
also have a Tom for a second cousin. But there was only one Uncle Tom
in my world growing up. He was my dad's uncle, one of my grandma's
four brothers.

Uncle Tom was quite a humorous character. In our family, the stories
abound. He was the sort of person who when told not to touch the
chocolate fudge cooling in the kitchen was known not just to brush
aside such cautions by taking a finger full but he was known to take the
whole tray with him to work. As a butcher he was known to cause a
couple of unsuspecting women to all but pass out by his sharp chop of
the cleaver followed by yelling and writhing as if he just chopped off a
finger or two.

My dad tells a story of Uncle Tom taking him and his sister fishing,
when they were still young, at a creek a short walk from their house.
Now this creek was lucky to have a couple frogs, some worms and a
stray snake or two. It majored mostly on mosquitoes. There were no
fish to be found in that creek. But my dad and Aunt Harriet were very
young, and they didn't know better. So off they went with Uncle Tom
and two fishing rods. He generated the sort of enthusiasm fit for a serious fishermen at a raging Montana stream. Once they got to the creek
he set them up and they started fishing. He didn't place them right next
to each other but spread them out a bit, "so that we can find out where
the fish are really biting." As Dad tells it, Uncle Tom moved back and
forth between the two of them for a bit.

And then he said, "Tommy, you'd better go see if Harriet needs
some help, I think they might be biting down there. Here, I'll hold
your rod."

After looking at Harriet's situation for a bit and without any results,
Dad walked back to his rod. Uncle Tom handed him the rod and
headed back to Harriet.

But as he left he said, "Tommy, you might want to reel back in your
line, I think I felt a couple tugs."

So, as the story goes, Uncle Tom walked back to see Harriet. And in
a short time, Harriet was sent over to find Dad reeling in the biggest

fish either of them had ever caught. Then Harriet ran back to tell Uncle Tom of "Tommy's great big fish," only to discover a whopper at the end of her own rod. What an absolutely wonderful afternoon for Dad and Aunt Harriet! And I suspect, for Uncle Tom as well. They grinned and bounced with joy, delight and pride, and headed home, carrying their catch and their rods, and walking with Uncle Tom. A strange and humorous sight it must have seemed to neighbors watching the threesome walking proudly back to the house with their miraculous catch.

It was not until years later that Dad learned of Uncle Tom's stop at the fish market before they headed down to the creek. But, by then, his memory had done its work and Uncle Tom's place in his heart was secure and fruitful and unrivaled.

Dad recounts another childhood discovery when he finally realized why it was that every time he returned home from a walk with Uncle Tom, his pockets would be full of change. Whenever he took a walk with anyone else—other uncles or aunts or his mom or dad—he might have found a chance penny or two, and that on a good afternoon. But his walks with Uncle Tom were profitable beyond a small boy's imagination. Everywhere they went together Dad spotted coins on the pavement, on the sidewalks, even on some lawns—pennies and nickels and even dimes filled and jingled and weighed heavy in his pocket by the end of their trek. Again, it was not until well through early childhood that Dad discovered Uncle Tom's skillful coin-flicking on their walks together. Walks with Uncle Tom were about far more than dollars and cents, they were, for a small boy, profound offerings of grace and life and care. There was a tremendous generosity about Uncle Tom's life. His spirit spilled over to everyone who knew him. His life shaped and occupied deep places in others' lives.

Uncle Tom and his walks have offered a portrait, perhaps even a parable, of what it is like to journey through life with certain people. Some people just seem to rub off on you. They are infectious with life and spirit and grace, and you cannot remain the same person, merely because you have been with them. They are like Jonathan to David, Jesus to Peter or John, Barnabas to Paul, and Paul to Timothy. Like a small boy taking a walk with his Uncle Tom, when you are with them, truly good things seem to happen *over and again*. And this *over and again* does its work, inviting, guiding and forming us in deep places we cannot reach on our own. We walk home and our pockets are full. We catch impossible fish. And much of the time it is absolutely inexplicable and delightful, because we have also taken these same walks alone and with others, and we know what it is to return home with *empty* pockets. We have discovered that every person does not take walks the same.

We find ourselves where we are today because at some point a person or a series of people have taken "pocket-full sorts of walks" with us. There are Uncle Toms in our lives. They intersected our lives full of life and grace and time and laughter and acceptance. For some it was a grandparent or a teacher early in our lives, for others it is was a neighbor or a coworker or a pastor. Their impact is written all over the stories of our lives. Their attention may have lasted for decades or it may have been a penetrating conversation at a critical time in our lives. Most often such relationships are unspectacular, but their effects are dramatic.

Keri Wyatt Kent uses a very helpful phrase to describe what happens as we allow the Spirit to lead us into sharing our lives in this manner. She writes:

> If we are led by the Spirit, we will increasingly imitate God and become people who are filled with "coming-alongside-ness." That is, we listen to God and people and then come into their story, get involved with them enough that we can point out where God is in their story and allow them to do that for us as well. When we are full of come-alongside-ness, we will be willing to walk with people through their pain; we will listen before we try to fix. We will be with people.[1]

COMING-ALONGSIDE-NESS

Beyond the routine of our lives, beyond the mere roles or functions that we play, the Spirit calls us to be *with* people in a way that honors both his purposes and our well-being. Testimonies of *coming-alongside-ness*

---

[1]Keri Wyatt Kent, *Listen: Finding God in the Story of Your Life* (San Francisco: Jossey-Bass, 2006), pp. 97-98.

are strewn through the Bible. Just think about Naomi and Ruth, Jonathan and David, Elijah and Elisha, Paul and Timothy, to name a few. It is in these relationships that we find women and men empowered and sustained for holiness and influence.

The Christian faith is an imitative faith. Sometimes little Tommys, who have taken walks with Uncle Tom, grow up to be Uncle Toms to others. Beginning with Jesus' earliest words to the men and women who would become his disciples, "Follow me," Christianity has understood itself to be *a faith imparted by one to another*. No matter what stage of development, we need spiritual companions—mentors and guides, friends and peers along the journey—in order to flourish over a lifetime of godly service. Moreover, we need to walk with others, guiding and helping them discover God's gracious activity in their lives and communities.

And in this regard, the life of Jesus must be seen and held as the unique model of worthy of imitation for Christians. For in Jesus we discover not only a model for the journey but an invitation to this life together. Jesus reaches out to us by his Spirit, speaking and sharing his stunning life with us.

JESUS' WAY WITH OTHERS

Frederick Buechner writes,

> A Christian is one who points at Christ and says, "I can't prove a thing, but there's something about His eyes and His voice. There's something about the way he carries His head, His hands, the way He carries His cross—the way He carries me."[2]

Jesus lovingly walked with men and women in a most unusual way, a way that was (1) deepening, (2) particularizing, (3) hospitable and (4) patient. Listen and ponder and learn yet again with his first disciples. Imagine yourself near him throughout his earthly ministry. What are you noticing about the way he moves in community and develops other people?

---

[2]Frederick Buechner, in *Celtic Daily Prayer: Prayers and Readings from the Northumbria Community* (San Francisco: HarperCollins, 2002), p. 640.

A deepening way with others. Jesus was very concerned with inviting people to greater spiritual depth in *every moment and facet* of their lives. He recognized that so much of their "righteous" living was simply scraping the surface of God's faithful way as revealed in the Law and the Prophets. Consider one table conversation recorded by Luke:

> While he was speaking, a Pharisee invited him to dine with him; so he went in and took his place at the table. The Pharisee was amazed to see that he did not wash before dinner. Then the Lord said to him, "Now you Pharisees clean the outside of the cup and of the dish, but inside you are full of greed and wickedness. You fools! Did not the one who made the outside make the inside also? So give for alms those things that are within; and see, everything will be clean for you." (Lk 11:37-40)

His poignant words unsettled those who sat around the table. He asked, "Did not the one who made the outside make the inside also?" Time and again in the Gospels, Jesus confronts those for whom the faithful life was defined by only a part of their life (e.g., behavior, right thoughts, religious experiences). Like the great prophets of the Old Testament, Jesus' hard words drive his community below the superficialities of their faith in order to draw their attention to the greater concerns of *justice and the love of God* (Lk 11:42).

— *Jesus' gift of a good question.* This Lukan dinner table scene clearly illustrates one of the primary methods Jesus utilized in this deepening way with others: question asking. In *Kindred Souls* Stephanie Ford calls it "the gift of a good question." She writes:

> Jesus was a master of the kind of question that took a conversation deeper. Moreover, he deflected many questions, realizing that the issue behind the seeker's question needed to be explored, rather than an answer provided. In fact, he often directed a similar question back to the individual. Jesus' questions pushed his followers and friends beyond where they had been to honesty before God and themselves that was vulnerable, and risky. Yet he knew that the right question could open the seeker to transformation, a new experience of grace, and greater congruity of life and faith.[3]

---

[3]Stephanie Ford, *Kindred Souls: Connecting Through Spiritual Friendship* (Nashville: Upper Room, 2006), p. 78.

Whether it is a brief encounter or a deep friendship, Jesus' questions consistently draw his listeners into a greater field of discovery. To the suspicious religious authorities who tried to trap him with a question about his authority, Jesus exposed their hearts by turning the question on them with a question of his own: "Did the baptism of John come from heaven, or was it from human origin?" (Lk 20:4). Or in response to the blind Bartimaeus's disruption and demands for Jesus' attention, Jesus pulls him into the vulnerability of his need with a question, "What do you want me to do for you?" (Mk 10:51). Jesus seems to prefer asking questions in order to invite deeper exploration and repentance rather than offering direct answers that invite little or no personal engagement.

Jesus' storytelling. Along with asking good questions, Jesus also told parables in order to cultivate a deeper dialogue and exploration into faithful living. Jesus' *storytelling* is strewn through the Gospel accounts. So distinctive is it that his disciples even ask at one point, "Why do you speak . . . in parables?" (Mt 13:10). Matthew even records that "Jesus told the crowds all these things in parables; without a parable he told them nothing" (Mt 13:34). Whether addressing opposition to his choice of unseemly meal partners (Lk 15) or communicating the nature of the kingdom of heaven (Mt 13) or unfolding what loving one's neighbors will actually mean (Lk 10), Jesus tells a story. And these stories or parables involve the listeners in a way that demands their response. Brian McLaren elaborates on the transforming power of storytelling when he points out that

> parables entice their hearers into new territory. If the goal is an interactive relationship (which is at the heart of terms like *kingdom of God* and *eternal life* . . .), a parable succeeds where easy answers and obvious explanations couldn't. With a clear and easy explanation, hearers can listen and achieve understanding and then go their way, independent of the teacher. But when a parable confounds them, it invites them to ask questions, so they continue to depend on the teacher himself, not just their independent understanding of his words. . . .
>
> Parables have a capacity that goes beyond *informing* their hearers; parables also have the power to help *transform* them into interactive,

interdependent, humble, inquisitive, and persistent people.[4]

Through his imaginative stories Jesus confronts his listeners with another way of living. And again they and we are forced into deeper exploration and experience of God's way in the world.

Jesus offered a sharply contrasting perspective to other leaders of the day. He walked the same streets, worshiped in the same synagogues, read the same Scriptures, observed the same festivals, and yet, when we listen to his teaching, we are immediately faced with a different sort of presence. We agree with Luke: "They were astounded at his teaching, because he spoke with authority" (Lk 4:32). In comparison to Jesus, the rest of his community seemed to have missed the whole point of this life with God. Jesus' way with others was a deepening way that called them to turn from their shallow, self-securing religiosity.

A particularizing way with others. Jesus *particularized* others throughout his earthly ministry—that is, he uniquely noticed them. His compassion toward others was not a one-size-fits-all approach. He singled people out amid the crowds and approached them for the unique persons they were. Just imagine sitting in the tree with the small and despised Zacchaeus, who was straining to see this Jesus, yearning to get a glimpse of this reputed "friend of tax collectors." And just as he is getting a good look, the whole scene turns toward Zacchaeus. Jesus looks up into his face and startles him with these words, "Zacchaeus, hurry and come down; for I must stay at your house today" (Lk 19:5).

Or imagine sneaking away with the shameful woman after she has just touched the trim of Jesus' clothing and been immediately healed of her decade-long bleeding illness, only to become caught at the center of the crowds' attention. "Who touched my clothes?" Jesus asked. Those closest to him are perplexed by the foolishness of the question, in light of the crowds pressing tightly in on Jesus. But this woman knows of whom Jesus speaks. She fearfully falls down before him and tells him *the whole truth.* "Daughter, your faith has made you well; go in peace, and be healed of your disease" (Mk 5:33-34).

---

[4]Brian D. McLaren, *The Secret Message of Jesus: Uncovering the Truth That Could Change Everything* (Nashville: Thomas Nelson, 2006), pp. 44-45.

Zacchaeus, the bleeding woman and the many others like them were all transformed by Jesus' particularizing attention. Their lives were never the same. Jesus had a way of seeing and believing in what people could become well beyond their capacity to do the same for themselves. They felt noticed, embraced, accepted, forgiven and invited into a wholly alternative way of living—God was seeking them out and calling them to a new life.

It is a powerful thing to be lovingly and particularly noticed by another person, let alone by Jesus. And in our culture today we hunger to be seen in this manner. As we mentioned in chapter 1, so many people carry a deep sense of unnoticedness from an early age. In Eugene Peterson's meditation on the relationship between Jonathan and David, he comments,

> Each of us has contact with hundreds of people who never look beyond our surface appearance. We have dealings with hundreds of people who the moment they set eyes on us begin calculating what use we can be to them, what they can get out of us. We meet hundreds of people who take one look at us, make a snap judgment, and then slot us into a category so that they won't have to deal with us as persons. They treat us as something less than we are; and if we're in constant association with them, we *become* less.
>
> And then someone enters into our life who isn't looking for someone to use, is leisurely enough to find out what's really going on in us, is secure enough not to exploit our weaknesses or attack our strengths, recognizes our inner life and understands the difficulty of living out our inner convictions, confirms what is deepest within us. A friend.[5]

We long to be befriended in this way. We long to be picked out of the crowd—noticed and invited, chosen and called, like Zacchaeus was by Jesus. We also long to befriend others in this way. Unfortunately, due to the high rpms of life and leadership today, both inside and outside the church, we more often overlook each other's unique person and context. This aspect of Jesus' way with others, which seems so inefficient considering everything we have to get done at home and at work, must

---

[5]Eugene H. Peterson, *Leap Over a Wall: Earthy Spirituality for Everyday Christians* (San Francisco: HarperSanFrancisco, 1997), p. 54 (emphasis in original).

continue to be instructive to traveling together in the Christian life. Jesus' way with others continues to be a particularizing way.

A hospitable way with others. Jesus' life and ministry reflect a spirit of hospitality. That is, as one person puts it, Jesus consistently creates a safe, open space where friends or strangers can enter and experience a welcoming spirit of respect, acceptance, and care.[6] And this was not simply common courtesy or good manners on display. In fact, what got Jesus in trouble often was that he befriended all sorts of characters whom most righteous people at the time thought were not deserving of such welcome (e.g., tax collectors, prostitutes, Samaritans, Gentiles). In a Jewish culture that drew clear categorizing lines, Jesus scandalously crossed all those lines. This was the gospel, God's loving and restoring way in the world, in practice. He looked across the whole scope of first-century Israel society and said, in essence, there is room at the table for you. For some this invitation was offensive; for others, "those with ears to hear," it was truly good news.

Jesus' practice of table fellowship. The Gospel writers repeatedly point out this hospitable spirit in Jesus' practice of table fellowship. Jesus was eating with all the wrong people. And sharing a meal during Jesus' day communicated far more than it does today. More than mere acquaintance or good manners, sharing a meal was an act of *mutual acceptance.* And Jesus was turning the first-century Jewish world upside down with his choice of meal partners. The contemptuous question that would be repeated by religious authorities, "Why do you eat and drink with tax collectors and sinners?" (Lk 5:30), reflected Jesus' alternative vision of hope and healing for those with ears to hear. Jesus put it this way when seated around Levi's table, "Those who are well have no need of a physician, but those who are sick. I have come to call not the righteous but sinners to repentance" (Lk 5:31-32). The common thinking and practice of the day could only offer hostility, contempt and fear for a tax collector like Levi, but Jesus offered loving attention and acceptance. This meal scene would be repeated throughout Jesus' lifetime. *There is room at the table for you.*

---

[6]Adele Ahlberg Calhoun, *Spiritual Disciplines Handbook: Practices That Transform Us* (Downers Grove, Ill.: InterVarsity Press, 2005), p. 138.

Jesus' practice of friendship. This spirit of hospitality was also expressed in the way Jesus befriended his disciples. Christine Pohl writes, "In hospitality, the stranger is welcomed into a safe, personal, and comfortable place, a place of respect and acceptance and friendship. Even if only briefly, the stranger is included in a life-giving and life-sustaining network of relations."[7] Her description is characteristic of Jesus' way with those closest to him. He made space for *a life-giving and life-sustaining network of relations* in which his followers would learn and grow, follow and imitate him. In short, he formed a learning community that would in time be released and sent out for kingdom purposes. His nurturing way—respect, acceptance and friendship—was a critical element in his inviting, challenging and preparing his followers to serve, lead and guide others down the road. David Benner writes, "Jesus was not just talk. He did not just speak of friendship; he actually offered it to his disciples and followers. . . . Reading the Gospels with a focus on the relationship between Jesus and the disciples is a powerful experience."[8] The Gospels portray Jesus offering a staggering level of intimacy with his disciples. He never reduced them to mere pawns on his chessboard. Nor were they simply means for his greater purposes. It was not their usefulness that was primary to him; it was each individual person. He honored them with dignity, treasured their company and developed them with great affection. They were his friends.

A patient way with others. "Better is the end of a thing than its beginning; the patient in spirit are better than the proud in spirit" (Eccles 7:8). Perhaps it is our cultural preoccupation with speed, efficiency and control that causes us to notice Jesus' patient way with others. Jesus is not conditioned by our constant search for shortcuts and getting the biggest bang for our buck as he moves through the world. His patient mentoring unfolds most clearly in the way Jesus treats his disciples. The Gospels repeatedly reflect the disciples' slow learning process. After just witnessing Jesus miraculously feed five thousand people (Mk 6:35-

---

[7]Christine D. Pohl, *Making Room: Recovering Hospitality as a Christian Tradition* (Grand Rapids: Eerdmans, 1999), p. 13.

[8]David Benner, *Sacred Companions: The Gift of Spiritual Friendship and Direction* (Downers Grove, Ill.: InterVarsity Press, 2002), p. 64. See Lk 24:13-45; Mt 13:36-52; 26:38; Lk 19:18-27; Jn 13:1-17; 14.

44), the disciples, when faced with another crowd, incredulously ask, "How can one feed these people with bread here in the desert?" (Mk 8:4). And Jesus yet again blesses the little food that they do have and amazingly stretches it into a meal for four thousand. On the eve of his death the familiar argument over the disciples' pecking order repeats itself, and Jesus graciously reminds them yet again, "But not so with you. . . . I am among you as one who serves" (Lk 22:26-27). The Gospels paint a picture of the disciples as a fellowship of slow learners. And we are invited to join this fellowship to encounter Jesus' gracious and patient way with us.

In particular, the Gospel writers draw attention to Jesus' development of the impetuous and determined Simon Peter. More is offered about his relationship with Jesus than any other person in the Gospels. We encounter a rhythm of affirmation and confrontation, affection and demand in this mentoring relationship (Lk 5:1-11; Mt16:13-23; Lk 22:28-62; Jn 21:1-23). Peter's ambitions and expectations are reshaped by Jesus' consistent support and challenge. A much older and wiser Peter would tell a suffering church in a letter years later, "Humble yourselves therefore under the mighty hand of God, so that he may exalt you *in due time*" (1 Pet 5:6, emphasis added). Peter knew firsthand the transformative power of Jesus' patient mentoring in his life.

Jesus' mission involved apprenticing others to faithfully share in God's way and work in the world. And Jesus knew that we can't rush the development of people. Repentance and conversion (turning *from* and turning *toward*) are lifelong processes. Projects can be crammed and hurried, but nurturing and challenging people to maturity cannot. There would be setbacks and differences and failures along the way, but Jesus kept the end in mind. And consequently, he never seems to be hurried or in a panic. For those of us who find ourselves frustrated time and again by the slow pace of change in our lives and in our communities we would do well to prayerfully study and reflect on Jesus' way of apprenticing his followers. Our imaginations, which have been largely shaped by a cultural addiction to speed and control and technique, must be confronted and retrained by the Gospels' images of Jesus' patient way with others.

Just a focused glimpse of his earthly life and ministry reveals that Jesus immersed himself within a web of personal interactions and relationships in order to live out his formational mission. He journeyed with others in a manner that we have characterized as deepening, particularizing, hospitable and patient. *How can we imitate this relational and developmental way of Jesus today?*

WALKING WITH OTHERS TODAY

In Matthew 7:24 Jesus says, "Everyone then who hears these words of mine and acts on them will be like the wise man who built his house on the rock."

We face tremendous pressure in our lives today to be spectators of this Jesus. But faithful living has never been a spectator sport. Over 150 years ago Danish Christian thinker Søren Kierkegaard emphasized this by drawing a contrast between being an admirer and being an imitator. He wrote:

> What, then, is the difference between an admirer and an imitator? An imitator is one who strives to be what he admires, and an admirer keeps himself personally detached, consciously or unconsciously does not discover that what is admired involves a claim upon him to be or at least to strive to be what is admired.[9]

We can become too self-satisfied in our admiration of Jesus and thereby keep his *claim* or demand on our lives at a safe distance. But Jesus is seeking something far different than mere admirers or knowledgeable spectators. Jesus calls us to appreciate who he is to such an extent that we seek to turn from our own way to life in order to imitate him day-in and day-out. It requires getting out of the stands and onto the field to follow him. This is, after all, what the Spirit is doing in our lives—inviting and mentoring us to move beyond spectatorship and to live into Jesus' loving way in the world (Eph 3:16-17). And at the heart of this invitation is the person of Jesus, both our Savior and our Teacher, who is calling us to follow and learn and imitate just as he did with Peter and

---

[9]Søren Kierkegaard, *The Essential Kierkegaard*, ed. Howard V. Hong and Edna H. Hong (Princeton, N.J.: Princeton University Press, 2000), p. 384.

Thomas and Mary and Paul. Jesus has much to teach us as disciples about life in general, and about his way of developing and mentoring people in particular.

A critical discovery in this apprenticeship with Jesus is that there is absolutely no substitute for seeing the gospel lived out by another. No amount of personal Bible study or sermons can replace our need to experience and envision up close the gospel incarnated in a person's life. Or as Timothy Jones observes, "Sometimes we need to see the Christian life lived out, we need to stand in the presence of the genuine article, not just be told about it."[10] Spiritual companionship is a necessity on the journey. Spiritual mentors are not gurus or advice dispensers or answer people to every situation or question, but rather they are ordinary people who offer a wise presence that shows interest in us by asking questions and listening, by discerning and praying with us.

Just after I (Randy) had become a believer in Christ I was introduced to a man whom I later discovered made a recommitment to the Lord because of a tragic death of a young man in the community, the same young man who was the primary witness to the gospel in my conversion story. Warren was a successful farmer who had the biggest farming equipment I had laid eyes on. It was the kind of equipment you wished you had the opportunity to play with if you come from a farming community. He was also a big man, the kind you would be glad to have on your side if need be.

I would come out to have coffee with Warren while he would be working the fields with his Versatile 875. Our conversations would always seem to turn to how each of us was doing in our walk with the Lord, and what might be hindering our walk. Amid the hilarious laughter, and at times through swelling tears, we discovered God in our midst, in the ordinariness of riding a tractor in the farming community of Yorkton, Saskatchewan.

Although Warren did not have a degree from a seminary or go to the latest spiritual mentoring seminar, he had an intuitive way of making

---

[10]Timothy Jones, *Finding A Spiritual Friend: How Friends and Mentors Can Make Your Faith Grow* (Nashville: Upper Room, 1998), p. 36.

> *space for my life, asking the right probing questions and allowing me to*
> *discover what we both believed the Spirit wanted to do in and through*
> *me as a newborn child of God. I became more aware of those things in*
> *my life that needed to be cut away, and to discover how my life may be*
> *used to serve God in the future. But I think more than all of that, I*
> *experienced the real and present love of God in my life through my*
> *friendship with Warren.*

Whatever we call what Warren was for Randy—and we are going to refer to it as being a "spiritual mentor," although others may aptly use the terms *discipler, soul friend, spiritual director* and so on—we recognize that our church communities need more folks like Warren. We need people who can confidently and humbly come alongside others, whether formally or informally, and make space for deeper discovery and guidance on our faith journey.

Spiritual mentoring is not a ministry for specialists or experts, but it belongs to the priesthood of all believers. It is an everyday means to our spiritual formation as individuals and as communities that can be practiced at kitchen tables, in offices and factories and fields, as well as in Sunday school classrooms and retreat centers. There is a great breadth to what these relationships can look like. Sometimes they will involve a relationship between a mature believer and a less mature believer, as in the case of Warren and Randy. Other times there will be more of a mutual mentoring relationship or friendship between peers. The dynamics we will explore can even be applied to a relationship of three of four people who meet together for the purpose of paying greater attention to their life with God and others.

Essentially, spiritual mentoring is a relationship between two or more people and the Holy Spirit, where the people can discover, through the already present action of God, three things: (1) intimacy with God (who is God?), (2) identity as beloved children of God (Who am I?), and (3) a unique voice for kingdom responsibility (What am I to do with my life?).[11] The three guiding questions serve as both launching points and

---

[11]Keith R. Anderson and Randy D. Reese, *Spiritual Mentoring: A Guide for Seeking and Giving Direction* (Downers Grove, Ill.: InterVarsity Press, 1999), p. 12.

signposts for the relationship. We never grow out of these questions; rather we grow into them. The questions mature amid the many challenges of our lives, stretching us beyond their individual framework into matters of relationship and community, beyond I to we. And along the way, these questions pull us into a field of greater discovery and faithfulness when asked in loving and accountable community.

FIVE DYNAMICS OF A SPIRITUAL MENTORING RELATIONSHIP

Two questions often associated with spiritual mentoring relationships are (1) What actually takes place in the relationship? and (2) Why are some relationships more effective than others? The following five dynamics seek to address these questions.[12] It is best to see them as processes that take place as the relationship progresses. They serve as guides to see what is taking place, and why the relationship may be working well or struggling to survive. For a more detailed treatment of a mentoring relationship using these concepts and dynamics we highly recommend Keith R. Anderson and Randy D. Reese's *Spiritual Mentoring: A Guide for Seeking and Giving Direction.*

As we briefly reflect on these processes, let your heart and mind shift back and forth between the realities of being mentored and of being a mentor. Where might God actually be inviting you to greater intentionality in your relationships for the sake of his kingdom and others' development?

Dynamic 1: Attraction and initiation (the art of beginning well). One Sunday morning Jill was in an adult Bible fellowship class and heard Sandy and Bill share very candidly about the struggles in their first ten years of marriage. Now thirty years into their marriage Sandy offered her perspective on what she learned from that time. Jill was all ears. There was something in Sandy's combination of honesty and hopefulness that sealed the deal for Jill. She wanted to get to know Sandy better.

These relationships will invariably begin because someone sees something in the life of another that causes him or her to desire a more intentional meeting together. Perhaps it is the person's character or

---

[12]The five dynamics of the mentoring relationship described are an adaptation of J. Robert Clinton and Richard W. Clinton's dynamics found in *The Mentor Handbook: Detailed Guidelines and Helps for Christian Mentors and Mentorees* (Altadena, Calif.: Barnabas, 1991).

wisdom or the healing in his or her story that draws us. Energy is stirred, a sense of curiosity or a simple desire to explore greater depth in the relationship more intentionally. This dynamic of attraction can start with either one or both parties. Most commonly, it is the more mature believer who is sought out by another. But we would love to see more mature people seeking out those persons they sense God leading them toward to invest in their formation.

Attraction or chemistry, rooted in prayerfulness, seems to have been Jesus' listening and discerning process before he chose twelve men to be his disciples. "He went apart to the mountain and waited on the leading of God, and, after a night in prayer, asked the twelve" (Lk 6:12-16). When seeking a mentor, or being the mentor, the following process may be helpful:

- *Ask* God if you are to enter into a mentoring relationship with this person. Listen for the confirmation from your thoughts, needs or stirrings within.

- *Seek* the heart of God, trust that God cares for the growth of you both, and consider how the mentoring relationship with one another could become good soil for that growth to take place.

- *Knock* on the door of the person's life. Take the risk to ask the person if they will mentor or walk with you more intentionally. If you are the mentor, take the risk and share with the person what you have noticed in them and that you think it would be good if the two of you spent time together.

Once there is agreement that we want to move forward in this mentoring relationship, then we need to discuss what we expect and hope for in the relationship. This is best done when we meet together for the first time. Some people develop a formal mentoring covenant in order unpack the expectations, while many choose to more informally address the concerns of establishing this relationship. In each case there is always a need to converse about your *purpose* (why you will be meeting together), *particularities* (answering the where, when, and how long you will meet together), and *parameters* (what you will do when you meet together). When there is more of a mutual mentoring relationship or friendship, covering these initial areas of concern will be a shared responsibility. This covenanting together, whether done formally or informally, contributes to cultivating a safe learning space in which the people involved can move freely amidst a set of clear expectations and hopes for the relationship.

Dynamic 2: Relationship (developing trust and intimacy). A critical work of a spiritual mentor is to cultivate a hospitable environment where trust and intimacy can naturally grow in the relationship. Without the creation of this safe space, honest and prayerful discovery will become frustrated. Developing trust requires a way of being with another that lovingly moves the relationship beyond the pretense and comparison that pervades so many of our daily relational interactions. Trust is not simply built by following a clear set of steps, but there are things we can do. In particular, the practices of listening, asking questions and prayerfulness serve to foster this trust and intimacy in a relationship that is concerned with helping one another "grow up in every way . . . into Christ" (Eph 4:15). Here are a few elements that will contribute to cultivating a safe and hospitable space for the relationship to grow.

A willingness to be vulnerable. Perhaps nothing is more destructive to a spiritual friendship than pretending we are something or someone we are not. One person has written, "To be a spiritual friend is to be willing to be oneself. Not a professional hiding behind a mask, but a struggler of flesh and blood, with our own gifts and talents, our burdens, doubts, fears, weaknesses, temptations and guilt."[13] In short, we must have the courage to be honest, open and transparent in the relationship. This certainly implies prudence in knowing what or when we share. Our vulnerability must not be self-serving, but rather it must be in the service of the other. We must be willing to bring our whole selves to the table if we are to connect deeply and be of help to another.

Listening. Listening is fundamentally about *being present and attentive* to another. It is a powerful experience to be listened to well. When we recall the experience of a friend's listening presence, we recognize the deep gift it was to us. We also can recall when we have not

---

[13]This is quoted from an unpublished document, Centerpoint/Stillpoint: The Center for Spiritual Development, Santa Barbara, California.

been heard or listened to well. This can be very painful, shutting our spirit down and leaving us feeling more discouraged and unable to move forward. Listening is critical to building trust, gaining understanding and fostering conditions for discovery and action. But being present and attentive to another is very challenging. Our mind can wander in so many directions away from the person sitting before us. Perhaps we are too absorbed in our own context to listen long and well to another. Perhaps we grow anxious and distracted by the reality that we might not be able to adequately help. Perhaps we think we already know the answer. Our need to be helpful can often blur and distract us from the task of simply being present and attentive. There are many factors that make listening well a challenge, yet it remains one of the most healing things we can do as guides on the journey.

Question asking. Simone Weil said, "The love of our neighbor in all its fullness simply means being able to say to him: 'What are you going through?'"[14] Good questions reflect a real interest and caring for the other—what is it like to be in his or her shoes? How is he or she making sense of life? As we learn to walk compassionately with others, we discover that people more often need honest and caring inquiry rather than advice or input. Is our relationship a safe place for people to come to struggle or wonder out loud about their relationships with God and others? Or out of our own anxieties do we smother them with the "right" answer? Do we put fixing them ahead of listening to them? We must learn to welcome and make space for the questions that are emerging from each other's lives. It is only in this sort of atmosphere that we can begin to pay attention and discern more confidently God's presence among us.

Prayerful discernment. We must honor our uniqueness and mystery through prayerful discernment and guidance. As we walk with the Lord over the years, certainly our capacity to discern wisely grows as we personally encounter the *truthfulness* and *grace* of the Lord. One wise man, when asked by a younger believer how it was that after ten or fifteen minutes of listening to him he could seemingly see so clearly and lovingly what he was going through, responded by saying, "The Lord sends a

---

[14]Simone Weil, quoted in *Secrets of a Good Life as Told by Saints and Sinners*, comp. Kathleen Stephens (Nashville: Upper Room, 2005), p. 57.

thief to find a thief. Get to know the thievery of your own heart and you will come to provide both the discernment and the grace to be of help with another's heart." Wisdom and *a deep trust* in the loving movement of God in the life of another develop over a lifetime of faithful attentiveness.

Dynamic 3: Responsiveness (a spirit of teachability). Proverbs 26:12 says, "Do you see persons wise in their own eyes? There is more hope for fools than for them." An unwillingness to learn or submit to one another is a sure indicator of trouble or struggle in a spiritual mentoring relationship (Eph 5:21). No amount of giftedness or insight can overcome a mentoree's unwillingness to learn. The possibility of growth requires receptivity, a type of childlikeness. Jesus' teaching called his disciples to be ready for growth. "Let anyone with ears to hear listen!" (Lk 8:8). And he responded to this readiness in those who became his followers. He captured most vividly this posture of readiness in his admonition to be *childlike.*

> People were bringing even infants to him that he might touch them; and when the disciples saw it, they sternly ordered them not to do it. But Jesus called for them and said, "Let the little children come to me, and do not stop them; for it is to such as these that the kingdom of God belongs. Truly I tell you, whoever does not receive the kingdom of God as a little child will never enter it." (Lk 18:15-17)

What do you think this means—*receive the kingdom of God as a little child?* What are the qualities of a child that Jesus is referring to? Children are curious, not afraid to ask questions, greedy for more, trust, get up when they fall, find joy in discovery, are playful and laugh, are still dependent even when wanting to be independent, and are usually not afraid to express themselves or try new things. Jesus knew that childlikeness, in all of these traits and more, is an essential requirement for our development. In contrast, an *unchildlike* attitude—one which is too easily satisfied or hoping to get by with what he or she already knows—will slowly shrink our visions and cause us to lose sight of our possibilities for growth and change. There must be an open heart, willing and receptive to the perspectives and processes of a mentor, in order for the relationship to flourish.

Hindrances to receptivity. In order to be responsive to spiritual guidance and accountability, a person must remain open, pliable and teachable. It is important to grow in an awareness of why a person may from time to time seem unreceptive or even closed off to the support and challenge of a spiritual mentoring relationship. Anderson and Reese point toward some possible reasons for this lack of positive responsiveness. Consistent hindrances or resistances include:

- *Some people simply do not see their need for help.* They are strong individualists, or at least determinedly private in their faith and have never considered that someone else might be of assistance to their spiritual formation.

- Some people have little confidence that they are worthy of the time of another person, especially if they perceive the mentor to be important or busy. Their own feelings of inadequacy block them from seeking what may be the most important step they might take for their spiritual growth.

- *Many, we believe, live behind the façade of spiritual adequacy and competence.* Afraid to let down the mask, they maintain a strong public image that greatly distorts their own interior pain, fear, weakness, inadequacy or history. Because they are already in positions of leadership or maturity, they believe they should have it all together and dare not show the weakness.

- *Some have good reasons for refusing the ministry of mentoring: they have had poor experiences with teachers, coaches and mentors in the past.* Their history of ineffective mentoring, hurtful relationships or even abuse at the hand of leaders creates a hesitation that hinders their involvement.

- *An unwillingness to submit to the authority of another.* Not only does this impede the work of a mentor, but it also impedes the work of the Spirit.[15]

We can bump into these resistances both before the relationship ever gets off the ground and once we have been meeting for a while. In athletics it is called coachability; a player will listen and learn from the

---

[15]Anderson and Reese, *Spiritual Mentoring*, p. 124.

coach or she will stubbornly insist on her way of doing it. Many extremely talented players' careers have amounted to very little because they were never open to constructive feedback or coaching. Similarly, in life are we really open to learn, regardless of our insights or talents, our setbacks or successes? Or do we fearfully grip onto our way of life out of a need for comfort or control, always insisting that we know better? It is important to grow in an awareness of why a person may from time to time seem unreceptive to the support and challenge of a spiritual mentoring relationship.

Dynamic 4: Accountability (exercises of grace). The spiritual mentoring relationship flourishes long term in a climate of both support and challenge. Typically, a supportive and trusting environment must precede the sorts of growth challenges that will emerge in the relationship. Sam discovered this when different people would inexplicably withdraw as he sought to deepen their spiritual friendship. He tried to make sense of this, but it wasn't until Curt shared honestly of how strong and sometimes even aggressive Sam came off in a relationship that clicked for him. Through Curt's feedback Sam began to recognize his own difficulty in patiently cultivating trust before diving into the deep end. Our capacity to graciously challenge one another to greater faithfulness will depend on our ability to build a trusting and safe climate.

In contrast there are some relationships that stall due to their inability to offer challenge. The mentor never risks moving the conversation beyond its safe confines. Nothing is asked of the mentoree. No invitation for greater honesty or challenge to look at things differently is ever offered. If we desire to grow then it will require some challenge to move beyond our comfortable securities.

As the relationship matures and we become more familiar with and trust each other, accountability becomes a natural part of our meeting together. A simple exercise of grace that we offer from week to week is our consistent presence and inquiry. We check in with one another, we explore progress or setbacks or updates since we last met, we discuss any aha moments in our Bible reading. We simply seek to discern together what God might be up to and how we can assist in this work of the Spirit. Anchored in trust and respect, our meetings together become opportunities in seeing and speaking truth. In all of this, accountability is a process more than it is a single action. Many spiritual mentoring relationships that have started out well have floundered over time because of inattention to the mentoree's growing edges. Thomas Merton captured this challenge so poignantly when he said, "If you want to identify me, ask me not where I live, or what I like to eat, or how I comb my hair, but ask me what I think I am living for, in detail, and ask me what I think is keeping me from living fully for the thing I want to live for."[16] If these relationships are not to be limited to an atmosphere of easy spiritual chatter, the mentor will provide a structure of learning and accountability that gently encourages the mentoree to stretch beyond their comfort zones and easy answers.

A good mentor or soul friend will be become increasingly aware that particular disciplines or directives will be needed to spur further growth.[17] These exercises of grace in all their forms provide new paths for discovery. They will undoubtedly need to be contextualized to each relationship. The aim of each is never to rigidly impose these exercises as an end in themselves. Their overarching goal is to further our maturity and worship, our "growing up . . . into Christ" (Eph 4:15).

Dynamic 5: Empowerment (the goal of mentoring). Whether structured or unstructured, formal or informal, the spiritual mentoring relationship is always intentional. There are certainly meeting times that will seem wandering or inefficient or unfocused. But often these times are spent cultivating context and building trust amid the ordinary, everyday details of life. The mentor though must always keep in mind the purpose of the relationship.

In this sort of dance of spiritual mentoring, a gentle process of leadership is the responsibility of the mentor. Being led is the responsibility of the mentoree. As a dance partner leads by guiding, gently moving, listening to the music and attending to the movements of the other, so spiritual mentoring requires a back and forth, a give and take. Account-

---

[16]Thomas Merton, quoted by Brian J. Mahan, *Forgetting Ourselves on Purpose: Vocations and the Ethics of Ambition* (San Francisco: Jossey-Bass, 2002), p. xxiii.

[17]Calhoun's *Spiritual Disciplines Handbook* is an excellent resource for us to consult as we walk alongside others. It can provide further breadth and rationale for the many sorts of disciplines, practices and exercises of grace found useful in the history of the church.

ability and leadership are required of the mentor. From the mentoree, responsiveness and teachability are necessary. Prayerful attention to each of these dynamics serves to foster an encouraging and challenging environment in which growth can occur.

Annie Dillard writes, "You were made and set here for this, to give voice to your own astonishment."[18] We engage in a spiritual mentoring relationship in an effort to assist others in discovering their unique voice, their amazement in who God is, who they are and what God has invited them to be about. So while the particular set of life circumstances in which a mentoree finds herself dictates where her mentor begins and builds the conversation, ultimately the goals of their meeting together develop along the trajectory of our three primary questions. As we introduced earlier in this chapter, it is in a faithful and honest exploration of three defining questions that our unique sense of calling or voice unfolds:

- *Who is God?* Living in a relationship of intimacy with a loving God

- *Who am I?* Coming to understand our identity as a beloved child of God

- *What am I to do with my life?* Discovering our unique voice in God's story

We then set out to help the mentoree discover how God wants him or her to embrace the Ephesians 2:10 reality: "We are what he has made us, created in Christ Jesus for good works, which God prepared beforehand to be our way of life." We are each invited into a life of partnering with God's creative and reconciling work in this world, but the way we express this cooperation is unique to who we are. The Spirit of God is shaping who we are—our particular mix of experiences and relationships, gifts and strengths, temperament and character, personality and passions—for unique kingdom purposes. Our hope as spiritual mentors is to play a modest part—for God is the primary worker—in awakening anew the mentorees' awareness of God's calling in their lives and empowering their unique voice for kingdom service and leadership.

John of the Cross put it so aptly a few centuries back, "God has so or-

---

[18]Annie Dillard, *The Writing Life* (New York: HarperCollins, 1989), p. 68.

dained things that we grow in faith only through the frail instrumentality of one another."[19] Coming alongside others requires a focused effort of expecting and noticing God at work in their lives. It is an exercise in paying attention expectantly to God's developing of another. How are we learning to pay attention expectantly to the good things God is up to in our neighbors' lives? Eugene Peterson speaks of this expectancy:

> A community of faith flourishes when we view each other with this expectancy, wondering what God will do today in this one, in that one. When we are in community with those Christ loves and redeems, we are constantly finding out new things about them. They are new persons each morning, endless in their possibilities. We explore the fascinating depths of their friendship, share the secrets of their quest. It is impossible to be bored in such a community, impossible to feel alienated among such people.[20]

Look around your network of family and friends, acquaintances and staff members. Pay attention to the margins of your surrounding community as well. Are we open to being surprised by what God might do next in our neighbor's life? *Are we willing to take an Uncle Tom's pocketful sort of walk with them?*

REFLECT ON YOUR LIFE

- What difficulties have you encountered in conversing with others about the things that matter most to them and to you? That is, what are the consistent challenges you experience in moving beyond superficialities in your conversations and relationships?

- Think back to one significant shaping relationship in your life (mentor, teacher, mentoree, etc.) in this light of the five dynamics of the spiritual mentoring relationship (*attraction, relationship, teachability, accountability* and *empowerment*). Describe the strengths and struggles of this relationship using these five dynamics.

---

[19]John of the Cross, quoted in Marjorie J. Thompson, *Soul Feast: An Invitation to Christian Spirituality* (Louisville: Westminster John Knox Press, 2005), p. 124.
[20]Eugene H. Peterson, *A Long Obedience in the Same Direction* (Downers Grove, Ill.: InterVarsity Press, 1980), p. 176.

REFLECT ON YOUR CONTEXT

- How does Jesus' intimate way of noticing and investing in others challenge your community's way of developing others?

- What are the ways you can encourage your communities' leaders to greater intentionality and care in their relationships? How can they learn to come alongside others like Warren did with Randy?

8

CHRISTIAN LEADERSHIP FORMATION
The Nature of Our Work

*Let us consider how to provoke one another to love and good
deeds, not neglecting to meet together, as is the habit of some,
but encouraging one another, and all the more
as you see the Day approaching.*

—HEBREWS 10:24-25

*Transformation is about altering the nature of our relatedness
and changing the nature of our conversation.*

—PETER BLOCK, *COMMUNITY*

*While there are of course some leaders who fail
in leadership due to lack of ministry skills it is probably
more true that the majority of failures in leadership come due to
failure in the area of spirituality. . . . As [Dallas] Willard . . .
has so aptly pointed out, your thoughtless and heretofore
unorganized theology of spirituality guides your life
with just as much force as a thoughtful and
informed one. Kingdom leadership
demands spiritual leadership.*

—J. ROBERT CLINTON, *LEADERSHIP EMERGENCE THEORY*

The thing I (Randy) like about a cathedral is that it lets you know that we are a part of something that has been going on for a very long time. The columns, high ceilings and length of the sanctuary give a sense of space and grandeur. The building itself is designed like a giant cross to hold the community who gather faithfully. The large altar invites us to remember and celebrate the Lord's Supper. Then there is the artwork: the fourteen stations of the cross remind us of Jesus' suffering and crucifixion; on some of the larger pillars near the altar the Gospel writers and the prophets are depicted; and high up alongside the large columns the saints from past ages look down from above. Then there are the old-school wooden pews whose job is to hold congregants and prevent them from falling asleep.

Some places help us remember that we are a part of a much larger story than we realize. And we must remember. In remembering we come to recognize all that we have learned, and we gain hope for our smaller stories that reside within the larger one. In remembering we also discover what we may need to unlearn in order to become more true to who God is, who we are, and the good works God has made ready for us to do. It is in remembering that we gain perspective.

From time to time, we hear the echo of Jesus' "but not so with you. . . . I am among you as one who serves. . . . [A]nd I confer on you, just as my Father has conferred on you, a kingdom" (Lk 22:26-27, 29-30). Jesus' words grab us. Facing numerous challenges, often including confusion about Jesus' way and opposition to Jesus' servant way, we seek to be faithful to God's mission within our unique set of circumstances and people. We continue to gather around tables, like the disciples who first heard these words, listening intently and responding cooperatively to Jesus' servant work in the world, in our communities and in our unique lives.

As long as God's word has been heard, Jesus encounters us in varied forms, seated around some very different tables. But we must pay attention because we are so forgetful. We need one another's encouragement and listening ears so that we will remember what God has done and is doing in our world, in our communities and in our unique lives. There is a tremendous need today for people who will seriously consider

Jesus' gracious service in their lives. We must continually ask one another, How is God cultivating servant communities in our world today? How is God cultivating servant communities in our local communities? How is God prompting such servant character in our unique lives?

Simply put, a servant community is a gathering of people (often a small gathering) who are gripped by the demand and the grace of Jesus and his servant way in the world. If we are grabbed by Jesus' servant way in the world, then what is the nature of our work to be wherever we are placed? And how does the nature of that work play itself out as we seek to guide the leadership formation of others? Our response is fourfold: we are involved in a *deepening* work, a *particularizing* work, a *hospitable* work and a *patient* work. The nature or way of our work will resist the conditions of the day: skimming the surface, one size fits all, means toward ends, faster ways.[1] Christian leadership formation is an act of cultural resistance. As we *stay true* to our work, we will naturally guide the leadership formation of others with greater particularity and care in Jesus name. It will become our nature.

A DEEPENING WORK

Ruth Haley Barton says, "In all this listening to my own life and the lives of others, I have become convinced that the More that we are looking for is the transformation of our souls in the presence of God. It is what we want for ourselves and it is what we want for those we are leading."[2]

One of the remarkable things about Jesus' ministry is the way he moved through the communities of Galilee, Samaria and Judea, and offered such a different vision of reality than his contemporaries did. Jesus saw things that everyone else apparently missed at the time. Tax collectors were transformed, lepers were engaged and healed, prostitutes were forgiven, religious authorities were confronted, and fishermen were empowered with kingdom authority. And his alternative vision and presence has for two thousand years continued to be distinctive of those who follow in his way.

---

[1]See the discussion of cultural conditions in chapter 1.
[2]Ruth Haley Barton, *Strengthening the Soul of Your Leadership: Seeking God in the Crucible of Ministry* (Downers Grove, Ill.: InterVarsity Press, 2008), p. 14.

Jesus' life and work persistently invited the community below the surface reality in which so many of them lived. Consider yet another meal Jesus shared with the Pharisees. Imagine what you might have been thinking and feeling if you sat with them.

> One of the Pharisees asked Jesus to eat with him, and he went into the Pharisee's house and took his place at the table. And a woman in the city, who was a sinner, having learned that he was eating in the Pharisee's house, brought an alabaster jar of ointment. She stood behind him at his feet, weeping, and began to bathe his feet with her tears and to dry them with her hair. Then she continued kissing his feet and anointing them with the ointment. Now when the Pharisee who had invited him saw it, he said to himself, "If this man were a prophet, he would have known who and what kind of woman this is who is touching him—that she is a sinner." Jesus spoke up and said to him, "Simon, I have something to say to you." "Teacher," he replied, "speak." "A certain creditor had two debtors; one owed five hundred denarii, and the other fifty. When they could not pay, he canceled the debts for both of them. Now which of them will love him more?" Simon answered, "I suppose the one for whom he canceled the greater debt." And Jesus said to him, "You have judged rightly." Then turning toward the woman, he said to Simon, "Do you see this woman? I entered your house; you gave me no water for my feet, but she has bathed my feet with her tears and dried them with her hair. You gave me no kiss, but from the time I came in she has not stopped kissing my feet. You did not anoint my head with oil, but she has anointed my feet with ointment. Therefore, I tell you, her sins, which were many, have been forgiven; hence she has shown great love. But the one to whom little is forgiven, loves little." Then he said to her, "Your sins are forgiven." But those who were at the table with him began to say among themselves, "Who is this who even forgives sins?" And he said to the woman, "Your faith has saved you; go in peace." (Lk 7:36-50)

Can you feel the embarrassment and even outrage that must have been shared by the people around the table? How socially inappropriate and morally disturbing was this woman's behavior? Yet Jesus sees things differently. He seems to see very clearly both the woman and Simon. So he draws the conversation into a deeper reality by telling this story of two debtors. Stanley Hauerwas argues that a good story or a compelling image pulls the listener or the reader into its field of reality, offering an alternative way of seeing and being in the world. Jesus' story offered Simon a field of reality other than his offense at this woman's actions and his judgment toward Jesus. The story provided a portrait of forgiveness and gratitude, thereby inviting the listeners into new possibilities for understanding Jesus' acceptance of the woman. Jesus' question decisively draws the Pharisees at the table into a consideration of the more critical concerns of genuine faith and love. Wherever Jesus traveled he seemed to be reinterpreting, in a *deepening* manner, the reality most people lived in. *How about us?*

Our culture tends to encourage action to the exclusion of reflection; hence the compulsive busyness that characterizes so much of our lives. Educator Parker Palmer points out the North American culture wants to externalize everything because it sees "the good life as a matter of outer arrangements rather than inner well-being." He goes on to say that we in North America

> have a long and crippling legacy of believing in the power of external realities much more deeply than we believe in the power of the inner life. How many times have you heard or said, "Those are inspiring notions, but the hard reality is . . ."? How many times have you worked in systems based on the belief that the only changes that matter are the ones you can measure or count? How many times have you watched people kill off creativity by treating traditional policies and practices as absolute constraints on what we can do?[4]

We must resist the temptation to view and approach our leadership challenges superficially. If we are grabbed by Jesus' servant way in the world, then *the nature of our work is to be a deepening work*. Our action in our communities must be accompanied by reflection. This is obviously not a simple matter. Richard Foster's words ring true again, "Superficiality is the curse of our age. . . . The desperate need today is not for a

---

[3]Stanley Hauerwas, *Vision and Virtue* (South Bend, Ind.: University of Notre Dame Press, 1981), p. 2. See also Eugene H. Peterson, *Under the Unpredictable Plant* (Grand Rapids: Eerdmans, 1992), p. 6.
[4]Parker Palmer, *Let Your Life Speak* (San Francisco: Jossey-Bass, 2000), p. 77.

greater number of intelligent people, or gifted people, but for deep people."[5] We must be willing to go below the surface of things today, not in order to impress anyone but rather that we may see and be more truthful and gracious in our communities. Our work must invite depth for others by *listening*, asking *questions* and providing *hope* as their stories continue to unfold toward a fuller awareness of who God is, who they are and what God desires to do through their lives.

Listening. We honor people by listening to the details of their past, their present circumstances and their future dreams. Our presence with them can remind them that God has called them by name and will be faithful to them. In doing so we will be loyal to them as we stick by them in their journey. In a world where people often feel they are not heard, listening to and being present with those developing under our care will help them perceive what the already present action of God is doing in their lives.

Asking questions. We also have the task of asking timely and discerning questions that invite an obedient response and move people to take the next step in the journey toward maturity in Christ. What might God be inviting by way of obedience? How do they describe their intimate relationship with God? Who are they at their particular place in the journey? What is God inviting them to do at this juncture in life?

Providing hope. We can be a voice of hope and encouragement by reminding people that God is in the process of making all things new. Providing hope means giving careful attention to and perspective on what is taking place during different seasons along the journey. Hope often comes from the life stories of those who have come before us.

A PARTICULARIZING WORK

Wendell Berry observes that

> love is never abstract. It does not adhere to the universe or the planet or the nation or the institution or the profession, but to the singular sparrows of the street, the lilies of the field, "the least of these my

---

[5]Richard J. Foster, *Celebration of Discipline: The Path to Spiritual Growth* (San Francisco: Harper & Row, 1978), p. 1.

brethren." Love is not, by its own desire, heroic. It is heroic only when compelled to be. It exists by its willingness to be anonymous, humble, and unrewarded.[6]

Besides being a Kentucky farmer, Wendell Berry writes novels, poems and essays. In an essay titled "A Good Farmer of the Old School," Berry gives us a lesson on paying attention while visiting with a friend named Lancie at a draft horse sale. Lancie was known and respected for his old-school ways of farming. Berry writes,

> At the next Columbus Sale, I hunted Lancie up, and again we spent a long time talking. We talked about draft horses, of course, but also about milk cows and dairying. And that part of our conversation interested me about as much as the hog story had the year before. What so impressed me was Lancie's belief that there is a limit to the number of cows that a dairy farmer can manage well; he thought the maximum number to be about twenty-five: "If a fellow milks twenty-cows, he'll see them all." If he milks more than that, Lancie said, even though he may touch them all, he will not see them all. As in Lancie's account of his corn crop and the 360 shoats, the emphasis here was on the importance of seeing, of paying attention. That this is important economically, he made clear in something he said to me later: "You can take care of twenty or twenty-five cows and do it right. More, you're overlooking things that cost you money." It is necessary, Lancie thinks, to limit the scale of operation, not only in dairying, but in all other enterprises on the farm because proper scale permits a correct balance between work and care.[7]

Are we paying attention to the proper balance between work and care in our spiritual formation efforts? It seems that so much of our effort today can lack care simply because we have not paid attention to this balance. Our concerns and the demands on our time drown out the necessary element of care, and consequently we overlook critical elements of our work. The importance of *seeing*, noticing the uniqueness of the persons before us and paying attention to God's movement in their lives, is not a very efficient way to operate in our one-size-fits-all

[6]Wendell Berry, *What Are People For? Essays by Wendell Berry* (New York: North Point Press, 1990), p. 200.
[7]Wendell Berry, *Home Economics* (New York: North Point Press, 1987), pp. 153-54.

world. A more relational approach to the formation of others will confront our ambitious ways of serving Jesus. Imitating Jesus' way of empowering others will require of us a work that particularizes others.

Throughout the pages of this book we have emphasized the importance of noticing people. Walking alongside others through mentoring, for example, is not a one-size-fits-all approach. We are more complex than that. Images of Jesus picking Zacchaeus out of the crowd, of the shepherd leaving the ninety-nine for the one lost sheep, of the good shepherd knowing his sheep by name have all given texture to our portrait of God's particularizing love for us. And they in turn challenge us to a certain sort of approach in our relationships. In today's world in which anonymous encounters with strangers are our most pervasive sorts of relational interactions, we hunger for the sustained attention and care of another who notices us.

In our reflections on the nature of Christian leadership formation, we want to expand this notion of particularizing to include not just people but places or communities. We are defining particularizing as *paying loving attention to the details of a person or place/community*. In this sense Christian leadership formation is a particularizing work. Whether working with individuals or communities, a one-size-fits-all approach is not sufficient. We need to be attentive to the details of our context. If we are going to serve in a Jesus-servant-authority sort of way, then we have to immerse ourselves within the complexity, the mess and the wonder of our particular context. This is what is involved in paying loving attention to the details of people and place. Consider one pastor's early experience in ministry.

> In my first congregation I decided within the first few weeks that I needed to confront racism. I went at it with hard-charging "thus sayeth the Lord" intensity. But after a lot of conflict and threats and near-brawls with a few people and good counsel from some wise ones, I began to pay attention to my congregation and to what God was saying through them as well as to them.
>
> I started learning how to do a hermeneutics of people-hood, sitting on front porches and working in gardens with the people and drinking iced tea afterwards while listening to their stories, including their stories

of race and fear. As a result, my preaching and teaching changed. I still talked about race, but how I talked about it was different. My sermons began to grow out of the conversation between the people and the Bible and the place where they lived. I learned to listen throughout the week in order to speak for 20 minutes on Sunday morning.[8]

What happened in this young pastor's experience? He discovered that it was not problems that sat before him but people. He learned that a necessary portion of his work was to know intimately the people and their contexts. And through this interactive dialogue the communities' problems, of race in this case, took on a more human and hopeful shape.

Jesus expressed his kingdom work amid the everyday challenges of friends and acquaintances, enemies and followers. He sat around fires, ate meals at tables, visited at wells, listened and taught in synagogues and fishing boats. He worked in the midst of leprosy and self-righteousness, social rejection and family deaths. *In short, he began where people were.* This is a hard work. There is always the danger of offering solutions to situations and people we do not understand well. Some of us are discovering that if we listen for an hour or so about an organizational predicament or a person's disorientation or perhaps hear someone's story, we can then begin to zero in on the conflict, or begin to connect the dots, and arrive at some sort of plan or suggestion for the situation. However, if we listen for another four or five hours to the same person with the same situation, we then begin to realize that we understand less clearly what to do. It is with this discovery that we begin to listen to the particular situation and place. This discipline of deep and reverent listening must be brought to each of our unique contexts. There can be so much presumption and generalizing of solutions in our ministry conversations without patiently attending to the unique conditions and details of a person's life or a communities' challenges. We so hurriedly adapt borrowed solutions or flippantly deal out advice without honoring the community or the person with our attention. Such presumption and generalization do not reflect a particularizing way with others in our unique settings.

---

[8]Kyle Childress, "Good Work: Learning About Ministry from Wendell Berry," *Christian Century*, March 8, 2005, p. 30.

Paying attention to people in our settings over time has a way of leaking out. Soon after someone is noticed, they have a way of letting others in on what has taken place in his or her life. And before long others want in. What we have noticed in our own context of helping local pastors, missionaries and others invest more deeply in the formation of their adult believers is that when they do so with a measure of care they soon have a small group of people within their communities who want to learn and serve. And that learning and serving community becomes a catalytic gift for change within the larger community.

A HOSPITABLE WORK

Jean Vanier says,

> Peace will come through dialogue, through trust and respect for others who are different, through inner strength and a spirituality of love, patience, humility, and forgiveness. Little by little, a culture of competition will be transformed into a culture of welcome and mutual respect.[9]

We have expressed the priority and concern for making space for others through this notion of *hospitality*. If we are grabbed by Jesus' servant way in the world, then the nature of our leadership formation work will be a *hospitable work*. Men and woman are never just a means to an end. *There is always room at this table for you*—this is the expression of a hospitable spirit. David Benner offers a memorable portrait that captures this spirit:

> I cannot think of soul hospitality without recalling a remarkable visit that I was blessed to have with Paul Tournier shortly before his death. Well into his eighties and frail at the time, this much-loved Swiss physician and author of numerous books on psychology and spirituality continued to receive guests who came to see him from around the world. Arriving with thirty eager university students, I was warmly greeted by Dr. Tournier at his home in Geneva. He invited us into his backyard. There he first spoke to each of us individually, slowly asking our names, where we were from and some questions about our lives. It was aston-

---

[9]Jean Vanier, *Becoming Human* (Mahwah, N.J.: Paulist, 1988), p. 4.

ishing. He seemed to be—and genuinely was—interested in each of us, all of us strangers to him until that moment.

But then he offered us a gift that really took our breath away. He slowly walked to a garden shed, steadied by the arm of his nurse. After several minutes he emerged with a pile of flags. Moving toward a flagpole that was in the center of his garden, he proceeded to hoist the flag of the country of birth of each of the thirty guests. As each flag was raised, he welcomed us and told us how honored he was to have us as guests in his home. This ceremony, lasting nearly half an hour, was one of the most moving acts of hospitality I have ever witnessed.[10]

There is something so deeply human and holy in this scene. Invitation and care, recognition and respect are graciously tied together in Dr. Tournier's welcome. Of such hospitality, Marjorie Thompson writes, "Hospitality is essentially an expression of love. It is a movement to include the guest in the very best of what we ourselves have received and can therefore offer. It is the act of sharing who we are as well as what we have."[11] There are various connotations for hospitality today. Many definitions seem to reflect notions akin to good manners, hotel management or a warm Thanksgiving table scene. For our purposes we want to remain firmly planted between Dr. Tournier's welcoming portrait and Thompson's description—*the act of sharing who we are as well as what we have.*

A central assumption in so much of our contemporary North American life is that our worth must be proven. "Prove yourself" is a motto that reaches to the depths of who we are. Individual dignity must be earned. Value endlessly fluctuates with performance. The powerful, the popular, the beautiful and the talented are given the highest line of credit. Worth is cashed out. We all trade, so to speak, on this market of personal worth, confronted and overwhelmed and motivated by the competition. As the performance dims, so does the respect. For many, this takes on the mood and plot of a Greek tragedy, fated to wake up each morning and toil with an impossible task of earning worth yet again.

---

[10]David G. Benner, *Sacred Companions: The Gift of Spiritual Friendship and Direction* (Downers Grove, Ill.: InterVarsity Press, 2002), p. 49.
[11]Marjorie J. Thompson, *Soul Feast: An Invitation to the Christian Spiritual Life* (Louisville: Westminster John Knox, 1995), p. 129.

Our Christian communities must challenge this cultural story of eroded personal dignity. Humans have been created in the image of God (Gen 1:26-28). God's personal thought, breath and touch impart dignity and bestow worth (Gen 2:7-8). The biblical narrative breathes fresh life into this weary cultural conversation and animates it with hope instead of burden. May we marvel with David, who cries out in awe of God:

> When I look at the night sky and see the work of your fingers—
>> the moon and the stars you have set in place—
> What are mortals that you should think of us,
>> mere humans that you should care for us?
> For you have made us only a little lower than God,
>> and crowned us with glory and honor. (Ps 8:3-5 NLT)

> You made all the delicate, inner parts of my body
>> and knit me together in my mother's womb.
> Thank you for making me so wonderfully complex!
>> Your workmanship is marvelous—how well I know it.
>> (Ps 139:13-14 NLT)

That God creates humans in his image offers radical implications for human life (*radical* in its original sense—*at its roots*). Such an understanding confronts all thinking and acting that grounds human dignity in what we do, what we say or what we have—individually or corporately. Any sort of human existence that conceives of dignity as something earned, rather than given, must be recognized as dehumanizing. When this demand is made, the person is demeaned. In her book *Making Room: Recovering Hospitality as a Christian Tradition*, Christine Pohl offers a historical context for hospitality within the church. Of John Calvin's contributions she writes:

> More than anything else, the conviction that all human beings were marked with the image of God undergirded Calvin's response to the stranger. Bearing God's image establishes for every person a fundamental dignity which cannot be undermined either by wrongdoing or neediness. But, for Calvin, the simple fact of our common humanity also provided a basis for recognition and respect. Humanness itself re-

quires that persons recognize others as like themselves. Each person is made for others and depends on others.[12]

Christians have passionately defended the worth of the person in human rights discussions and abortion debates, but how has such an understanding affected our common life together?

One of the central ways we can be the church in our context (i.e., an expression of God's reconciling life in this world) is through a welcoming respect for one another. In the supermarket, the office hall or at the kitchen table, are we agents of grace, patiently accepting the other—the friend, the coworker, the stranger? Do we demand "prove yourself," or do we make a caring space for the other? This is important because when we sit across from someone and respect him or her as a person created by and in the image of God, we express grace to that person. By our lives together we remind each other who we really are.

When we are grabbed by Jesus' way in the world, we will honor the dignity of the people with whom and for whom we serve; they will be dignified by being viewed as an end, not as a means to our vision and activity. Our leadership formation work must create hospitable spaces where people will become aware of their worth. When we do so we cultivate a community of belonging where people flourish.

In his book *Community: Structure of Belonging*, organizational consultant Peter Block describes what enhances transformative change within local communities. He discusses how we can lower the bar for leadership in order to allow more people to contribute toward a common good. Hospitality plays a critical role in organizations becoming places of cohesion, where recognizing and empowering people is the norm. These become communities that learn, serve and stick together. Block says,

> The key to creating or transforming community, then, is to see the power in the small but important elements of being with others. The shift we seek needs to be embodied in each invitation we make, each relationship we encounter, and each meeting we attend. For at the most

---

[12]Christine D. Pohl, *Making Room: Recovering Hospitality as a Christian Tradition* (Grand Rapids: Eerdmans, 1999), p. 65.

operational and practical level, after all the thinking about policy, strategy, mission, and milestones, it gets down to this: How are we going to be when we gather together?[13]

How are we going to be when we gather together? If we are concerned with hospitality, then we will make space for one another and the Spirit of God in such a way that vulnerability, honesty and hopefulness become the norm. The result is a group with awareness, respect and love for one another—a powerful community who can hardly conceive of not being together.

Is this vision of a hospitable community possible in light of the many challenges and obstacles that surround us? In our own VantagePoint[3] ministry context, we provide resources and processes that help local church communities and organizations invest more deeply in the formation of their adult believers. The processes we have developed have come from many of the perspectives we have been exploring in this book. We have discovered along the way that if *paying attention* is the first step in the leadership formation of others, then *setting the table* for learning and change to take place is the second. Without it, we would simply be inviting pastors and teachers in local settings to be "information dispensers" rather than facilitators concerned about the cultivation of life transformation. Hospitality plays a critical role.

Thousands of people in local settings have gone through our process—men and women serving in a leadership capacity, others who reflect a potential to lead, and those who don't think they have much to offer but sense God is doing something in their life. They have been guided by facilitators in their context through processes in which they are invited to pay attention to God's shaping activity by *editing* their life stories. We know that what we have developed would be dead in the water were it not for the ability of these facilitators to create safe spaces of hospitality. This is a key to life transformation.

Katie's story represents hundreds of others who have gone through the process, paying attention with others to what God has been up to in their lives. When Katie was first invited to join the group she was re-

---

[13]Peter Block, *Community: The Structure of Belonging* (San Francisco: Berrett-Koehler, 2008), p. 10.

luctant because of past small groups that turned out to be a disappointment. Her life was full with work, family and activities in her church community. But something within her hoped this group might be different. After eight months of gathering together two to three hours a week, Katie and her peers celebrated the journey at a "graduation." When Katie stood up before the hundred or so people at the celebration, she began with these words, "It has felt like I've experienced church for the first time." We have heard this response time and again. The resources we've developed have certainly been helpful for Katie and others like her, but the work of hospitality has made the difference.

A PATIENT WORK

If we are gripped by Jesus' way, we will more clearly recognize that our leadership formation of others is not only a deepening, particularizing and hospitable work, it is also a *patient* work. Walking with those in our communities will require a long-haul perspective—trusting that the good work in their lives and the life of the community will unfold in due time. It is an illusion to think we can change people quickly—*it is a slow and deep work that takes time.* When we slow down, we begin to notice God's shaping work in the lives of those around us. This is where the action really is.

This patient work will be hindered unless we allow its truth to confront our own preoccupation with faster ways. So much comes to us with the expectation that reality can be controlled and sped up. Technology saturates every area of our lives. It isn't that technology is so problematic; it is its all-pervasiveness that results in a myth. We believe that all of reality can be controlled (even should be controlled) with careful observation, analysis, application and replication of results. This myth causes confusion and delusion in our work, for much in this world is not within our control. Longer hours and harder work will not resolve many of the deepest problems we encounter. Our relationships with creation, with people and with God cannot be controlled. For example, M. Robert Mulholland illustrates how control can shape our expectations on spiritual maturity. He writes in *Invitation to a Journey,*

Just sit near a vending machine and watch what happens when people do not get the product they have paid for. They will complain to anyone handy or even begin to abuse the machine. This silly example illustrates a deeper dimension of our culture. We have generally come to expect immediate returns on our investments of time and resources. If we have a need, we have only to find the right place, product or procedure and invest the right amount of time, energy and resources, our need will be met. It is not surprising that we, as members of an instant-gratification culture, tend to become impatient with any process of development that requires of us more than a limited involvement of our time and energies. If we do not receive the desired results almost instantly, we become impatient and frustrated.

Often, our spiritual quest becomes a search for the right technique, the proper method, the perfect program that can immediately deliver the desired results of spiritual maturity and wholeness. Or we try to create the atmosphere for the "right" spiritual moment, that "perfect" setting in which God can touch us into instantaneous wholeness. If we can find the right trick, the right book or the right guru, go to the right retreat, hear the right sermon, instantly we will be transformed into a new person at a new level of spirituality and wholeness.[14]

Hidden within Mulholland's portrait is our preoccupation with control. Our own inflated sense of control often lies at the root of our life and leadership frustrations. We cannot get this senior elder to change, the young manager just will not step up, our daughter refuses to "just care a little more" about her brother, the organization will not buy into our vision. In spite of all our well-meaning efforts toward the person, he or she doesn't change. And we are frustrated. In spite of all our hard work and planning on the project, it doesn't succeed. And we are frustrated. The whole situation begins to feel very much like a vending machine that will not give us the drink we paid for.

The interrelationship between the cult of speed *(do everything faster)* and the myth of control has given significant shape to the way we address the deepest concerns of our lives. So whether they are questions of happiness or justice, identity or vocation, leadership or even God's kingdom,

---

[14]Robert J. Mulholland Jr., *Invitation To a Journey: A Road Map for Spiritual Formation* (Downers Grove, Ill.: InterVarsity Press, 1993), pp. 19-20.

we must realize that our approaches to these concerns are conditioned by our preoccupation with control and speed. This conditioning must be resisted. To approach life and the leadership formation of others in Jesus' way, we must be retrained regarding pace and control. A patient approach to leadership practices will be learned only after much frustration and disappointment with our more conventional ways. What does it mean then for us to develop the leadership of others in a more patient way? And what effects might this have? We want to again seek out the help of Wendell Berry. Sink into his vision of good work in this poem.

> Whatever is foreseen in joy
> Must be lived out from day to day.
> Vision held open in the dark
> By our ten thousand days of work.
> Harvest will fill the barn; for that
> The hand must ache, the face must sweat.
>
> And yet no leaf or grain is filled
> By work of ours; the field is tilled
> And left to grace. That we may reap,
> Great work is done while we're asleep.
>
> When we work well, a Sabbath mood
> Rests on our day, and finds it good.[15]

Is the farmer responsible for the field's growth? There is a yes and a no response to this question. In one sense the farmer is deeply responsible. Berry writes of the "ten thousand days of work" in which "the hand must ache, the face must sweat." Without the many early mornings' efforts there will not be a good harvest. The farmer's hard work is required. Yet clearly his or her work is only part of the process. Berry concludes, "no leaf or grain is filled / By work of ours." It is foolish for a farmer to believe the harvest is the result of his solitary efforts. The wise farmer understands that "the field is tilled / And left to grace." The farmer recognizes the limits of his or her efforts and respects the mystery of the work. The farmer's responsibility stands in the light of Another's responsibility.

---

[15]Wendell Berry, "Whatever Is Foreseen in Joy," *A Timbered Choir: The Sabbath Poems 1979-1997* (Washington, D.C.: Counterpoint, 1998), p. 18.

Here we encounter the lesson of this farmer. And this lesson stands in stark contrast to the myth of control. Implicit in this farmer's work is the reality of trust. The farmer does not control the process but rather participates in it. There is no guaranteed result attached to farming efforts. A myriad of factors may frustrate the farmer's work and deny the vision of the harvest. At best the farmer offers conditions in which growth may occur. He or she creatively cooperates with the givens of soil and seed and seasons and weather—and so many other things. And then the farmer waits for the "great work" of Another. This working and waiting and trusting and receiving constitute the nature of the farmer's responsibility. This is faithful, patient and good work.

The farmer who works well recognizes both the necessity and the modesty of his or her part in the whole. The posture is not one of control but of cooperating with the Maker of all things. This trust or faith resonates through all the farmer's labors and rest, all successes and failures. It is a blend of trust and effort, foresight and reverence, resolve and patience.

Herein lies an image for our leadership formation work. Just like the farmer, our work is skewed when we have an inflated view of our responsibility, when we ignore the "great work" of Another and become preoccupied with controlling the results of our actions, when we resist the tension inherent in our work and attempt to control what is not ours to control, when we forget the trust implicit to our work. The Greeks would have called it hubris—an offense against the gods (the good ordering of things). We may call it pride or arrogance or delusion. In such cases, we resist the good ordering of things. We work irreverently. We must resist the notion that the development of others needs to keep pace with the normal, frenetic pace we keep. Good work of this kind must be reverent and patient.

God's work is primary. Our effort responds to and participates with God's ongoing work. God goes ahead of and behind us in creation, in redemption, and in the stories of those who have come before us. We must remember that *paying attention* is fundamental when guiding the formation of others. Thankfully, our noticing comes from learning how God has been at work shaping the lives of those who have come before us. With wonder and fidelity and patience we pay attention to the

Worker already laboring in our own lives, the lives of those in our communities and in the world at large.

A PORTRAIT

Pella, Iowa, is a community well familiar with farming. It's the community where Keith lived and served as one of the pastors at Third Church. Several years ago Third Church needed a way to prepare people in their midst who felt a call to pastoral ministry. I (Randy) met with Keith at a bookstore coffee shop in Sioux Falls, South Dakota, for a conversation about this need at Third Church and to see if I might be able to help Keith think through a few things. Keith was in a hurry to get something going for his people. But what he lacked in patience he made up for with a heart and vision for what God could do through the people at Third.

After a lengthy chat I encouraged Keith to think more critically about what he was going to do with the majority of his adult believers who did not have an obvious call to pastoral ministry. Imagine what could happen if they received a little more ignition or attention or encouragement. Because of his determination to get things going "yesterday," I wasn't sure Keith would have the perseverance to cultivate a more foundational approach for those in his community. So I challenged Keith: if he could bring together a few key people from his church, and perhaps a few other people from other churches in his area who shared a similar concern, I would meet with them and see how together we could develop a process for the discipleship and leadership formation of their adult believers. I was wrong in my assessment of Keith. A month later we met again, only this time Keith had brought with him four other pastors and five leaders from his denomination, all of whom shared the same concern: *How can we become more effective at the formation of our adult believers?*

It has now been seven years since my initial encounter with Keith. Since then, dozens of people have gathered together in small groups to take inventory of what God is doing in their lives. Most of them were good, upstanding church folk who had a certain familiarity with the church scene and yet had not paid attention to what God had been up to in their lives. Among one of Keith's first groups was Bev, a retired professor of education who had a passion for helping others discover the gift of learning. Together, Keith and Bev identified those called to invest in the formation of others and prepared them to walk more closely with newcomers to the process. They seemed to stumble into a way of engaging learning described by Parker Palmer as a "community of truth." This manner of learning honors both the "teacher" and the "student" as colearners rather than the traditional approach where an "expert" dispenses content to an "amateur."[16] Although Keith, Bev and other facilitators knew what they wanted to happen when their groups gathered, mutual learning took place within the context of their groups.

The learning process that was taking place at Third Church was just as significant as the subject matter, which in their case was a blending of their formation as adult believers and their formation in the work of leadership. Keith and Bev helped cultivate deep and meaningful conversations about their relationships with God, what they were learning about each other as they shared their personal narratives, and how they were going to support one another in the various endeavors in which God seemed to be calling them to serve. The conversations turned to groups of conversations as the word spread at Third Church about the sorts of life change taking place through their "Leaders for the Harvest" ministry. The change within individuals and within small groups expanded to new groups of changed persons.

After a few hundred people have come together to pay attention to what God is doing in their lives, Keith and Bev found that not only did more people from Third Church, and the broader community, want to go through what others had experienced, but those who had gone through the learning process wanted to continue gathering in order to grow in their followership and learn to become more effective in their leadership and service. People continued to gather to talk and pray about what they cared about. The authors of *Cultivating Communities of Practice* discuss the importance of providing people with opportunities to congregate around shared concerns, and what that can do to enhance their ongoing learning.

---

[16]Parker J. Palmer, *The Courage to Teach: Exploring the Inner Landscape of a Teacher's Life* (San Francisco: Jossey-Bass, 1998), pp. 100-102.

These people don't necessarily work together every day, but they meet because they find value in their interactions. As they spend time together, they typically share information, insight, and advice. They help each other solve problems. They discuss their situations, their aspirations, and their needs. They ponder common issues, explore ideas, and act as sounding boards. They may create tools, standards, generic designs, manuals, and other documents—or they may simply develop a tacit understanding that they share. However they accumulate knowledge, they become informally bound by the value that they find in learning together. This value is not merely instrumental for their work. It also accrues in the personal satisfaction of knowing colleagues who understand each other's perspectives and of belonging to an interesting group of people. Over time, they develop a unique perspective on their topic as well as a body of common knowledge, practices, and approaches. They also develop personal relationships and established ways of interacting. They may even develop a common sense of identity. They become a community of practice.[17]

What's the next step for Keith and Bev and the folks at Third Church? They are developing a center to address the learning of clusters of people—*communities of practice*—within their larger community who share a common interest and a common desire to steward the good work God has done and is doing within them. What began as a concern to pay attention to the discipleship and leadership formation of a few folks has ignited into an ongoing desire to learn and serve within their unique community. Such deepening and empowering communities over time cultivate unimagined kingdom impact.

> We are what he has made us, created in Christ Jesus for good works, which God prepared beforehand to be our way of life. (Eph 2:10)

A FINAL INVITATION

In the introduction we invited you to consider what we have come to believe as we have sought to help others notice more particularly the persons in their settings. We would like to share with you again these

---

[17]Etienne Wenger, Richard McDermott and William M. Snyder, *Cultivating Communities of Practice* (Boston: Harvard Business School Press, 2002), pp. 4-5.

convictions. We hope that you will add to this list what you have and will come to learn as you invest in the *slow and deep work* of guiding the leadership formation of others.

Shape the person and you stand a much greater chance of shaping everything else. This was a challenge given to us by Dr. James Houston, founder and chancellor of Regent College in Vancouver as we set out on our work. After a dozen or so years of experience, we have noticed repeatedly how change in a small group of people leaks out of the group and influences their local community.

Discipleship and Christian leadership development are inextricably linked and together make a slow and deep work. Those who promise impressive growth through simple and easy steps are selling an illusion. Some things simply cannot be learned quickly. Apprenticing others toward Jesus' way eventually presents a set of learnings around what it means for them to influence others toward God's purposes. In this regard, discipleship and leadership development are seamless.

Igniting a grassroots way toward renewal is possible. Although there are important things to be said for "vision from the top" or a "speed of the leader, speed of the team" approach, these have become overrated, especially if we wish to witness the work of the Spirit in our midst. Igniting more people toward an Ephesians 2:10 way of life will precipitate significant movement in a local setting.

A Christian approach to leadership formation requires a ministry of paying attention. If it is true that God uses people, events and particular circumstances over time to shape us, then our role in guiding others toward growth and maturity becomes a ministry of noticing where God is at work and then partnering with him in the learning endeavor.

Conditions can be cultivated in order for local communities to become significant places of learning and growth. Although formal education has its place in the learning process, it is not the only place. Igniting a thirst for learning happens when we help people make a connection between truth and life—in the ordinary places where life is lived.

> When I heard of the solid trust you have in the Master Jesus and your outpouring of love to all the followers of Jesus, I couldn't stop thanking God for you—every time I prayed, I'd think of you and give thanks.

But I do more than thank. I ask—ask the God of our Master, Jesus
Christ, the God of glory—to make you intelligent and discerning in
knowing him personally, your eyes focused and clear, so that you can
see exactly what he is calling you to do, grasp the immensity of this
glorious way of life he has for his followers, oh, the utter extravagance
of his work in us who trust him—endless energy, boundless strength!
(Eph 1:15-19 *The Message*)

REFLECT ON YOUR LIFE

We have covered much ground in this book. *Noticing, learning* and
guiding are the three macrothemes we have invited you to consider in
this work of leadership formation. At this point, a good question is,
What have you found yourself saying as you read the book?

We invite you to convert your response to this question into a
written prayer.

REFLECT ON YOUR CONTEXT

Step back from what you have been reading and give particular attention to the people within your own setting and respond to the
following questions:

- What do you need to *think* clearly about regarding the leadership
  formation of the persons in your setting?

- What do you need to *design* in order to invite adults into an honoring
  learning process?

- How will you *cultivate* the learning process so that it bears the fruit
  of individual life change and change within your community?

APPENDIX 1

LESSONS FROM THOSE WHO HAVE COME BEFORE US

What contributes to the flourishing and finishing well of many Christian leaders? It seems that being skilled and strategically minded are not the only criteria. God's shaping work is of greatest value. A person's willingness to respond faithfully to the Spirit's work in his or her character—the inner life—is an essential factor.

J. Robert Clinton's leadership studies reveal some persistent patterns or lessons from those who in the long term ignored character concerns in their development. These lessons can be viewed as barriers to a faithful and thriving life. Clinton also compiled characteristics of the leaders who finished well. Our own personal formation can be significantly instructed by looking at these negative and positive lessons. As the proverb reminds us, "A prudent person foresees the danger ahead and takes precautions; / The simpleton goes blindly on and suffers the consequences" (Prov 22:3 NLT).

LESSONS FROM THOSE WHO FINISH POORLY

1. They misuse, mismanage and abuse finances. Richard Foster points out that money was Jesus' second most recurrent theme in his ministry (the kingdom of God being first). Jesus seemed to emphasize money's use and abuse in a way not so common in our spiritual conversations today. Yet certainly there are plenty of contemporary examples of financial misuse and abuse. Such mismanagement and irresponsibility continues to trip up many leaders.

A leader's inability to manage money is often an expression of deeper problems, such as an unwillingness to respect boundaries, a refusal to submit to another's authority or perhaps simple greed. In any case, the result is often a poor finish to the leader's life.

> Such is the end of all who are greedy for gain;
> it takes away the life of its possessors. (Prov 1:19)

2. They struggle with issues of power. Leaders who are effective in ministry must use various power bases in order to accomplish their ministry. Unfortunately, a tendency to abuse this power often is present. Because of their perceived status, privileges can be assumed by those in positions of power. Usually leaders at the top in a hierarchical system have no counterbalancing accountability.

Leaders who struggle to properly manage power may also fail to listen to wise counsel, because power wielded for personal gain takes no one into account but the one who possesses it. For so many leaders the exercise of power over the years can result in a certain sense of superiority that leads to the misuse and abuse of people. The leader who flourishes over the long haul learns to exercise and express his or her power generously in the service of others.

3. They become trapped in their own pride. Pride and the insecurity that walks hand in hand with it refuse to trust what God thinks of us (rather than what other people think). A first step or response in trusting God with our lives is honestly admitting that we don't have it all together, that we cannot solve our own deepest problems. Until we learn this rhythm of honesty and recognition, confession and grace, we will continue to resist God's shaping action in our life. Moreover, we will persistently ground our lives on a faulty foundation and will direct others out of a shell of leadership, masking both our arrogance

---

Lessons from Those Who Finished Poorly

- They misuse, mismanage and abuse finances.
- They struggle with issues of power.
- They become trapped in their own pride.
- They struggle with boundaries related to sex or issues of sexuality.
- They fail to deal with family of origin issues.
- They simply plateau in their development.

and insecurity. Such a mask hides who we really are and our tremendous need. At the root of several other character concerns, pride certainly has led to the downfall of many leaders and the erosion of many communities.

> All those who are arrogant are an abomination to the LORD;
> be assured, they will not go unpunished. (Prov 16:5)

4. They struggle with boundaries related to sex or issues of sexuality. There seems to be a persistent connection between sexuality and power. Those whose thinking becomes skewed in regard to power often express this confusion in sexually inappropriate ways. Repeatedly we hear of Christian leaders who have been snared in sexual and relational infidelity. As in all other areas, there must be significant accountability for those in leadership.

It is clear that past sexual experiences, especially those that took place during the formative years, have a lasting effect on a person. If someone was sexually abused as a child, he or she might lean toward or be trapped by that behavior as an adult. Sexual intimacy confusion often has its roots in past sexual abuse. A wise response will involve addressing these past experiences with a good counselor or therapist. It is critical for individuals to deal *thoroughly* and *patiently* with whatever past sexual issues they may have if they are to continue living an emotionally and spiritually flourishing life. A leadership context will be a very dangerous place for a person who has not addressed his or her sexual intimacy concerns.

5. They fail to deal with family of origin issues. Much of who we are and have become is a result of the context we grew up in. As children and then adolescents we consciously and unconsciously pick up on both helpful and unhelpful habits and behaviors. When we are young, learning is much like catching an infection. Character is more often caught than taught. Parents spread the infection, a combination of good and bad elements, which come to characterize much of their children's way of seeing and being in the world. In adulthood if we don't recognize and address these unhelpful things from our past, we can often infect, unknowingly so, the people and contexts in which we live and work.

Addressing our family of origin issues early in our development as a leader is critical to finishing well. This involves an unlearning of our old patterns and ways of seeing the world. It also will involve learning new ways of seeing and being in the world. Thankfully, this is one of the things the Spirit of Jesus does in our lives—a patient process of unlearning our old ways, many of which derive from our family of origin.

6. They simply plateau in their development. A final characteristic of leaders who respond negatively to God's shaping action is that they plateau in their development. This trait may not seem as striking as the previous five, but it can be just as destructive to our goal of finishing faithfully and well as leaders. People's own competence can cause them to minister without really having a Spirit-empowered effect. In essence, their very strength becomes their weakness.

Formation must continue in our life if we are to become all that God has destined us and is shaping us to be. Such development requires a lifelong commitment to running the race.

> Do you not know that in a race the runners all compete, but only one receives the prize? Run in such a way that you may win it. Athletes exercise self-control in all things; they do it to receive a perishable wreath, but we an imperishable one. So I do not run aimlessly, nor do I box as though beating the air; but I punish my body and enslave it, so that after proclaiming to others I myself should not be disqualified. (1 Cor 9:24-27)

LESSONS FROM THOSE WHO FINISH WELL

1. They maintain a learning posture throughout life. Poet Archibald MacLeish is said to have written, "There is only one thing more painful than learning from experience, and that is not learning from experience."

Leaders who finish well have learned to continually apply their experiences to their lives. It's as simple as that. However, experiential learning is only part of the learning posture. Leaders who finish well have an insatiable desire to learn through directed activities. They value lifelong education, and although they may not all be *A* students, they are all *A* learners. They often have a variety of interests, and they see those interests as avenues to a rich and meaningful life. They have learned to enjoy the process of picking up new skills and developing new areas of their lives. And in those learning habits are the seeds of both the flexibility and purpose needed for a lifetime of consistency.

2. They value spiritual authority as a primary power base for leadership. J. Robert Clinton found that people who finished well in Christian leadership operated with spiritual authority. This became the basis for their influence. And this spiritual authority flows out of a life of integrity, a life that is primarily concerned with listening to the voice of the Spirit. And listening to the Spirit in today's world is not an easy task.

The eroding tide of secular culture can blur truth. Instead of engaging the culture with spiritual authority, many leaders quietly and subtly acquiesce to it, often using the need to be relevant as their excuse. It's the difference between telling the truth in terms that are sensitive and persuasive, and molding the truth into something it's not.

How do we cultivate this sort of authority? A voluntary attitude of submission on the leader's part is a prerequisite. As we learn to submit to the directives of others in authority, we will also become more open to submitting to God's shaping activity in our lives, which is a crucial lesson for us to learn. Our submission to God's shaping will enable us to maintain integrity when we help others consider how God is shaping them, which is a primary task for Christian leaders.

3. They recognize leadership selection and development as important. Good leaders help select and develop new good leaders. They see far enough beyond themselves to recognize that the people they lead need two things from their leaders: variety and continuity. When those who lead with us have a variety of personalities and skills, the chances are good that those who are called to follow will be able to find someone in our leadership group they feel comfortable following. This is why variety in leadership selection and development is so important. We also should develop people who can provide positive leadership after we are gone. As Peter Drucker says, "There is no success without a successor."

Leaders who finish well have an intuitive ability to recognize the shaping actions of God in others. Because of this, they are able to notice and specify those in their midst who need further development. They view this development primarily (1) as an opportunity for God's kingdom purposes to be unleashed through that emerging leader, (2) not as an opportunity to pad their own ongoing ministry with competent people. Leadership selection and development is important to the furthering of God's kingdom, whether or not there is personal benefit to be had by those leaders by engaging in the activity.

> ### Lessons from Those Who Finished Well
>
> - They maintain a learning posture throughout life.
> - They value spiritual authority as a primary power base for leadership.
> - They recognize leadership selection and development as important.
> - They work from a dynamic and focused ministry philosophy.
> - They lead from a growing awareness of personal destiny.
> - They perceive their ministry from a lifetime perspective.
> - They prioritize mentoring relationships for themselves and in developing others.

4. They work from a dynamic and focused ministry philosophy. Billy Graham's daughter once indicated that her father's good ministry was largely accomplished through his habit of asking, "How important will this be in 50 or 100 years?" Billy Graham was able to avoid the fads of the day that trapped so many people. Instead he concentrated on things that had more long-range significance.

In other words, Graham knew what he had been called to do and kept his eyes on that calling. He also knew what worked for him and what didn't. So along with his strong sense of call he had a strong sense of style and method. His willingness to stick to a consistent way of doing things showed that he had a good handle on the way God had wired him to operate as a leader. Billy Graham has a dynamic and focused ministry philosophy, and he is in the process of finishing well because of it.

5. They lead from a growing awareness of a personal sense of destiny. God destines us for kingdom purposes. Leaders have a sense that God has his hand upon them for special purposes. This personal sense of destiny means that they base their ability to influence others on their identity as children of God first, and then on their specific call to ministry. They do not base their leadership on personal charisma, knowledge or skill. Instead, their leadership flows out of who they *are* and who they are *becoming*. And this anchor keeps them focused for the long haul.

6. They perceive their ministry from a lifetime perspective. We are not all what we wish to be. And yet God chooses to see us from a long-term perspective, as loved ones made worthy of his sanctifying influences because of the death and resurrection of his Son. And this requires a great deal of patience.

We need to see our lives as under God's shaping and transforming power over the long haul. Successes and failures (at least by the world's count) will come and go, and yet we must never take our eyes off of the work God is doing within us. We must never stop asking What next, Lord? There may be times when life seems to be coming apart at the seams, but having a lifetime perspective helps us to see that "this too shall pass!" Such a lifelong perspective honors the journey with God we are on as we serve him in this world.

7. They prioritize mentoring relationships for themselves and in developing others. Leaders who do not participate in mentoring relationships lose one of the most significant shaping tools available to them. Mentoring relationships can provide gracious contexts within which existing and emerging leaders can share the joys and sorrows of life and ministry. They also bring some accountability to bear on the lives of Christian leaders. Mentoring relationships help keep leaders from leading in a vacuum, and they empower them to become more faithful leaders. Developing a balance of mentoring relationships can help keep leaders on track through a lifetime of unexpected experiences and ensure a good finish.

APPENDIX 2

BIG PICTURE
Getting a Lifelong Perspective

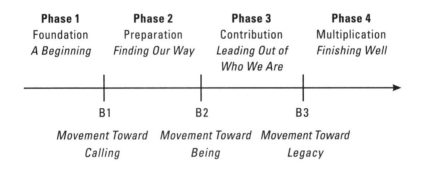

Phase 1	Phase 2	Phase 3	Phase 4
Foundation	Preparation	Contribution	Multiplication
A Beginning	*Finding Our Way*	*Leading Out of Who We Are*	*Finishing Well*

B1   B2   B3

Movement Toward Calling   *Movement Toward Being*   *Movement Toward Legacy*

Figure A2.1

PAYING ATTENTION TO CUES OF DEVELOPMENT

• personal history
   • desire to learn
      • willingness to submit
         • surrender to follow

           • growing discovery of giftedness and fit
              • growing maturity in competencies
                 • relational, authority and organizational insights

                    • willingness to face limitations and embrace brokenness
                       • questioning of issues of identity
                          • deepened sense of calling
                             • courage to lead out of values and convictions

                            • reconsideration of life purpose
                               • review of effective methods
                                 • scanning for role and fit
                                     • desire to empower others

WHY IT MATTERS

- Intimacy with God is primary to godly leadership.

- God is the primary agent of our development.

- Godly leadership flows out of who we are, moreso than what we do.

- Integrity is foundational to the foundation of character.

- Seasons of boundary are heightened times of learning in our formation.

- We can appropriately move from descriptive to prescriptive approaches.

- A balanced approach to development is more likely to foster leadership maturity.

APPENDIX 3

TEN MACRO-OBSERVATIONS FROM CLINTON'S LEADERSHIP EMERGENCE STUDY

1. Ministry flows out of being.
2. A lifelong perspective is critical in order to move toward finishing well.
3. We need to anticipate God's shaping activity for our formation.
4. A timeline process can have a powerful life-changing impact.
5. Few leaders finish well.
6. Understanding boundary times can aid in navigating through them.
7. Awareness of destiny helps bring about confidence and perseverance.
8. Understanding social base (life management) can help navigate and live proactively in light of one's social base.
9. Understanding giftedness, life purpose and unique personal methodologies can direct a person toward his or her major role.
10. A focused life is dedicated to exclusively caring out life purpose, unique methodologies, major role and ultimate contributions.

FIVE PRACTICES FOR
THE LONG HAUL

1. Spiritual Reading

Forming the habit of prayerful scriptural reading can tune our ability to listen to the indwelling shaping work of the Holy Spirit. Prayerfully reading some of the Christian classic writers (e.g., Augustine, Bernard of Clairvaux, John of the Cross, Teresa of Ávila, Jean Guyon, John Calvin, John Wesley, Martin Luther) or biographies and autobiographies (e.g., Henrietta Mears, Charles Simeon, Billy Graham, Mother Teresa) can also help us recognize parts of our own story where the Spirit may be at work.

2. Spiritual Mentoring

Spiritual mentoring (a relationship which helps us pay attention to the already present action of God) can help those in leadership discover blind spots, such as too much dependence on one's own abilities. This type of mentoring can help discern one's movement toward living a more focused life.

3. Solitude and Silence

Solitude helps us get away from the many responsibilities we carry; silence in the solitude helps us listen and receive what the Lord wants us to discover. Solitude and silence can be practiced over extended periods of time and in the moment.

4. Sabbath

Observing a sabbath means stopping, pausing for rest, relaxation and remembering the God who saved us, continues to conform us, and invites us to remember the essential mission we are a part of is not ours but God's. Sabbath can also be practiced over extended periods of time or in the moment. Regularity is key.

5. Self-Care

We have unfortunately paid little attention to caring for our bodies, and we seem to do so only after we have hit some hard times. We experience erosion of our bodies because we neglect our diet, sleep and exercise. Even small steps toward implementing self-care can move us toward a healthier lifestyle.

ABOUT VANTAGEPOINT³

VantagePoint³ is a nonprofit ministry that cares about the deepening and empowering of adult believers in local settings by providing resources and processes that have been developed from what has been articulated in *Deep Mentoring: Guiding Others on Their Leadership Journey.*

WHAT WE LONG TO SEE

Individuals particularized, awakened and ignited for kingdom life and influence—many long for a way of life reflective of the good works God has prepared for them to be about.

Christian leaders who are paying attention to the people around them—intentionally walking alongside others in their communities, patiently investing in their development and maturity.

Churches and organizations becoming vital places of learning—communities where men and women are consistently invited and mentored into a life of apprenticeship with Jesus amid daily life.

A tribe of Christian leaders—a fellowship of learners gripped and bound together by a more relational way of doing life and ministry—caring about an economy of "leaving the ninety-nine for the one" (Mt 18:10-14) that honors the uniqueness of who God has created and redeemed each person to be.

WHAT WE OFFER

- Developmental processes, resources and consultations

- Facilitator training retreats and events

- "VP3 Readings & Leadings" blog and webinars

- Explore more at our website: www.vantagepoint3.org.

A helpful place to begin is with "The Journey," a life-changing discipleship and spiritual formation process for adult believers. This process is guided by three questions: Who is God? Who am I? and What does God desire to do through me? It blends many of the concepts presented in *Deep Mentoring* and focuses on shaping each person in the context of an eight-month small-group experience.

Name and Subject Index